Dead Celebrities, Living Icons

Dead Celebrities, Living Icons

Tragedy and Fame in the Age of the Multimedia Superstar

John David Ebert

PRAEGER

AN IMPRINT OF ABC-CLIO, LLC
Santa Barbara, California • Denver, Colorado • Oxford, England

Library of Congress Cataloging-in-Publication Data
Ebert, John David.
Dead celebrities, living icons : tragedy and fame in the age of the multimedia superstar / John David Ebert.
p. cm.
Includes bibliographical references and index.
ISBN 978-0-313-37764-8 (hard copy : alk. paper)—ISBN 978-0-313-37765-5 (ebook)
1. United States—Civilization—1945– 2. United States—Civilization—1918–1945. 3. Celebrities—United States—Death. 4. Popular culture—United States—History—20th century. 5. Popular culture—United States—History—21st century. 6. Tragedy—Social aspects—United States—History—20th century. 7. Tragedy—Social aspects—United States—History—21st century. 8. Fame—Social aspects—United States—History—20th century. 9. Fame—Social aspects—United States—History—21st century. 10. Tabloid newspapers—Social aspects—United States—History. I. Title.
E169.12.E24 2010
973.9—dc22 2010003460

ISBN: 978-0-313-37764-8
EISBN: 978-0-313-37765-5

14 13 12 11 10 1 2 3 4 5

This book is also available on the World Wide Web as an eBook.
Visit www.abc-clio.com for details.

Praeger
An Imprint of ABC-CLIO, LLC

ABC-CLIO, LLC
130 Cremona Drive, P.O. Box 1911
Santa Barbara, California 93116-1911

This book is printed on acid-free paper ∞

Manufactured in the United States of America

To my beautiful son, Julian Samuel Ebert, with love

"The cult of stars is the last great myth of our modernity."
—Jean Baudrillard

Contents

Acknowledgments

This book would not even be remotely what it is without the help of a handful of brave souls who undertook the task of reading the manuscript and offering their advice and criticisms for improvement.

First and foremost, I would like to thank John Lobell, as always, for his suggestions and insightful commentaries. And then also William Irwin Thompson for his enthusiastic support for the project.

In addition, I would like to thank the following: Gershon Reiter, John Lawrence, William Doty, and Dan Harmon.

Introduction: Saints in the Age of Electronic Stained Glass

> Worshipped as heroes, divinized, the stars are more than objects of admiration. They are also subjects of a cult. A religion in embryo has formed around them. This religion diffuses its frenzies over most of the globe. No one who frequents the dark auditoriums is really an atheist.
>
> —Edgar Morin[1]

On the night of August 30, 1997, Dodi Fayed came up with a plan to elude the paparazzi who had been stalking him and Diana. They would send a decoy car out the front of the Hotel Ritz while he and Diana would escape out the back in their black Mercedes. Henri Paul, the acting security manager of the Hotel Ritz, was selected to drive the car, although he was not Fayed's chauffeur and did not even have a chauffeur's license. In addition, autopsies by French authorities later concluded that he was legally drunk at the time of the accident and also had antidepressants in his system. They departed from the Ritz Hotel at about 12:20 A.M. with Henri Paul in the driver's seat, Trevor Rees-Jones—Dodi's bodyguard—beside him, Dodi himself sitting in the back behind the driver, and Diana beside him on the passenger's side.

Before leaving, Paul had gone around the front of the hotel and taunted the paparazzi that they would never catch up, thus revealing the whole plan. Hence, when they pulled away from the curb, a handful of paparazzi on motorcycles were already in pursuit. Paul traveled south on the rue Cambon and then turned right on the rue de Rivoli. Instead of turning on the Champs-Elysees where streetlights would have required him to slow down, Paul sped west down the Cours La Reine/Cours Albert I er, which ran parallel with the Seine. This was a long stretch of road that would enable him to pick up speed and, indeed, he did so, for by the time they had reached the mouth of the tunnel at the Pont de l'Alma, the paparazzi had fallen behind and Paul was doing about 70 miles per hour (mph) in a 30 mph zone.

None of the four occupants of the Mercedes was wearing seatbelts, an interesting psychological detail, for one would think that at any moment in which it was important to put on a seatbelt, it would be at the start of what one knew very well was going to be a high-speed chase. This fact should be highlighted, because any psychologist worth his salt would recognize a collective death wish at work here.

There was a dip at the mouth of the tunnel and a slight bend to the left, and apparently Paul grazed a white Uno fiat, which caused him to oversteer to the left to get out of its way, but he did not steer far enough back to the right (and here is where the alcohol writes *its* fatal signature) and the car, consequently, slammed with full impact into the 13th column of the tunnel's interior. According to Diana biographers Clayton and Craig, this was not exactly a safe tunnel, as 34 accidents had occurred there in the past 15 years, including eight deaths.[2] There were no buffers between the pillars, and so the car slammed into the 13th pillar with immense force and was then spun about to the opposite wall where it glanced off and came to a stop pointing in the opposite direction from which it had come. The whole front of the car had accordioned back in on itself, instantly killing the driver and Dodi Fayed. Though both airbags had deployed, only the passenger, Trevor Rees-Jones survived, although with major head injuries.[3]

Diana was found by the paparazzi after they caught up, illuminating the tunnel with a barrage of lightning flashes while the sound of the car's horn remained stuck, blaring. Diana was sitting on the floor with her back to the passenger side, one leg underneath her, while the other was forward onto the seat. She was apparently still conscious, although in shock, and her external injuries were surprisingly mild. She could be heard to mutter the words, "Oh my God," over and over like a mantra, and her eyes were open and blinking, so she seems to have been aware of the horror that had befallen her. When the emergency crew arrived, they claim that they heard Diana mutter, "Leave me alone." It took them an hour to pry her from the wreckage. Her injuries were mostly internal and they were fatal: her heart had been pushed to the other side of her body, severing the pulmonary vein and rupturing the pericardium. She had a heart attack on the way to the hospital, at which point the ambulance had to stop for nearly an hour to try and massage her heart back into beating on its own. Inside the hospital, she had another attack and they massaged it once again, using electroshock, but it was unavailing, for her heart would no longer beat on its own.

She was gone.

Her death was announced at 4 A.M. Paris time.

Diana's car crash immortalized her by transforming her life into the stuff of Shakespearean tragedy. Projected on a mass scale around the globe via electronic screens, the whole drama is given a sort of mythical exemplarity about it, as though it were a parable for the kinds of dangers that lie in wait for those who wish to become megafamous in the age of real-time video screens and satellite technology. Electronic media conferred on Diana's life a mythical quality that renders it difficult to forget. Her life has become as haunting as that of Hamlet's or Oedipus's or Ophelia's, for the interaction between the modern self and electronic media has created a new myth for our age, one of the *last* great myths still standing after the analytical gaze of science has banished all the rest from the field of contemporary consciousness.

Make no mistake about it, the cult and culture of the media superstar, as the French philosopher Edgar Morin was one of the first to realize, *is* a modern religion, a religion in which we are all unwitting hierophants waiting to gobble up the latest sacraments in the form of tabloids. Tabloids that allow us to devour every little piece of the celebrity's mediatic corpus through the absorption and accumulation of information about them.

The crash of Princess Diana in 1997 was the climax of an epoch that began with the car crash of James Dean in 1955. This is the period during which the myth of the media superstar came into being, flourished, and began to die out. The exemplary patterns for the attainment of fame via the media were created during this period, and what is going on in our culture right now, and what is waiting to unfold in the future, is but a collection of reruns and repetitions of these exemplary, mythical patterns. No one, nowadays, can attain to fame—and particularly to the type of tragic fame about which I have written in this book—without in some way embodying the ghosts of Marilyn Monroe, Elvis Presley, James Dean, Jim Morrison, and others. They are the Platonic Forms of our media culture, and they are the means by which all 21st-century celebrities must be measured. This book, then, is an attempt to investigate the precise nature of this myth of the media celebrity through an examination of the lives of its most archetypal practitioners.

The names of such individuals need hardly be mentioned to conjure up the particular qualities of charisma and tragic fatalism that I am talking about. Indeed, the very connection between the life patterns exemplified by these individuals was suggested in a kitschy way by Gottfried Helnwein. In his 1984 painting *Boulevard of Broken Dreams*, he takes over the basic staging of Edward Hopper's noirish masterpiece *Nighthawks* and substitutes for its brooding personages James Dean, Elvis Presley, Humphrey Bogart, and Marilyn Monroe. The interesting thing about this painting, though, is how Helnwein transforms Hopper's diner into a visual pun on both a movie screen and a television set: the rectangular shape of its window, within which all four personae are carefully framed, reminds us of a theater screen, but the flow of light is moving in the opposite direction of a theater screen, which normally receives its light from an exterior source in the movie projector. The diner in Helnwein's painting—as in the case of a television set—is radiating its own interior light, which spills out across the sidewalk in a pale-blue wash like the glow inside a darkened living room with the television set on. Helnwein, in a subtle way, is suggesting that the very source of the shared misery of these four icons is to be found in the nature of their electrically generated avatars. These avatars captured and confined them to their own stereotypes from which, try as they might, they could never free themselves.

The stereotypes of electronic media, no matter how fascinating, are ultimately only two dimensional, for at the speed of light, everything collapses into two-dimensionality. Once imprisoned within their flat electric icons, the real James Dean, Humphrey Bogart, Marilyn Monroe, and Elvis Presley had no idea what to do with the rest of their three-dimensional personalities. Marilyn Monroe, for instance, was a literate woman who enjoyed reading Tolstoy and Dostoevsky, but the flatland nature of her ditzy blonde icon was not complex enough to allow room for this side of her personality to surface into public view. The whole tragedy of her life, therefore, lay in this tension between the anxiety generated by attempting to rid herself of her own clichés, while remaining true to her own complex personality.

Something similar happened to Elvis Presley, as well. At some point in his life he began reading books on Eastern mysticism and New Age spirituality, devouring them hungrily for days at a stretch. This behavior was strongly discouraged by his circle of paid "friends," as well as by his agent, Colonel Tom Parker, because such conduct was not thought to be "Elvisian." Surrendering to this peer pressure, Elvis dropped the books and held his own book-burning rally to purge his heretical thoughts; however, in doing so, he remained beholden to the prison of his own icon, for light-speed acceleration reduces complexity to mere stereotype.

And it does more than that. The fatal quality shared by these particular celebrities was an effect of accelerating their personae to light speed via the electronic media of their day. For the process of exposing the personality to electronic replication and duplication tends to have a disintegrative effect upon it by splitting it asunder into multiple egos—like the thousand-fold Malkoviches in *Being John Malkovich.* These egos can proliferate with such bewildering speed that the accelerated individual soon finds himself thrust into playing roles—and donning masks—that he had no idea would be required of him. These clones and doppelgangers are like golems, for they are nearly impossible to kill once awakened to the light of day. Their originators tend, more often than not, to become unwitting victims in a war of images and icons that often require them to sacrifice their lives.

The phenomenon of "celebrity" per se is nothing new, but the concept that this book sketches out, that of the tragic electronic media superstar, is a recent development within U.S. culture, going back only about as far as World War II. Although the 1950s can be regarded as the period of its classic formation, we do find forerunners in the 1920s and 1930s. Such celebrities as Rudolph Valentino (around whom the first early warning signs of cult hysteria, especially at his funeral in New York, which caused riots, began to gather) and Jean Harlow (who seems to have been reincarnated as Marilyn Monroe) can be regarded as precursors. But it was primarily during the aftermath of World War II that Western society—and America in particular—underwent an enormous structural transformation that was tantamount to the creation of a new society with emergent properties. American society before World War II simply was not the same society that emerged out of the ash heap of that war.

The metropolitan landscape of shopping malls, interstate highways, theme parks, and fast food restaurants that have been part of U.S. culture ever since, at that time, was entirely new. Although suburbs, drive-in movies, motels, and automobile culture generally predate this development, these things nonetheless attained to a kind of apotheosis at that time. Levittown in Long Island, New York, for instance, was built between 1947 and 1950 as the great archetype of the first mass-produced suburb for the middle classes. Cheap, small tract housing backed by the Federal Housing Authority (FHA) and the G.I. Bill, the Levittown houses were more or less clones of one another and were as rapidly produced as Big Macs.

In 1956, the Interstate Highway Act was passed, and this set the process in motion of creating the world's finest and most elaborately interwoven system of roads and highways, all of which was subsidized by the U.S. government (at the cost of cutting funds to public transportation systems, that is).[4] This system became crucial to the success and spread of fast food restaurants, as such restaurants were normally located (as they are to this day) at the entrance and exit ramps to freeways. Also located near such ramps to this day are indoor shopping malls, the prototype for which also was first built in the same year, 1956. This was the Southdale Shopping Mall in Edina, Minnesota, designed by Austrian architect Victor Gruen, who had originally conceived the idea for shopping malls while living in Los Angeles.[5] The basic design of the Southdale Mall, with its climate-controlled bilevel interior set down into an ocean of parking that surrounded all four of its bland, featureless sides is the prototype of the very same malls that U.S. consumers patronize into the 21st century.

If the automobile and the shopping mall decentered the city by creating the new structure of the metropolis with multiple centers, then it was the explosion in electronic technology at this time that created the similarly diffuse human personality with multiple egos, precisely the type of being who would be typified by modern celebrity.[6] The saturation of U.S. society by the television, the computer, radar, and satellite technology laid the foundations for the creation of a paranoid society. The Cold War brought into being a new world of "open skies" in which Russian satellites battled with American U2 spy planes for access to information. With electronic eyes watching over everyone, and with the Central Intelligence Agency (CIA) listening in on everybody with their new world of sound recorders, no longer did a place on the globe exist where "they" were not present. This hypersaturation of the human nervous system with electronic signals and pulse fields became visible in popular culture with a new wave of paranoid characters like James Bond and paranoid science fiction films like *Invasion of the Body Snatchers* and *The Thing from Another World.* These films were attempting to convey the idea that no one could now be trusted to *be* who they said they *were*. This new ontological uncertainty regarding the status of the simulacrum versus the real became a permanent feature of U.S. society, spawning such celebrity urban legends as the replacement of Paul McCartney or Howard Hughes with doubles.

These developments in electronic technology, furthermore, began to make possible the advent of new kinds of celebrities, for the domestication of television opened a pathway for the rise of Elvis Presley—the first televised rock star—and John F. Kennedy—the first televised president, while the geosynchronous satellite technology of Howard Hughes in the 1960s began to cover the earth with an electromagnetic dome of real-time broadcasts of events.

But above all, it is the blandness of a synchronized society in which everybody thinks alike and acts alike and in which every city looks alike that was manufactured and exported to the rest of the world at this time. It was out of this bland synchronization, moreover, that the multimedia celebrity of the 1950s arose as an anomalous irruption, tantamount to a discontinuity, in the homogenized sameness of this utopia. Just as Andy Warhol's discovery of the cult of the celebrity with his serialized Liz Taylors and Marilyn Monroes represents a sudden discontinuity that opened up a crevasse into the world of his blandly repeated soup cans, so too, did the birth of the charismatic electric celebrity come about in the 1950s at just the point at which American homogenization was beginning to close the world down around us, sealing off its edges with an air-tight dome of hyperreality.

Thus, Marlon Brando, James Dean, Marilyn Monroe, and company emerged as larger-than-life figures projected on the screens of the 4,000 drive-in movie theaters then in operation. Such an image of a charismatic human being projected against the stars of the night sky could not have failed to make an impression upon the masses who went to see their movies when the drive-in was at the height of its popularity. And in the cool, cavernous grottoes of the movie theaters, such sharply defined and idiosyncratic personalities must have stood out with a reassuringly human relief against the backdrop of the cookie-cutter suburbs.

Amid the colossal gigantism and bureaucratic impersonality of the "edge node" cities then coming into being, these iconic humans would have loomed as larger-than-life billboards advertising the charisma and power of the human personality that had been buried beneath all the asphalt, steel, and glass of the glittering new megalopolitan postwar metropolises.

The real significance of the emergence at this time of the megacelebrity is that the celebrity is a human life that has been scaled up to properly gigantic magnitudes to make the human presence visible amid all this machinery. The megacelebrity is so huge because the industrial landscapes of our cities demand that he be large enough to stand up to them on behalf of the rest of us mortals. The megacelebrity is therefore the human equivalent of an industrial engineering project, large enough to be discernible amid the towers and bridges of a civilization of truly colossal proportions. Such an age requires larger-than-life human beings to reassure ourselves that we are still here, and that the scale of our civilization, by means of which we have inadvertently dwarfed ourselves to the size of ants, cannot rob us of the potentiality for effecting and realizing our lives. In an age of impersonal institutions, it is important that a lone individual can be thought of as being powerful enough to stand up to the huge bureaucracies that increasingly have come to dominate our lives.

In his book *The Image*, Daniel Boorstin points out that the very notion of "celebrity" is a rather recent development in U.S. culture, which he traces back to about the middle of the 19th century with the rise of what he calls the Graphic Revolution, in which the new media of the press—telegraph, Associated Press, newspapers, magazines, and so on—simply could manufacture ersatz fame whenever it needed a good story. Boorstin says that the idea of the celebrity in this sense is different from the older idea of the hero, the justly famous man who slowly came to fame over the years while generally avoiding the public spotlight: men like Napoleon, Lincoln, Washington, Robert E. Lee, and so on. The idea of the celebrity as the individual who is famous for being famous came along and began to displace this older idea of the hero in which fame was identical with greatness. The disjunction between fame and greatness, Boorstin says, took place when the new media of the Graphic Revolution began to manufacture heroes by means of press agents whose job it was to keep their clients constantly in the news.

The main characteristic of the celebrity in contrast to the hero, Boorstin says, is that the hero becomes more famous with the passage of time, while it is precisely the passage of time that destroys the celebrity. Nothing is forgotten so quickly as yesterday's celebrities. Ask your parents who the celebrities of their time were and you are likely to hear some obscure names. Indeed, celebrities are often forgotten even in their own lifetimes. Hence the existence of columns such as "Where Are They Now?"[7] Boorstin does have a point here. If I dared mention the celebrities from my own youth—Debbie Gibson, for instance, or Tiffany, or Terence Trent Darby, or Max Headroom to a 20-year-old, I would almost certainly draw a blank stare, and one can easily imagine that such a fate lies in store for Britney Spears, Paris Hilton, and Anna Nicole Smith. Try mentioning *them* to your children in 20 years.

Hence, though it is difficult to argue with many of Boorstin's assertions, the existence of this book is predicated on a crucial type of celebrity that Boorstin overlooks, and, that I have chosen, somewhat arbitrarily, to designate the "electronic media superstar"—namely, that species of celebrity that does *not* become less famous with the passage of time, but rather *more* so. John F. Kennedy, Jim Morrison, Ronald Reagan, and John Lennon: such figures exist in an almost timeless realm while the news of the day and the newer celebrities, the ersatz ones, come and go. But these individuals stand above all the others. Like demigods. Or saints.

This book examines why our society is haunted by such individuals and will not let go of them. Indeed, with each passing year, they take on more and more the aura of the legendary and the fabulous. In fact, it is my contention that the reason why we cannot forget these particular celebrities is that they are slowly being transformed into a modern electronic equivalent of saints.

It is worth pausing here for a moment, then, to glance back at the significance of the cult of the saints as it emerged in the fourth century B.C.E., at about the time of Augustine. The cult was a largely popular attempt on the part of the rustic masses—though not exclusively so—to replace the magical healing powers and supernatural abilities of the vanishing pagan gods with a new collection of invisible patrons who could be worshipped with the same type of piety as Christ or Mary. Thus, the old hilltop shrines and classical temples of the Greeks and Romans gave way to the emergence of two types of church: the classic basilica, and a special type of building called martyria. These martyria were at first erected in cemeteries outside Roman cities over the tomb of this or that saint. These saints could then become invisible companions who took the place of the earlier genius or guardian angel, their names identified with human individuals by bestowing them on the newborn. In this way, they became lifelong protecting spirits, watching over the living and acting as divine intercessors on their behalf. The relics of these invisible companions—pieces of their skeletons or tiny splinters from the cross kept in gold vials—were thought to be particular concentrations of divine power. It was normally a major civic event, celebrated with proper festivals, for the relics of a saint—such as those of Zecharia that were translated to the city of Constantinople—to arrive at a certain place.[8] These relics were guarded jealously by such cities and their saints would become their patrons.

The saints were models of Christian suffering and perseverance in the face of great opposition from the Roman Empire. Their deaths were usually bizarre and bloody, and indeed, it is almost the only thing about them that our present society retains. Classic works of art portrayed the beheadings of virginal Saint Agnes or pious Januarius; the pale, frozen body of Saint Eulalia, tortured to death on a Roman scaffold, but subsequently dusted with a light covering of preservative snow; the stoning of Saint Stephen, the first of the martyrs; or the shooting of Saint Anthony with an impossibly complex latticework of crossed arrows. Indeed, through Medieval and Renaissance iconography, the lives of these saints have come down to us with all their broken bones and bleeding limbs, preserved particularly in the artwork of the cultures of Spain and Italy.

But in the 21st century, it is Los Angeles—born as a tiny Mexican village around 1780 within the once-great zone of the Spanish empire of the southwest—where the new electronic cult of the multimedia celebrity finds its Vatican City. Indeed, the same dichotomy that characterized the unfolding of European civilization—with its word-based Protestant north versus its image-based Catholic south—seems to have been replicated in the New World, with the image-dominant Mexican-American Southwest set against the book-dominated Northwest Pacific Coast, Front Range, and Midwestern regions. In these two cultures, movies and Hispanic mural art tilt their lances against the printed page of cities like Seattle, San Francisco, Denver, and Minneapolis, which are consistently ranked as among the most literate in America. It is, consequently, in the center of iconic Los Angeles that the cult of the electronic saint is flourishing, although it must be said that the cult has spread across the entire North American continent.

Indeed, no one better typifies the nature of the cult of the electronic saint than Elvis Presley—as the famously kitschy Velvet Elvises of 1970s Mexican Tijuana suggest (Tijuana in the 1970s has been called the "Florence" of velvet painting)—for Elvis has been designated by some as the first Protestant saint. This is scarcely an exaggeration, for Elvis bears nearly all the trademarks of a Catholic saint: his mansion Graceland is a sort of modern equivalent to the martyria of the saints, which, we recall, were buildings resembling churches that had been erected over the tomb of a particular saint. When he died on August 16, 1977, Elvis was at first buried in Forest Hills Cemetery in midtown Memphis, but a few months later, his father Vernon had the coffin dug up and reburied at Graceland, thus making it function exactly like a Christian martyrium complete with relics and walking tours. Those who deny that Elvis ever died, meanwhile, such as the proprietor of the Elvis Alive Museum, confer on him the special power to defeat death that one would associate with a saint, or even better, with Christ himself.

In the early days of Christianity in the fourth century B.C.E., when the cult of the saints was first crystallizing, it was a common practice for people to name their children after particular saints. As Peter Brown remarks, "In Syria, for instance, we can follow the name Sergius, spreading through the towns and villages along routes that radiate from the baptisteries that flanked the shrines of the saint."[9] Likewise, since Elvis's death in 1977, there have been 76 children in Queensland, Australia, alone who have been named after the King. This is true not only of Elvis, but also of several of the other celebrities studied in this book. A quick search on Google will reveal the numerous people who have been named after James Dean, some of them relatively well-known musicians like James Dean Bradfield and James Dean Hicks. Many children have been named "Diana," in deliberate invocation of the Princess of Wales.

The relics of these latter-day electronic saints, when they are not highly sought after and bought by collectors at auctions—such as the lucky coin that Kennedy rubbed to get him through the Cuban Missile Crisis, or James Dean's iconic red jacket—are displayed proudly at museums, such as the 1961 Lincoln Continental in which Kennedy was assassinated, which is on display at the Henry Ford Museum in Dearborn, Michigan; or Howard Hughes's gigantic H-4 Hercules cargo plane, which is displayed at the Evergreen Aviation Museum in McMinnville, Oregon. Weird urban legends of magical powers associated with some of these objects have turned up, as well, such as the stories associated with James Dean's postcrash automobile, the Porsche Spyder 550, which is supposed to have caused a number of other deaths and human injuries before finally disappearing entirely as of 1959.

Furthermore, whereas the Catholic saints became saints—at least in the early days of Christianity—as a result of suffering bizarre and violent deaths at the hands of persecution by the Romans, we may say that in the present case, these new saints of electronic culture are becoming saints precisely because of enduring the *passios* of their descent into electronic culture. They are the ones who have undertaken the dangerous experiments of descending into the electric plasma pool and allowing themselves to be cloned, replicated, duplicated, and shot around the planet at light speed.

Their deaths, moreover, have largely been the result, one way or another, of the image dynamics of this new electro-iconic culture. The shootings of John F. Kennedy, John Lennon, Andy Warhol, Ronald Reagan, and Gianni Versace were direct results of the sorts of psychological fallout that is left behind in the wake of the acceleration of their personae to light speed, for their electronically generated doppelgangers are like viruses capable of infecting and destabilizing disoriented minds. Mark David Chapman did not set out to kill the real John Lennon, but rather to unleash the same kind of iconoclastic war against his image as the Taliban did when they destroyed the Buddhist sculptures at Bamyan.

In the case of the overdoses—Jim Morrison, Elvis Presley, and Marilyn Monroe—the reader of the subsequent chapters will take special care to note how the years of these people's lives preceding these "accidental" overdoses were filled with attempts to "kill" their own media-generated personae. Marilyn Monroe, at the time of her death, was still struggling—and losing the battle—against the celluloid image of herself that she had generated and that prevented her from stepping very far outside the limitations of her own stereotypes. Jim Morrison, at the time of his death, had only recently arrived in Paris as a desperate attempt to flee from his rock star persona, which he wanted to be rid of. In overdosing on heroin, it is almost as though he had intentionally tried to "drown" his own image. Elvis Presley, likewise, had fought for many years a battle with his own image, a battle he ultimately lost.

What you are about to read in the chapters which follow, then, is a series of "hagiographical" studies—a sort of *vita celebratori*, as it were—of the sufferings of the martyrs of electronic culture who lost their lives in battle against their own electrically generated images. These are individuals who had no idea that the price of their rise to global fame would involve a struggle against images of themselves brought weirdly to life by the power of electronic mirrors. Myths and tales throughout history are filled with dire prognostications of what happens when one encounters one's own doppelganger or else comes up against the power of the strange and otherworldly technology of mirrors. What follows here is a series of portrait studies of 14 individuals who found themselves in precisely such an ancient situation, caught unawares.

But before we begin, we must first ask one more question: why *these* 14? Are there *only* 14 such examples of tragic celebrities?

And the answer, of course, is no. I have chosen these 14 celebrities to study because it seems to me that they best exemplify the myth of the tragic celebrity. I could have added others, Marlon Brando or Elizabeth Taylor, for instance. But as I have confined myself only to discussing dead celebrities, this would eliminate the latter as a possible choice. And in the case of Brando, it is really only the *young* Brando who fits the pattern of the mythical celebrity who opens up new pathways for others to follow. Brando was indeed the prototype, as Camille Paglia remarks, for at least half the male actors currently working in Hollywood, from Billy Zane to Hayden Christensen. Nothing, however, is tragic about Brando's death, and by the time it had occurred, he already had become a ghost of himself, anyway. If Brando had been killed after doing *The Wild One*, then we would have had *two* James Dean figures on our hands, and a chapter on him would have been mandatory for this book.

Which leads me to my main criterion for selecting these particular celebrities: all of them—or nearly all—died in tragic ways, usually at young (or at least premature) ages. Ronald Reagan, Howard Hughes, and Walt Disney are exceptions to this pattern, but in their cases, the final personae they projected of grizzled old men was essential to the retinal image we now have of them, for there is something of the archetype of the old wizard that hangs about both Disney and Hughes—even as young men—and their attainment of a respectable age actually added luster to this image of the priest of the machine they both projected. In Reagan's case, we only remember him as an old man, and even when watching one of his early Hollywood movies, we still see him as an old man, when his character was already fully formed (unlike, say, Brando, whom we always see in our mind's eye as the young rebel of *The Wild One* or as Stanley Kowalski, even in his later roles).

So, these 14 celebrities embody a tragic dimension in their lives. But, of course, plenty of celebrities have come to tragic ends, and the list of such demises is quite long: Brandon Lee, Anna Nicole Smith, John Belushi, Jimi Hendrix, Natalie Wood, and so on. So it is not just a tragic ending that defines the pattern exemplified by these 14. It is also the fact that this particular group embodied something uncanny, something almost otherworldly, for their auras were absolutely unique and utterly irreplaceable. Hundreds have tried, for example, to imitate the aura of Marilyn Monroe, and not one of them has succeeded in capturing her strange mixture of beauty, innocence, naïveté, and doom. Elvis's magnetism was so fascinating that it has spawned a virtual industry of Elvis impersonators, caricatures all, of the unique mix of guilelessness, charm, and charisma this man possessed. And James Dean's on-screen personae has been replicated a thousand times with little or no success: as we watch him onscreen in *East of Eden*, he conveys a bizarre scattering of contradictory emotions, as though he were uncertain of, and conflicted about, his own impulses.

And finally, the particular celebrities I have chosen are the most persistently imitated celebrities in the history of electric culture. Just as

Plato insists that we move from the particular imitations to the ultimate forms that inspired those imitations, so too have I traced these celebrity patterns back to those individuals whom I believe to be the source for all later celebrity-hood. These, then, are the Platonic Forms, the mythic protagonists, in other words, of celebrity culture. Just as in the arts—in which, for example, no one can aspire to *be* a great painter without the shadow of Picasso hovering somewhere in the back of his mind; or a philosopher without Immanuel Kant or Heidegger lurking at the periphery of consciousness—so too, no male actor can aspire to Hollywood without being thought of by executives as cut from either one of the two molds established by Marlon Brando or James Dean. Thus, if Marilyn Monroe had never existed, then neither would Anna Nicole Smith; if Madonna had not existed, then neither would Britney Spears; and if the rich American heiress Jacqueline Kennedy Onassis had not existed, then neither would Paris Hilton.

So, although I could have discussed more than 14 case studies, 14 will be sufficient to establish in the reader's mind the basic contours of the myth.

1

Birth and Rise (The 1930s)

Howard Hughes and Walt Disney

INTRODUCTION

We preface our journey with a detour through the strange architectural landscapes invented by Walt Disney and Howard Hughes, the Master Builders, as it were, of the epoch we will be studying in this book. Howard Hughes created the technoscapes of our heavens as we know them in the 21st century, for his path-breaking flights had the effect of turning our cities upside down, of lifting them from the ground and placing them into the sky, where they have flourished ever since as floating fortresses among the clouds. His geosynchronous satellites, moreover, transformed the earth into a gigantic theater in which, as McLuhan put it, "there are no spectators, only actors," for satellite technology brought about the death of the spectator by creating a universal Lebensraum in which absolutely anyone who stepped in front of a video camera could become famous. In an age in which anyone can become famous for no special reason at all, no longer is there any such thing as an "audience," for the audience has now become part of the play.

Walt Disney, meanwhile, sculpted a new kind of city out of blocks of historic time, creating the notion of the city as a phantasmal dreamworld at the very moment that electronic technology was rendering history obsolete. For with our descent into "real time" and the vanishing of the past, cities lost the anchors that kept them from floating away into an *Italo Calvinesque* fantasia of dreamlike spires and chimerical forms; from henceforth—at least in America—they would become permanent World's Fairs perpetually exhibiting superfluous technologies whose function is actually closer to the realm of myth, dream, and metaphor than to the needs and exigencies of real living spaces. Las Vegas, for example, becomes a fantasia of the city-as-Golden-Goose, perpetually laying its eggs for those clever enough to find the Goose's lair, while a sprawling monster such as Phoenix becomes the fantasia of the megalopolis without people, an autopoietic machine that builds machines to make other machines like a nanotechnology experiment gone awry.

Although neither of these men fits exactly into the pattern of the violent dying and reviving celebrity demigod that forms the central thematic of this book, both are forerunners of the development that begins in the Cold War, for taken together they can be seen as having restructured the surface of the earth to prepare it for the coming of the celebrity melodrama to be enacted on its stage.

Both men were persistent idealists who fought against huge impersonal corporate powers to realize their dreams, and the ironic result for both was to create exactly the kinds of corporate megamachines they had spent much of their lives fighting against. Thus, while they represented the voice of the lone individual who could, through persistence, battle against bureaucratic powers and win, they ultimately were swallowed up into the machinery of the very corporations that had sprung, myth-like, from out of their own minds.

Both men, finally, were products of the west coast and spent their most creative years in Los Angeles, with Hughes in his later years relocating to another theme park city, Las Vegas. It was in the milieu of 1930s Los Angeles—the Los Angeles of Raymond Chandler and James M. Cain—that both men became famous, the one for his Mickey Mouse cartoons and the other for his movies and airplane flights. Los Angeles in the 1930s thus reveals itself as the archetypal Vatican City of the celebrity demigod, its primary breeding ground and mythical cavern and manger.

And now, without further ado, here they are . . . Walt Disney and Howard Hughes.

1

Howard Hughes, the World's First Serial Crash Artist

ASCENTS SUBLIME

Howard Hughes was the prototype for a new kind of human being: nomadic, uprooted, cityless, and wandering. Hughes prefigured the coming inhabitant of our global aeropolis, the transurban world of "no-place" that has come to displace the traditional container of the geographically bounded cities that have, for the most part, composed the textile of human history. This new world of "no-place," however, is history-less, for in dislodging the human being from the city that has formed his environment for millennia, the airplane has carried him up into the substratosphere beyond the reach of the temporal metabolisms of civic life, where he has entered a quiet but frenetic world of shopping mall airports, Styrofoam meals, and plastic coffee cups in which everything, everywhere is denuded of local identity and cultural authenticity. Furthermore, the substratosphere into which the human being has been relocated—for at any given time at least 100,000 people are up in the air—traditionally has been regarded as the realm of the gods and the home of the winged eternal soul exempt from the changing vicissitudes of corruption and generation that take place on the surface of the earth below. To live in the world of the skies, then, is to exist in a landscape carved out by eternity, beyond the reach of historical rhythms of change, culture, and ethnic identity.

In the 1930s and 1940s, Howard Hughes was the first man who could legitimately call this heavenly frontier "home," and he was therefore its single and (almost) sole pioneer occupant. Whenever Hughes wanted to go anywhere, he flew, and in those days, he flew everywhere, all the time, every day. The airplane was for him what our automobiles have become for us: a miniature environment that we carry with us on our backs like a tortoiseshell. Hughes, in becoming the world's first global citizen, also became a kind of aviation equivalent of the Flying Dutchman, who was cursed to wander the seas and never put in at any port for long.

In Steven Spielberg's film *The Terminal*, based on a real-life story, a man spends his days living inside an airport as the result of a loss of citizenship from his mother country. Such a story is merely a startling metaphor for the way we actually live our lives today, for as the French philosopher Paul Virilio has remarked, the airport has become the new city.[1] We no longer live in cities, for the incessant screeching of airplanes across the sky above us has effectively sealed us off *inside* a gigantic airport in which the dome of the sky is composed of the flight paths interwoven by air craft of all kinds and shapes.

The overall architecture of air travel as it exists today, furthermore, would not even be remotely what it is without the pioneering flights of Howard Hughes, for he was the mythic prototype of the haggard and gangly inhabitant of the transurban "no-place," which has encompassed the planet today. And since it is well known that bad things happen to pioneers, we may suspect that the loneliness and isolation of being the only occupant (relatively speaking) of this substratospheric "no-place" may have been the very thing that drove Howard Hughes to become the world's first case of pressurized cabin fever.

One day, in the early 1930s, Hughes gathered his staff in a field in Glendale, California, and told them: "I want you to build me the fastest airplane in the world."[2] The result of this directive was the creation of a sleek, burnished aircraft that resembled something out of a science fiction film and that was nicknamed the Silver Bullet. The plane officially was known as the H-1 racer, and it was Hughes's first aviation masterpiece. Its mirror-smooth gloss was partially the result of a new technique of eliminating friction and wind resistance by setting the rivets flush with the surface of the plane's aluminum skin. The cockpit was small, scarcely large enough for a single pilot, and the plane was equipped with a powerful motor. It was also the first plane in aviation history to feature retractable landing gear (as though Hughes had intuitively sensed the truth of McLuhan's point that the airplane renders the wheel obsolete).

On September 13, 1935, Hughes set a world record for the fastest flight over land: 352 miles per hour (mph), which beat the earlier record of 314 mph. Hughes ran out of gas going back and forth while the authorities clocked him on the ground below, and he crashed the plane into a beet field. He limped away mostly uninjured, insisting that the plane would go even faster.

It would also go higher. On subsequent flights, Hughes took the plane up into the substratosphere at 15,000 feet, where he realized that his instruments were giving him inaccurate readings, for they had been calibrated at sea level and recorded him as traveling 15 miles per hour slower than he actually was. Hence, the pioneer's dilemma: old tools will not work in new worlds and have to be reinvented to suit the new environment. In outer space, for instance, every man becomes an individualist, for the pressurized cabin of the airplane—designed to create a small world for a small group—becomes the individual space suit, in which each man carries his own ecosystem along with him. In the frontier of the Old West, likewise, the cowboy had to become an all-around generalist, completely self-sufficient in every respect, with each fireside camp becoming a sort of miniature town, for he could not rely on the city as a uterine environment to meet his needs. Like the astronaut and the cowboy, Howard Hughes, too, was coming to realize that he was in a new environment that would call forth new strategies for survival:

> "I realized," he said later, "that by climbing up to the substratosphere, and taking advantage of the westerly wind created by the motion of the earth, I could reduce the time of crossing the continent." It followed that airplanes traveling at high altitudes could fly faster and farther on less fuel, and therefore at less cost, than other planes.[3]

Hughes, then, was the pioneer of high-altitude flying, for his experiments with the H-1 racer would later lead to the creation of the first pressurized cabins for his TWA airplane the Constellation. The pressurized cabin is a miniature environment unto itself, enabling passengers to fly comfortably at 20,000 feet, an altitude above the weather and above most turbulence, for at such altitudes, one otherwise would require oxygen masks, and the temperatures would drop below zero.

Ever higher, ever faster. It is as though Hughes were palpating here the very curvature of the spaces around the earth, feeling out its contours to determine the limits of the heavenly ceiling. He is a wayfarer in the torqued cosmos set up by Einstein, in which light travels not in straight lines but along geodesic paths bent and curved by massive objects like planets and stars.

If the H-1 flight in 1935 was his fastest, his 1938 flight around the world in a Lockheed Model 14 twin-engine transport was his longest. Leaving from New York and traveling in the direction of the earth's rotation on its axis, counterclockwise, he flew over the Atlantic to Paris, and then went onward from Paris to Moscow, Siberia, Fairbanks, Minneapolis, and ultimately back to New York. With this flight, Hughes set the new world record for circumnavigating the globe via airplane. The earlier record had been set by Wiley Post, who had been the first to fly solo around the world in eight days in 1931. But Hughes accomplished the same feat in three days, 19 hours and 17 minutes.

His flight was tantamount to an embracing of the earth with artificially elongated arms, extended by mechanical wings. Such an embrace, however, was not without purpose, but was specifically intended to overpower and intimidate the planet.

Hughes's circumnavigation, moreover, was the modern technological equivalent of a motif out of ancient mythology in which a birdman or a god swoops down to pick up some hapless female and makes off with her. In Hindu mythology, the giant bird Garuda occasionally rapes a Nagini, one of the female serpents of the race of the nagas; in Greek myth, Cupid carries Psyche off to his magical castle (the earlier equivalent of this image had been Zeus in the form of an eagle making off with the cupbearer Ganymede); in comic book mythology, Superman is forever dropping down out of the skies to extricate Lois Lane from one or another of her predicaments. With his flight around the world, then, Howard Hughes, too, swoops down and picks up the earth, as it were, carrying it off to his kingdom like one of the Hollywood starlets he was forever romancing and then abandoning.

Indeed, one cannot help but see an analogy to Hughes's womanizing during the period of these heroic flights in which, following the collapse of his relationships with Billie Dove (note that the dove was sacred to Aphrodite, goddess of love) and Katharine Hepburn, he dated a series of women who became ever younger, more naïve and hence, more susceptible to his charms: Ginger Rogers, Bette Davis, Olivia de Havilland, Joan Fontaine, Gloria Vanderbilt, Faith Domergue, Ava Gardner, and so on. He went from one woman to the next in a long, long line of successive conquests.

Hughes regarded these women with all the detachment and objectivity of the lepidopterist carefully placing pins into his butterflies. Indeed, he was collecting these women in an attempt to shrink them down to the size of dolls to build up a collection of tiny miniature women, like the Melusine in Goethe's short story. As he told 15-year-old Faith Domergue, whom he gave the *real* Bluebeard treatment: "Remember, you belong to me now, so don't even look at another man."[4]

His attempt to shrink these women down was a microcosmic analogue of his effort to shrink down the earth through his various aviation feats to cast his shadow over it, just as he towered over Faith Domergue. Hughes, it seems, was at war with the goddess, for many of his actions can be seen as attempts to overcome the Great Mother, his own mother, who had smothered him with her suffocating presence during the early years of his life until her death when Hughes was 14. He was her only child, and she never let him out of her sight, reacting obsessively whenever he showed the slightest signs of illness. Indeed, she infected him with the bacteriophobia with which he would later become obsessed.

Thus, Hughes's symmetrical attempts to shrink women down to dolls on the one hand and the earth down to a plaything on the other were part of an effort to free himself, once and for all, from the suffocating all-inclusive body of his mother, with whom he seems to have identified the cosmos.

As I have said, Hughes carried around in his psyche an archaic image of the heavens as female. Hence, in Martin Scorsese's film *The Aviator*, Hughes remarks to his meteorologist on the set of *Hell's Angels* that he wants clouds as white as mother's milk so that the airplanes will be visible against a contrasting background on film. (Note that Jean Harlow, the film's leading lady, had bleached her hair to be nearly the same color as the clouds.) Scorsese, furthermore, shows Hughes in scene after scene drinking milk as his preferred beverage, as though he were imbibing it from the sky goddess herself (in ancient Egypt, the cow goddess Hathor was identified with the sky). And in the scene in which Hughes appears before the censors who have accused him of shooting too much of Jane Russell's breasts for *The Outlaw*, it is significant that Hughes appoints, of all people, his meteorologist to defend him by mathematically demonstrating the width of the cleavage shots of famous movie actresses using a pair of calipers.

Thus, for Hughes—according to our present idea of him—the sky was female, and therefore something to be conquered, for he viewed all women as potential conquests. But the earth, too, as we have seen, was female in his mind, and Hughes's bacteriophobia, which he acquired from his mother, was tantamount to a war on Gaia's offspring. According to scientist Lynn Margulis, bacteria are the immune system of Gaia and as such, they are her offspring, just like the various Titans and Giants she produced in Greek myth as extensions of her rage against Zeus, the sky god whose sacred bird was the eagle.

Hughes's bacteriophobia, then, was part of an overall desire to be free of earthly entanglements. It is the same anxiety that drove his fear of marriage as being possessed by a single woman, for after his first brief marriage, he did not marry again until very late in life. He was just as afraid of being possessed and suffocated by a woman as he was of being poisoned by bacteria, for he insisted that his second wife, Jean Peters, live in a residence separate from his own and confined his communications to her largely to the telephone, as though afraid her presence might somehow contaminate him.

Thus, Hughes's mighty aviation deeds of the 1930s and 1940s are a phallic thrust into the wide blue yonder of Mother Sky from out of which will come into being the embryonic Space Age. Hughes paved a path in the air for the American journey to the moon (his own corporation, Hughes Air, would construct the Surveyor spacecraft that first landed a manned mission on the moon in 1969), a deed of the great eagle of Zeus itself.

As the French theoretician Paul Virilio has written, the invention of every new technology of transport brings into being along with it a particular type of accident. With the invention of the train, for instance, the derailment is simultaneously invented; with the invention of the ship comes the shipwreck; with the automobile comes the car crash; and with the airplane comes the plane crash. It is not possible to have the one without the other, as the faithful of the religion of progress would have us believe, for a direct relationship exists between speed and accidents. The faster we go, the greater and the harder we crash. Hence, the breakneck speed of technological production throughout the course of the 20th century—the century in which more manmade catastrophes have occurred than at any other time in history—would seem to be a preparation for the coming of some kind of a technological catastrophe, a catastrophe that, Virilio insists, will, for the first time in history, occur on a planetary scale.

The Greek myth of the invention of flight by Daedalus seems to prefigure Virilio's point of view, for in it, Daedalus makes wings for himself and his son to fly out of the labyrinth from Crete and across the waters to the mainland. While Daedalus's successful flight confirms the efficacy of his invention, the downward arcing parabola of Icarus's flight is a crash that kills him and simultaneously makes visible the shadow side of this new technology. The myth seems to recognize that the invention of flight brings the plane crash, like a dark twin, into being along with it, and, it should be remarked, not as a mere possibility, but rather as a dead certainty, because the crash itself is inextricably entwined with the very nature of the technology.

As Howard Hughes's life was a miniature version of the technological unfolding of Western civilization—for his descent into the machine is a perfect encapsulation of the West's descent into its machines, and thus, his ultimate ruin through stasis, madness, and immobility can also foreshadow the coming end of technological civilization.

Thus, the crash of his reconnaissance spyplane, the XF-11, was far from being his only plane crash, but rather the last and most dramatic of a series of great crashes. Like James Dean, Hughes was addicted to speed, and the possibility of crashing that it generated was merely a stimulus to the thrill of physical acceleration. Hughes was involved in *five* separate plane crashes, three of which nearly killed him, as well as a string of automobile accidents. On one occasion, he even killed a man in a hit-and-run episode. He had crashed his first plane on the set of *Hell's Angels*, which resulted in a crack in his skull and a coma. The rugged landing of his H-1, by comparison, was a light crash and so was the one that followed, but the crash of his Sikorsky S-43 into Lake Mead in Nevada on May 17, 1943, very nearly killed him. (Two other men who were onboard with him died.) Thus, the crash of the XF-11 on July 7, 1946, was the fifth, and last, of a long string of "accidents" generated by his desire for ever faster forms of physical acceleration and speed.

The XF-11 had been commissioned by the military as a reconnaissance spyplane, and it was a forerunner of the later U2 spyplanes that created the Open Skies Policy of the Cold War. In peeling off the rooftops, as it were, of the world, the spyplane stepped up the intensity of an overall background noise of paranoia that has been characteristic of U.S. society ever since. (In the days of the ancients, men believed that their actions were watched over by gods who looked down on them from the skies above; thus, once again, we have used technology to recreate the scenarios of ancient myth.) Although Hughes had contracted for a whole series of such planes, he built only two, for the plane ultimately was rejected by the military on account of structural and design flaws.

Indeed, this was Hughes's Icarus crash, for he was warned by the military not to fly for longer than 45 minutes and not to retract his landing gear and not to carry more than 600 gallons of fuel in his tank. He ignored *all* these warnings and, hence, 75 minutes into the flight, the right rear propeller suddenly went into reverse, creating a drag that pulled the plane's wing down and sent him crashing into a Beverly Hills suburb. Here is how Barlett and Steele describe it:

> With a deafening noise, the right engine and landing gear crashed into the second floor of the house, at 803 North Linden Drive. The impact sent the plane yawing to the right, with the right wing slicing into the house and garage next door, at 805 North Linden. As the plane turned sharply right it hurled sideways through the air, shearing off a utility pole, then bounced and skidded through an alley before finally coming to rest in a heap between two houses at 808 and 810 North Whittier Drive. A fire broke out, engulfing the wreckage and one of the houses.[5]

Improbably, no one was killed. Hughes, though, was a mess: he suffered fractured ribs and bones, third-degree burns, cuts, bruises and abrasions, and a collapsed lung, and his heart was pushed to the opposite side of his body.

But, like the phoenix bird, Hughes emerged from the ashes to rebuild his life, although it would never be the same again, for the crash created a sucking vortex that went on pulling him down into the abysses of madness and drug addiction for the rest of his life. As the direct result of this crash, his doctors put him on morphine, and then later substituted it with codeine, to which he would forever remain addicted.

The rhythm of Hughes's life as an aviator, then, was precisely that of the rise and fall of the old Near Eastern dying and reviving gods. It is the phallic rhythm of the vanishing male, and of the great vertiginous towers of Babel that mark the rising and falling contours of the evolution of civilization.

A year later, in 1947, there was one last great mythical flight, that of the Hercules, the so-called flying boat. In the early 1940s, Hughes had contracted with the military to produce two kinds of planes that might be used during the war: the XF-11 and a fleet of flying boats that were designed to carry troops, tanks, machines, and war materiel to soldiers, because many of the ships carrying supplies were being sunk by German submarines. But Hughes produced only two prototypes for the XF-11, and since the astronomical costs involved in the construction of the flying boats were prohibitive, ultimately only a single HK-1 was constructed.

Hughes called it the Hercules (popularly known as the "Spruce Goose"), thus indirectly invoking the myth of Hercules holding the sky on his shoulders while Atlas fetches the apples of the Hesperides for him. It was the largest plane ever built, and into the 21st century, it remains the largest. At five stories tall, it had four engines mounted on each wing, and its wingspan was the length of a football field. Indeed, it was so large that nobody ever believed it would fly. But Hughes, under investigation by the Senate for wasting taxpayers' money on planes that were not finished until the war was over, did indeed manage to get this behemoth up into the air like a flying elephant out of Hindu mythology. It rose up 70 feet above the water off the shore of Long Beach for just under a minute. This was the shortest of all Hughes's great flights, but it astonished everyone, immediately terminating the Senate's investigations.

The Hercules was not only a flying boat; it was the aviation equivalent of the mythical great ark out of ancient flood stories, in this case, a specialized ark that would gather up all the machines, weapons, and materiel to be used in the apocalyptic War of the World, the first war to involve the entire human species in an attempt at racial suicide. Its failure to be mass produced, therefore, is not an accident, for it is an undertaking of such mythic scale that it is incapable of desecration by the mere banality of industrialization. It is a mythic spectacle designed for a unique apocalyptic event, and thus it defies the assembly line, for its value belongs ultimately to the realm of ideas, not to the history of aviation as such. It is U.S. civilization's equivalent of a great ark for surviving a world catastrophe, a sky ark for an age of machines, and its preservation in a museum in Oregon is as natural and inevitable as the relics of the saints.

Conceived in 1942, the Hercules was a vestigial holdover from the great age of gigantism in architecture and engineering of the 1930s, the same age that built the Empire State Building, Hoover Dam, the Golden Gate Bridge, the Los Angeles aqueduct, and saw the transformation of New York City under the direction of Robert Moses into an autopolis girded and surrounded by a latticework of bridges and expressways. By the 1940s, this gigantism had faded, and other than Hughes's great winged behemoth, only the atomic bomb would be suitable for rivaling the Hercules as the world's largest and greatest work of scientific monumentality.

This monument, however, was the swan song of Hughes's great aviation achievements, for after 1947, his flying days were mostly over (precluded by his drug addiction). Hughes's epoch of mighty feats, then, lasted for about 12 years (1935–1947), one complete cycle of the planet Jupiter around the sun, for Jupiter is the Roman equivalent of Zeus, whose sacred bird was the eagle. In Thomas Mann's novel *Doktor Faustus*, the composer Adrian Leverkuhn makes a deal with the devil for precisely 12 years of great creative composition, at the end of which time he descends into a madness induced by tertiary syphilis. Hughes, too, had syphilis, and from this point on, he would gradually descend into madness and isolation.

Hughes had made his Faustian pact, and now the bills were about to come due.

AZIMUTH OF DESCENT

The intense and erratic mobility of the first half of Howard Hughes's life is a startling contrast to the sedentary isolation of the second half. During the 1930s and 1940s, no one on the planet had as much freedom to move about the surface of the earth as Hughes, but during the 1960s and 1970s, no one was stricken with greater immobility than he. In these later years, Hughes confined himself to hotel rooms, where he instructed his aides to blacken out the windows and keep him supplied with codeine and Valium. He would rarely meet with anyone beyond his immediate circle of aides, and many of his top executives never even met with him face to face. Gradually, Hughes retreated to his bed, where he eschewed clothing, avoided baths, and allowed his hair, fingernails, and toenails to grow to absurd lengths. In his bed, he shot up with his beloved codeine and slept strange hours, usually awakening in the late afternoon and spending all night watching movies played on his projector.

In J. G. Ballard's novel *Concrete Island*, a man whose car goes off a freeway overpass leaves him stranded on an "island" surrounded by ministacks and cloverleafs, where he proceeds to make his home as a castaway of industrial society. The novel is a postmodern reworking of Robinson Crusoe, but it is also a perfect analogue of the later years of Howard Hughes's life, during which he became a castaway stranded in the midst of technological society.

In the early 1960s, however, Hughes's mind was still productive, and he continued to chisel away at the contours of the electronic cavern within which he lived in the 20th century. Hughes had become interested in electronics in the late 1940s, and he developed complex weapons control systems based on a fusion of radar and computers, as well as the first air-to-air remote controlled missile (known as the Falcon), which he mass produced for the military, which now was very happy to be in business with him.

In the early 1960s, Hughes Air signified its affiliation with the newly emerging aerospace industries by sending the first geosynchronous satellites into orbit around the planet. These were the prototypical commercial telecommunications satellites, and they made live broadcasts for radio and television possible (a branch of the technological tree leads from these satellites to today's DirecTV and Sirius radio). Syncom 2, launched in July of 1963, relayed the first satellite telephone call between President Kennedy and Nigerian prime minister Abubakr Tafawa Balewa. Syncom 3, the following year, enabled Americans to watch the Olympics in Japan live on television, the first such broadcast. Thus, the very technology that made it possible for Elvis Presley to wrap his own image around the planet during his 1973 Aloha from Hawaii concert—the first planetary-scale concert—was created by Howard Hughes scarcely a decade earlier.

These satellites, furthermore, laid the groundwork for the cocooning of the earth with an electrospheric otherworld populated by the disembodied ghosts of celebrities, television icons, and radio voices that continuously have covered the planet in a sheath of light-speed phantoms ever since. Hughes's satellites, in other words, enabled the actual physical creation of the old mythological cosmologies of the Arabs and the Greeks, in which the earth was thought to be enveloped by etheric spheres made out of delicate subtle matter infected with the ghosts of angels, spirits, and dead ancestors.

With the launching into orbit, furthermore, of another satellite, the ATS-1, Hughes created the first electronic double of the entire earth, for this satellite, equipped with a camera, was able to photograph huge strips of the earth, which could then be synthesized to create an electronic duplication of the planet as a whole. For the first time, meteorologists could actually *see* the cloud formations that they hitherto merely had talked about. Hughes's technology resembled a god holding up a gigantic mirror to the planet, in which it saw itself reflected for the first time. Hughes, then, was the first man to accelerate *the entire planet* to light speed. This moment begins an important epoch in our culture, in which the replacement of the real, which French theoreticians like Jean Baudrillard and Paul Virilio have been talking about for the past three decades, now takes place. From this point on, the planet is substituted by its own double, as with everything and everyone else in electronic society.

Appropriately, then, it was at about the time Hughes was working on the technology for the very satellites that would create a simulacrum of the earth and its etheric envelope of disembodied electric ghosts when he generated his own doppelganger. This mythical idea took on corporeal form in the personage of one Brucks Randell, who was hired by Hughes to help him dodge process servers during the years of his legal battles with TWA.[6] Brucks Randell, it seems, looked exactly like Howard Hughes, for Hughes's men found him working in a drugstore one day complaining that he could not get a job as a movie actor precisely because he looked so much like Hughes. Randell was hired on the spot, and Hughes made use of him to create false Hughes sightings to keep the process servers off his trail.

The double is a staple feature of electronic society, and so it seems appropriate that although Hughes never accelerated himself to light speed through video monitor playback, he did nonetheless rather mysteriously generate his own doppelganger at just the time when he was working on creating a clone of the entire planet through the encircling of the globe with his geosynchronous satellites. The timing of the man's appearance, around 1961, is eerily appropriate, and confirms Hughes's standing as an electronic icon.

Later, urban legends arose to circulate the myth of Hughes's murder and replacement by a double during the 1970 episode when he disappeared from his Las Vegas hotel room under mysterious circumstances. In reality, his aides had merely spirited him off to the Bahamas—for reasons that remain obscure—while they took over management of his Vegas properties and real estate. The episode is significant, however, since Hughes never again returned to the United States.

The falsehood of such urban legends is entirely beside the point of their significance, for they represent the play of mythology in a society under electric conditions. In such a society, it is part of the mythology surrounding electric technology that it generates doppelgangers—doppelgangers that, like the celluloid copy of Jeff Daniels in Woody Allen's film *The Purple Rose of Cairo*, can detach themselves from the physical lives of their owners and become self-aware. Thus, the urban legends of doppelgangers that hover around the lives of Howard Hughes, Paul

McCartney, Lee Harvey Oswald, and others are part of the architecture of human consciousness accelerated to light speed.

Like Elvis Presley, Howard Hughes, too, had his Vegas period. During the late 1960s (between the years 1966 and 1970, roughly coinciding with the city's legendary Elvis concerts), Hughes abandoned Los Angeles as the center of his kingdom and relocated it to the even more ersatz Vegas (for whereas it can be said of Los Angeles that it *has* theme parks, Las Vegas *is* one). Hughes took up residence together with his staff on the entire top floor of the Desert Inn Hotel and Casino for several months until their presence began to annoy the hotel's owner, for neither Hughes nor his Mormon staff gambled, and their presence was precluding those rooms from being occupied by high rollers. Hughes simply decided to buy the hotel outright, and this act seemed to inspire him, for shortly thereafter he began collecting hotels and casinos just the way he once had collected women.

He began to develop the idea that he might actually *buy* the entire city of Las Vegas and transform it into his own personal Disneyland, for he wished to rid the place of its mobsters and clean up its Coney Island–style seediness, just as Disney's ideal for *his* theme park had been to eliminate the dirt and grime of the Coney Island–type amusement park. (In reality, Disney did not so much create an amusement park as a permanent World's Fair, for the 1939 World's Fair, organized by Robert Moses, with its themed attractions, made a significant impression on him.)

Hughes then began buying Nevada real estate and properties, ranches, and vacant windblown lots across which twirled dust devils; he even bought KLAS, the local television station, just because it went off the air at night too early for his taste and reprogrammed it to play his favorite movies into the wee hours. At one point, he proposed to Nevada state officials that he would build the world's largest hotel in Vegas and also one of the largest and most high-tech airports. Although these plans fell through, they are a testament to the kind of scale upon which he was thinking, for Las Vegas was Howard Hughes's Epcot City, a place that he was increasingly coming to see as the center of a kingdom that he could design and redesign at will. He thought of the city's gangsters the same way he thought of germs and bacteria, as something disgusting and vile, to be gotten rid of at all costs.

As he had done with the earth itself and the women he had dated, Hughes was attempting to shrink Vegas down to the level of a play set.

He even begged Lyndon Johnson to stop the nuclear testing that went on in the deserts nearby and that jittered the walls of the hotels like an artificial earthquake. Johnson, needless to say, ignored him.

It was during this period that Hughes began to isolate himself in his hotel rooms, blacking out all the windows and eating Hershey bars and surrounding himself with reels of celluloid. Sometimes, he even urinated in the corners. For four years, he languished in Las Vegas attempting to shrink down the city, until one day his aides simply packed him up—he had withered to just under 90 pounds—and absconded with him to the Bahamas. No one knows why. But the event coincided with Hughes signing over control of his Nevada properties to his most trusted aides who, meanwhile, were happy to keep him doped up on codeine and Valium while they ran his empire.

They packed him up and carted him off to the Caribbean, just as Hughes had once tried to pack the earth up into a suitcase and make off with it. Thus, as in the ironic circle of Disney's life in which the mouse in the maze ended by becoming the white-coated lab technician pushing all the buttons, so too, the life of Howard Hughes had undergone an ironic reversal as he became the planet's wealthiest prisoner.

Nothing better illustrates the extent to which Hughes, in these final years, had lost control of the megamachine that he had set in motion than the parable of the *Glomar* explorer. In the early 1970s, the Central Intelligence Agency (CIA) contacted the Hughes organization to enlist its help in something they called "Project Jennifer." This was an attempt to salvage a sunken Russian nuclear submarine from its watery grave three miles down on the floor of the Pacific Ocean. To accomplish this feat, they arranged for Hughes's engineers to construct one of the world's largest boats, the *Glomar*, but the world was told that Hughes had constructed the first ship to be used for mining minerals from the bottom of the ocean, thus pioneering yet another technological frontier.

The irony is that Hughes had no idea what was going on. He believed what his aides told him, and he thought his organization was about to go into the ocean-mining business, for he could no longer perceive reality behind the veil of his drug-induced stupor.

The CIA recovered its submarine, or half of it, anyway, since the sub broke in two while it was being hauled up into the *Glomar*'s cavernous belly, where it was promptly digested for its secrets.

Thus, the creation of the *Glomar* by the Hughes organization in alliance with the CIA is a caricature of a Hughes achievement. It had the scale and the magnitude and the apparent audacity of something Hughes would have envisioned for the furtherance of technology, but its stated purpose was entirely contrary to its real purpose, which was a one-shot mission that had nothing to do with the future of technology. The *Glomar* was a technological mule.

Even before he was dead, Hughes's achievements were already being spoofed in grand *MAD* magazine style.

Thus, the giant who had once tossed the planet around like a toy was himself physically shrinking in size as he imploded inward, regressing to a state of total infantile helplessness.

For one last time, in 1973, Hughes took to the skies again (for the first time in 13 years). A friend of his named Jack Real got him excited about flying and arranged for him to test pilot a Hawker-Siddely 748 out of England. Hughes spent a couple of weeks sobering up, and between May and July of that year, performed four flights in London, two in the Hawker-Siddely and two in a De Havilland 125.

But as if to underscore the relation between his earlier years of flying and his later years of sedentarization, the Fates arranged it so that in August Hughes broke his hip one night while getting out of bed and making his way to the bathroom. No one is sure how the accident happened, for none of Hughes's aides were present, but British surgeons placed a pin in his left hip and proclaimed the operation a success. Then the drugs were resumed.

Hughes never walked again. He crawled back into his bed, where he curled up with his drugs, and continued with the process of dying. He had fallen into the nadir of captivity and utter immobility. The doctors who had operated on him were horrified at his condition, claiming that his skin had "a parchment-like quality" and that he had "long toenails and fingernails."[7] He was totally emaciated, malnourished, dehydrated, and neglected.

He had been hamstrung, like the Germanic smith Volund who is taken captive by an enemy king who has his leg muscles cut so that the smith can never escape from the island to which the king has confined him. There, Volund spends his days making weapons and tools for the king, but one day the king's sons go to visit him, and he kills them and transforms their skulls into bowls and their eyes into jewels, which he sends to the king as "gifts." Then he makes a pair of wings for himself and flies away from the island.

On April 5, 1976, Hughes, too, flew away, for he died on an airplane that was carrying him from Mexico to the United States to get medical attention for an apparent overdose of codeine.

As in the case of Marilyn Monroe, suspicions arose that Hughes may have been murdered by a conspiracy, in this case planned by his Mormon aides. The aides, after all, seemed dead set on stealing his empire from him, and they may have decided that it was no longer necessary, and indeed, even burdensome, to have him around.

But, as with most things in life, we will never know for certain.

2

Walt Disney Builds the Cosmos Electric

OF LANDSCAPES AND ICONOSCOPES

Walt Disney was one of the first men to hook up the comic strip to an electric battery. In so doing, the flow of current created a whole new world of forms as stylistically distinct and unique as the broad, syncopated spaces of Chinese landscape paintings. For the cartoon universe obeys its own laws, laws that are similar to those of non-Euclidean geometry, in which physical and mechanical forms bend and curve and warp. And, just as Relativity subsumed the laws of Newtonian mechanics, so too, in the realm of cartoon cosmology, machines are reabsorbed into the substrate of an animistic worldview in which locomotives transform into hungry, coal-devouring dinosaurs, while suburban tract houses change into airplanes and automobiles grow layers of human skin, their headlights gazing with the milky, nictitating membranes of reptiles. In the animated world, human and animal bodies bend and stretch like Silly Putty, while domestic objects such as pianos or tables and chairs grow legs and arms to move about with their own misguided wills.

Such a world, though unique, did not just emerge full blown out of the head of Walt Disney, or even out of the heads of his predecessors in the genre, such as Winsor McCay ("Gerty the Dinosaur") and Otto Messmer ("Felix the Cat"). Indeed, from as far back as Mary Shelley who, with her 1817 novel *Frankenstein*, imagined the animation of a living creature by means of an electric current, to Lewis Carroll who, in 1865, with his novel *Alice in Wonderland*, was the first to take a character out of the containing walls of Euclidean space and put her into the non-Euclidean world of a landscape of shifting fields, throughout the course of the 19th century the rate of incursion of electrically inspired tropes into Western literature gradually increased.

Lewis Carroll's two Alice novels, in particular, provide us with a glimpse into the coming world of animated cartoons, for when Alice takes her plunge down that rabbit hole, the world that she encounters is one that bends, stretches, and flattens as though it had been accelerated to the speed of light. Alice herself undergoes many spatial distortions, now shrinking to the size of a mushroom, now expanding to the scale of a giant, while the world around her remains disproportionate to her metamorphoses. Alice, in short, no longer occupies the universe shared by the makers of the mechanical cosmos of Newton and Laplace, in which space was conceived as a homogeneous container within which objects were placed, all subordinated to the same dimensions, for Alice's world is decidedly the electromagnetic universe of James Clerk Maxwell and Einstein, in which multiple spaces and times coexist simultaneously without bearing any necessary relationship to each other. Indeed, the form of Carroll's narratives demonstrates this, for each chapter is a self-contained episode that bears scant relation to any of the others: the Mad Tea Party has little bearing on what precedes it or on the Croquet Game that follows it, which in turn has almost nothing to do with the Mad Trial that succeeds *it*. In short, *Alice in Wonderland* is a mosaic of disconnected spaces and relations all juxtaposed beside one another like articles in a newspaper. Such spaces exist in a field of simultaneous relations, exactly like the fields of Einsteinian Relativity, in which each observer moves in his own frame of reference while carving out his own space and his own time relative to all others.

The disconnected landscapes of Carroll's novels were presupposed by Disney as basic vectors charting the universe within which his imagination roamed. From his early Laugh-O-Gram cartoon shorts, in which a live-action Alice wanders about a cartoon realm, to his 1951 adaptation of Carroll's novel, and even further, to the building of Disneyland with its aperspectival theme park in which disparate worlds wholly unconnected with each other are set side by side, the world of the Alice novels provided Walt Disney with the requisite maps for charting his navigations through the New Worlds created by electric society.

OF MICE AND MEGAMACHINES

At the conclusion of *Through the Looking Glass*, there are two, nearly identical illustrations by Tenniel, one of which shows the hands of Alice holding her cat, while the other, which is meant to be the cat's reflection in the Looking Glass World—for it is in exactly the same position—shows her holding the Red Queen chess piece instead of the cat. Thus, through the iconic world of the Looking Glass, Alice's cat becomes the Red Queen (just as her other kitten becomes the White Queen) for the Looking Glass World reflects not images of the physical body but masked apparitions of the imaginal body. Likewise, when Walt Disney gazed at himself through his own particular looking-glass equivalent, the image reflected at him bore the strangely distorted features of a mouse. For Mickey Mouse was the mask worn by Walt Disney as he ventured through the early years of his cartoon Wonderlandscapes. (Mickey Mouse really *was* Walt Disney, for Walt even provided Mickey's voice in the early black-and-white cartoons until his habit of smoking caught up with him and changed his voice.)

Mickey Mouse was conceived by Disney during one of the darkest periods of his life, when his school of animators had defected to a rival power and his character Oswald the Lucky Rabbit had been taken away from him through legal chicaneries. The mouse figure that surfaced out of his imagination was a response to this period of despair, for it was the mouse that saved his career and put him back on the path toward success as an animator.

That he happened to conceive specifically of a mouse at just this time does not appear to have been accidental, either, for mice in ancient myth are traditionally thought of as having great powers out of all proportion to their size. Indeed, they are often able to bring down the mighty in cases in which more apparently formidable powers fail. Apocryphal accounts describe the devil as having taken on the form of a mouse and attempting to gnaw a hole through Noah's ark, stopped only by a lion. McLuhan quotes Alexander Pope to the effect that "the *Dutch* stories somewhere relate, that a great part of their Provinces was once overflow'd, by a small opening made in one of their dykes by a single *Water-Rat*."[1] And though mice in *Aesop's Fables* tend to fare badly, in at least one famous story, that of "The Lion and the Mouse," the mouse's diminutive size enables it to perform the mighty feat of liberating the lion from the hunter's net that has ensnared him. The mouse is even able to strike terror into the heart of a beast so mighty as the elephant, which is perhaps why Ganesha, the elephant-headed Hindu god of pathways, is depicted as riding on the back of a mouse.

So the mouse is apparently a force to be reckoned with. Thus, Walt Disney's cartoon doppelganger, Mickey Mouse, was called forth out of the depths as a mythic figure traditionally capable of battling successfully against overwhelming odds to help him survive the early loss of his first studio. But it so happened that this character appeared at a time when America as a whole was about to enter the Great Depression, and the image of an indefatigable mouse appealed to the imagination of the country as metaphoric of the little guy overwhelmed by circumstances spiraling out of control around him while just barely managing to stay afloat.

In the cartoon shorts made by Disney and his animators (the first Mickey Mouse cartoon was "Plane Crazy" in 1928), Mickey Mouse is forever battling for control over an environment that threatens to undo him. Whether he is fighting a recalcitrant piano in "Ole Opry," or a house full of spooks in "Mickey and the Haunted House," or a train that has gone out of control in "Mickey's Choo Choo," Mickey is perpetually attempting to bring order to an environment that is nearly beyond his grasp. Thus, the tiny mouse fighting successfully against the powers of the almighty megamachine was an image that appealed to the entire country and explains the popularity of Mickey Mouse during the early 1930s.

Over time, Disney was to become more and more obsessed with controlling his environment, and in these early images of Mickey Mouse fighting for control over a world that nearly destroys him, we can see Disney himself fighting desperately for control over his career, a control that he would, by the end of his life, come to take for granted.

OF DWARVES AND MOUNTAINS

If Disney's first two masks were the Alice character of his Laugh-O-Gram shorts in the 1920s, followed by Mickey Mouse in the early 1930s, then with his creation of the first feature-length animated movies, *Snow White and the Seven Dwarves* in 1937 and *Pinocchio* in 1940, the problem shifted from the personae of his alter egos to that of his relationship with his muse, for Snow White *is* Disney's muse, and her stay with the seven dwarves is highly symbolic of a number of initiatory processes all rolled up together into one tapestry.

On the face of it, the story of Snow White as found in the Brothers Grimm is a tale of the transformation of a naïve young girl into a sexually receptive and mature adult woman ready to bear progeny, of which the seven dwarves, with their child-like stature, and Snow White's matronly attitude toward them, are a foreshadowing. However, if we dig deeper, we recall that dwarves are smiths, and since smiths in mythology are normally associated with the magical power of transmuting raw ores into metals, and of metals into weapons with mysterious and dangerous properties, it cannot escape notice that Snow White's temporary stay with the dwarves in their cottage must have something to do with this process. As Jung has pointed out, there is an analogy between the maturation of the psyche and the transmutation of base metals into gold, and the dwarves must be regarded symbolically as "obstetricians" whose responsibility is to bring about the birth of Snow White's mature personality.

Snow White's stay in the cottage of the dwarves is analogous to Persephone's journey to the underworld, for dwarves are workers in the underworld of caves, where they are thought to dwell (since exposure to sunlight would transform them into stone), forever digging up precious gems and minerals. Snow White, then, in taking up her residence in their cottage, really has gone down with them into their cavernous underworld, where they are able to weave their magic upon her simply by their presence.

According to tradition, metals were associated with the planets: the sun with gold, the moon with silver, Mercury with quicksilver, Jupiter with tin, Mars with iron, Venus with copper, and Saturn with lead. By naming each of the dwarves, something that does not occur in the original Grimm tale, Disney underlines the fact that each dwarf, like each of the planets, is associated with a different archetypal quality. Mars, for instance, was associated with courage, Venus with Eros, Jupiter with regality, Saturn with melancholy, and so on. Hence, Dopey, Sleepy, Grumpy, Sneezy, and so on each embody a separate archetypal quality that is in process of being imprinted on Snow White's soul.

In the classical world, the soul at the moment of its incarnation on earth was thought of as having arrived at the end of a journey through the seven planetary spheres where it has picked up a different archetypal quality at each one. When, in the Mesopotamian myth of "Inanna's Descent to the Netherworld," the goddess must carefully and deliberately remove a different article of clothing for a total of seven pieces in all before standing naked in the underworld at the throne of the Queen of the Dead, we realize that we are in the presence of the Near Eastern prototype of this classical myth, only here it is reversed, for in death, the soul must *shed* each layer of archetypal clothing within which it had been cocooned at birth.

Snow White's sojourn among the dwarves is really an image of the transformation of Disney's muse into a new and complex entity that, at the moment of its rebirth by way of the Prince's kiss, will be ready to inspire him with creative children of his own. The dwarves, on this analogy, have multiple layers of reference, too, for they are analogues for the animators of Disney's new studio, whose task it was to bring Snow White into vivid Technicolor life through the craft of their laborious art. In doing so, they created a great work of celluloid art, Disney's first feature film, and possibly also his best.

Thus, with *Snow White and the Seven Dwarves*, Disney's animators animated Disney's muse, and in doing so, transformed the raw materials of the Grimms' tale into the gold of the world's first great feature length cartoon.

OF PUPPETS AND GODS

The story of *Pinocchio*, based on an Italian children's novel by Carlo Collodi, is essentially a reworking of the myth of Pygmalion and Galatea, although with the presence of Shelley's *Frankenstein* looming like a mountain over the literary landscape of the 19th century, the role of lover and beloved has been changed to that of father and son. In Collodi's novel, Gepetto carves Pinocchio from a block of wood that is already animate with Pinocchio's presence—which hurls insulting and abusive comments at him—as though it were Gepetto's task merely to free the imprisoned child from the block of wood. But Disney changes the opening sequence, as he changes most of Collodi's novel, so that when the film opens, Gepetto has assembled an inert and inactive Pinocchio who rests on the workbench waiting for the finishing touches of eyebrows and mouth. Gepetto puts himself to bed, wishing that his creation were a real boy, and as he sleeps, his prayer is answered—by a pagan divinity—when the Blue Fairy shows up and brings Pinocchio to life. In making this change, Disney actually brings the story closer to the Pygmalion myth, for in that story, Pygmalion carves the statue of a beautiful woman and then prays to the goddess Venus to bring her to life, which she does.

We note that the Blue Fairy resembles a Hollywood movie actress, for she is actually another version of Disney's celluloid muse who has come to bring his animation cels to life by the power of electricity. The spark that she confers on Pinocchio is not like the spiritual pneuma given by God to the outstretched hand of Adam in Michelangelo's Sistine Chapel painting, but rather it is the current of electricity that powers the very movie cameras and projectors that will conjure forth the illusion of

Pinocchio's Technicolor existence. Thus, Gepetto's toyshop is really Disney's animation studio within which his dreams are brought to life by his animators, and Gepetto himself is now Disney's alter ego, the new mask that he has put on to assume the role of creator of animate illusions. (Later, Disney will don the Gepetto mask once again for the forging of his Audio-Animatronic robots by means of which he will create his own artificial human beings.)

In the novel, the very moment that Gepetto finishes carving his creation, the boy springs out the door and runs off, leaving Gepetto to be thrown into jail on accusations of child abuse. The wooden boy thereupon undergoes a series of very un-Disneyesque misadventures that Disney was careful to eliminate from his version of the story. Pinocchio, for instance, rests his feet on a burning brazier and falls asleep only to awaken and find them burned off. The talking cricket, which serves as the prototype for Jiminy Cricket, is immediately smashed by Pinocchio with a mallet when the cricket reminds him that he is on a wayward path. Later, when Pinocchio falls in with bad company, the Fox and the Cat, they manage to trick him out of his gold coins and try to kill him by hanging him from an oak tree, where he nearly chokes to death. None of these episodes are suitable to the spirit of a Walt Disney film, but they are consistent with the Punchinello-Harlequin world of Italian puppetry.

Thus, with his second film, Disney moves from the world of the Gothic, Germanic north, with its Brothers Grimm and their creepy fairy tales, to the bright, sunny Mediterranean realm of Italian puppet plays and carnivals.

Both films open by paying homage to the very Gutenbergian Galaxy that Disney's work is saying farewell to, for they display images of books whose pages are turned to begin their stories proper. This is a vestigial relic of the Gutenbergian world, like the ornate and florid capital letters that traditionally began each chapter of a printed book and that were carryovers from the illuminated manuscripts and incunabili displaced by the printing press. Disney soon drops the allusion, however, and by the time of *Dumbo*, the references to the printed book are gone (although they resurface in *Cinderella* and *Sleeping Beauty*). But Disney's films resemble not so much animated books as moving stained glass, for Disney is attempting to immerse the viewer inside an electronic cathedral in which he gazes upon the lives of fairy tale figures just as, once upon a time, the pious worshipper would have attempted to mentally animate the stories of the lives of the saints which towered above him in the tracery of Gothic windows. (Witness the climax of

Fantasia, in which Disney consciously places the viewer inside a cathedral made out of a forest of stylized trees set to the music of Schubert's *Ave Maria.*)

The point here is that Disney's aspirations all along have been of a religious nature, although most likely this was not conscious on his part. Nevertheless, as his career unfolds, he slowly and methodically sets about the creation of an electronic religion, casting himself in the role of prophet and messiah. By the end of his career, this role would enlarge to become that of a creator deity whose avatars occasionally descended into his own dreamworlds to tinker with them, now as a Gepetto, now as an Alice, now as a Mickey Mouse.

In the end, Disney would strive to become a god.

OF LOST BOYS AND WONDERLANDS

Disney's first three feature length films, *Snow White and the Seven Dwarves, Pinocchio,* and *Fantasia* were his best. They are, in a real sense, masterpieces, but the same cannot be said of any of the other films that followed. From *Dumbo* onward, all of his films are on an inclined plane downward in terms of the integrity and quality of his vision. Due to the budgetary problems resulting from the financial failures of *Pinocchio* and *Fantasia*, and then with *Bambi*, which was a total flop, he was plunged into an eight-year period of financial compromises that nearly wiped out his studio. This took place during the early 1940s, Disney's dark years, when the U.S. government conscripted his studio into making technical and educational films. When the war ended, Disney was so disoriented by the failure of his mythic vision that he seems not to have had any idea what sort of film to make, and so a string of bad movies followed.

It was not until the release of *Cinderella* in 1950 that he was to make a comeback, but by this time, his vision had been so diluted and compromised as to be virtually unrecognizable. He had become removed from the making of his own films, generally delegating them to his staff, and his lack of interest is evident in *Cinderella*, for though the film was a financial and critical success, its animation is lackluster, basically no different from the average Bugs Bunny cartoon, and the story was almost completely garbled by Disney's staff, who obviously did not understand the fairy tale. Disney, by this point, had routinized his own charisma.

With his 1951 adaptation of Lewis Carroll's *Alice in Wonderland*, which followed *Cinderella*, he nearly achieved a return to form. This film, contrary to popular opinion, is one of Disney's best, and hearkens back to the early years, inviting comparison especially to *Fantasia,* to which it alludes at a number of points. With this film, Disney returned to the cartoon Wonderland that had inspired his initial vision and created a film that is entirely faithful to the spirit of Carroll's book.

Peter Pan, which followed *Alice in Wonderland* in 1953, though technically inferior in terms of its animation, is nonetheless one of Disney's better films, for it represents his vision in a way that is archetypally Disneyesque. Here, Peter Pan has traded places with Alice as Disney's alter ego, for Disney *is* the boy who never grew up, and Neverland is another version of Wonderland, for it too is a realm of mythical archetypes in which nothing ever changes, no one ever ages, and where the shadow of Time never falls.

OF MODEL TRAINS AND GIANT DOLLHOUSES

If Disney, by the early 1950s, had become less interested in making films, it was because a new project was draining off all his creative energy into its own reservoirs. In the late 1940s, Disney had become fascinated with model trains, beginning first with electric trains, and then moving on to more expensive miniature steam locomotives. Indeed, he had become so obsessed with them, that he moved his family to a new property with a backyard that was large enough to accommodate the train upon which he was able to sit as it carried him around the perimeter, and through the tunnels, of the yard.

Then he began experimenting with recreating doll house–size movie sets of vanished epochs of turn-of-the-century Americana. He gathered a collection of these sets and put them into an exhibition that he called "Disneylandia." Then he started thinking about the possibility of blowing up these dollhouse miniatures of a vanished world to life size, and so put his mind, and some members of his staff, to work on planning the creation of an amusement park that would be based on a reconstruction of the small towns of early 20th-century America. Thus, the first drawings for Disneyland show what would later become scaled down to occupy merely one quadrant of the amusement park, Main Street, USA, with its general store and quaint shop fronts.

Once again, as is always the case with Disney, the problem was a matter of scale. He thought in terms of the spatial discontinuities of *Alice in Wonderland*, for at first he blew up his electric trains to the size of miniature steam locomotives; then he enlarged his dollhouse displays to the size of a theme park, to be circumscribed by a *real* locomotive as its boundary. These maneuvers are virtually an imitation of the scalings up and down of Alice at the beginning of her Wonderland adventure.

Such spatial discontinuities, furthermore, are characteristic of the cosmos electric, which is aperspectival and discontinuous, and in which each object occupies its own space without any relationship to adjacent objects. Here in Einsteinland, each clock moves at its own pace, for clocks that are closer to the ground move more slowly than clocks that are higher up in the air, while objects, as they approach light speed, contract in the direction of their motion and become weirdly elongated. Cause and effect are turned upside down such that the effect may even precede the cause, just as the Mad Hatter's incarceration actually precedes his trial and sentencing.

With the creation of Disneyland, then, Disney enlarges his miniature playsets and model trains so that everyone can play these games along with him. However, in the spirit of Lewis Carroll, it is perhaps just as true to say that Disney actually shrank the rest of us down to the level of Alice in the garden talking to the blue caterpillar on a mushroom so that we could enter his playsets while he loomed above us like a god, controlling now this effect, now that.

OF MANDALAS AND WORLD HISTORY

The early maps of Disneyland resemble a mandala, divided into four quadrants: the southern quadrant is Main Street, USA, the first thing one encounters upon entering the park; to the north, the miniature castle that terminates the vanishing point of the view along Main Street, indicates the quadrant of Fantasy Land; to the east, there is Tomorrow Land, with its 1950s imagery of rockets and spaceships; and to the west, is Frontier Land. Looking down at this microcosm from above, it becomes evident that we could divide it diagonally in two: for both Frontier Land and Main Street are based on historical realities, while Fantasy Land and Tomorrow Land represent imaginary worlds (those of the past and future, respectively).

Casting a backward glance at the now rapidly diminishing horizons of history, we note that the world of the small town—Main Street, USA—came into being directly as a result of the shutting down of the frontier with the near simultaneous arrival of two profoundly opposed technologies, the railroad and the telegraph, for the railroad had a strongly centralizing effect that tended toward the creation of cities and towns, whereas the telegraph was rather decentralizing, for at light speed all center-margin relationships are scattered. The telegraph, furthermore, put the Pony Express out of business and, along with the railroad, accelerated culture to a speed that was faster than what any Pony Express rider could keep up with. The world of Main Street, USA, furthermore, was a domesticated society based on the rule of law and order, unlike the Old West, and it was lit by electricity and powered by coal and gasoline.

With the arrival of the automobile, the small town was eventually torn apart by freeways and interstate highways laid out in the 1950s which gave birth to the imagination of big cities within which the world of Tomorrow Land, of rockets and space exploration, was dreamed forth upon the fluorescent-lit blueprints of the new frontier. The small town, during the Cold War, became as quaint as the antiquated frontier, as titans like Howard Hughes and Werner von Braun led us into the world of the skies.

Way, way back behind all of these worlds lay the realm of fairy tales and folklore as an archaic preserve in which the old myths that had built and sustained the ancient civilizations were recycled through the domestic imaginations of grannies and nannies who recounted these stories to their children. In this way, pagan divinities and ancient myths were kept alive, even if only scaled down to the level of dollhouse castles and imaginary kingdoms of once upon a time.

Thus looked at, Disneyland becomes a recapitulation of the major epochs of American history, each ripped from its temporal container and placed beside one another to create a newspaper mosaic of disconnected worlds.

OF VISTAS AND VICISSITUDES

The various optical tricks and spatial distortions that Disney utilized in the making of his theme park are not entirely without point, for they often conceal philosophical views about the world. Take, for instance, the spatial distortions of Main Street, USA. "Main Street was a function of clever foreshortening," Neal Gabler writes in his biography of Disney.

> The lower floors of the shops were nine-tenths scale, the second floors eight-tenths, and the third seven-tenths. As for the rest of the park, Walt wrote an old acquaintance that the "scale of objects varies according to what and where they are"—what he called a "matter of choosing the scale that would be practical and still look right." This kind of miniaturization

> underscored the sense of nostalgia because it associated the past and the fantastic with the small and quaint. "[P]eople like to think their world is somehow more grown up than Papa's was," he said.[2]

Disney has here provided us with a comment upon how the gradually increasing scale of technology has had the effect of reversing the mythology of grand historical cycles. For the Greeks, the world of *their* ancestors was anything but small and quaint, for they believed that the heroes of the Mycenean world that had preceded them were actually giants. The Greeks were forever finding the fossils of extinct species like dwarf elephants and other large Pleistocene mammals that they assumed were actual physical evidence that giants had once walked the earth before them. Pliny, for instance, insisted that a 35-foot skeleton of Orion had been found on Crete, while the giant bones of Ajax were said to have been discovered at Salamis. All this was consistent with the Hesiodic myth of a gradually declining and shrinking world in which the age of the Homeric gods was followed by the Mycenean epoch of great warriors like Achilles and Odysseus, which was followed in turn by the age of mere men in which the Greeks saw themselves as living.

It is only in the 20th century, as a result of the gradually increasing scale of our own technologies, that the world of *our* ancestors has come to seem small and quaint, for that world has been dwarfed by nuclear reactors, atom bombs, skyscrapers, and jumbo jets. In a roundabout way, then, we have come by means of the path of ever larger forms of technology to reversing the mythology of history, so that now *we* have become the giants looming over the shrunken old men of our Norman Rockwell past.

Thus, the visual effect as one strolls down Disney's Main Street, USA, is to subtly make one feel like a giant who has outgrown his parents' limited horizons and narrow vistas. This feeling is not an accident, either, for it is part of Disney's vision of the unlimited path to progress of technology that he naively believed would make better human beings out of all of us. He was almost completely unaware of the shadow side of technology and the damage it has done, not only to the environment, but to the humanities and the arts, which have been left in a state of near total disarray, like a trawler in the wake of a *Titanic*. Indeed, his faith in the unlimited vistas opened up before us by the potentialities of new technologies is so naïve that it is almost charming.

And yet, the disconnected tableaux of Disneyland lay right there in front of him as evidence to the contrary, for as Neil Postman was always fond of pointing out, the one thing we forget to ask whenever any new technology comes along is, "What way of life will this new gadget *un*do?" For just as the advent of the printing press heralded the twilight of the Middle Ages and brought about the erosion of the use of Latin as a language of international learning—while also decentralizing the Church's power by mass producing the Bible in vernacular tongues—so too Frontier Land, with its Romantic cowboyism and its Fenimore Cooper heroics, was undone by the arrival of Main Street, USA, with its quaint barber shops, drug stores, and *Weekly Bugle* newspapers. And Main Street, USA, in turn, was undone by the huge freeway systems of the 1950s that made small towns irrelevant and burst open the seams of the city to spill forth a massive sprawl of decentralized suburbs and shopping malls.

All of these changes, without exception, were brought about by the advent of new technologies, the yearly proliferation of which has continued to change the norm of society. Disney's nostalgia for his vanished small-town America moved him to create Disneyland as a museum of vanished worlds whose disappearances were brought about by the very sorts of technology that Disney enthusiastically endorsed in the creation of his theme park.

OF AUTOMOBILES AND PARKING LOTS

Disney actually was aware of one aspect of the shadow side of technology, and that side is implicit in the very structure and layout of Disneyland itself. When we pay close attention to the world that Disneyland *excludes* by means of the boundary established by the railroad that formed the park's original perimeter, we notice that it is precisely the automobile that must remain on the outside and that is not allowed to enter the park's interior. "Walt had always intended to transport his guests to a separate place," Neal Gabler writes, "and he once scolded a publicist who had parked his car where it could be seen from the Mark Twain because passengers in 1860 could not possibly imagine an automobile from 1955."[3]

Thus, one of the unintentional creations of Disneyland is the Mother of All Parking Lots (12,000-car capacity), the world's largest up to that time. Indeed, this may be the first parking lot in the world so large as to actually have vanishing points between the car lanes as they disappear into perspectival space along the blue horizon. The automobile is the enemy of the various worlds captured and preserved in formaldehyde by

Disney, because the automobile has an inherently decentralizing effect on cities and communities everywhere.

It is significant in light of this that Disney's plans for the creation of his artificial city, Epcot, did not allow for automobiles inside the city. "Here, the pedestrian will be king," he said, "free to walk and browse without fear of motorized vehicles," and so he exiled automobiles to a level underground from which they were never to be allowed to emerge. Thus, the disintegrative impact of the automobile on cities may be the one example of the shadow side of technology that Disney ever recognized.

OF UTOPIAS AND COSMOCRATORS

During the last years of his life, Walt Disney decided that he wanted to become a god. He bought some real estate in Florida, roughly 27,000 acres worth—twice the size of Manhattan—with the intention of erecting upon it an entire city. He called this city Epcot, an anagram for "Experimental Prototype Community of Tomorrow," and announced to the world that it would have a population of about 20,000 people. The city was to be built on a radial plan; that is to say, in the shape of a circle, with concentric bands of development radiating outward from a central hub of skyscrapers, including belts of suburban residences, schools and churches, parks, and so on. Monorails would bring commuters from the outlying areas to the central hub of the city to work, where People Movers would then shift them about from place to place. Automobiles and trucks would be confined to lower levels beneath the city. And, for a final touch of megalomania, the entire city would be enclosed by a huge dome of glass to provide climate control. As Disney's friend Robert Moses described it, Epcot would have been the "first accident free, noise free, pollution free city center in America."[4]

Disney did not live to see his experimental community built, but it is likely that had he lived another 15 or so years, he would somehow have found a way to bring it into being. And it is equally likely that the city would have been a monumental failure, for its utopian dream of the elimination of all forms of pollution is unrealistic in the extreme. Human beings are messy creatures, and they bring their messes with them wherever they go. They cannot live in laboratories, or in macroscale versions of laboratories like space stations and Martian colonies, for very long. Epcot was nothing if not a prototype Martian colony, like Biosphere II in Oracle, Arizona, a similar experiment inside a sealed environment that, I note, was a complete failure.

Disney's dream is an antiseptic one, as purged from contamination by the senses as Plato's fantasy of the soul's flight from the cave to the heavenly sun. It is a disguised dream of building the New Jerusalem on earth, for in the Book of Revelation, the New Jerusalem was essentially a spaceship that descended from the heavens to the top of a mountain to pick up its cargo of Christian passengers for the new millennium. Disney's vision is an attempt to build the New Jerusalem by means of technological progress, for if all history has been tending toward a goal, it is that of the perfection of technology to such a point of ethereal subtlety that it could enable the realization of the City of God on earth. Disney's plan to build a city beneath a glass dome is a macroscale version of the modelmaker's dream of placing a ship inside a bottle. Indeed, the city inside a glass dome is a vision nearly identical to Hieronymous Bosch's painting *Creation of the World* (c. 1466), which depicts the earth as a flat disc sealed off inside an enormous glass sphere, over which Yahweh broods in the outer firmament above. With the glass dome, Disney even thinks he can control the weather, something that only a god could do, which truly reveals him in his last fantasy as aspiring to an apotheosis.

For his final act, then, Disney wished to put on the mask of cosmocrator and to shrink his fellow human beings to the size of lab rats. Thus, the ironic arc of his career had taken him from playing the mouse in the maze battling obstacles at every turn to becoming the white-coated man who hovered over the maze and pushed the buttons.

OF DEATH AND SLEEPING KINGS

The urban legend that Walt Disney was cryogenically frozen at death and merely awaits the hour when science will come round at last with the proper technology to resurrect him, though factually false—since Disney was actually cremated, not frozen—is nevertheless inwardly true. Such a belief, if Disney had professed it, is perfectly consistent with his almost religious faith in the ever-ascending perfection of science. But more important, the urban legend suits the mythical contours of the life Walt Disney lived, which, as we have seen, was a gradual ascent toward a self-apotheosis as cosmocrator. The legend is a translation into the language of science fiction of the myth of the return of the sleeping king—or the god who has died—and merely awaits the proper moment when he will come forth once again. The Celts, for instance, believed that the warrior hero Fionn never really died, but rather had gone to sleep in a cave and presently awaits the moment when Ireland will summon him forth once again in her hour of need. A similar legend concerns the prophesied return of the German ruler Frederick I Barbarossa, in which it is said that he is not dead but sleeping with his knights in a cave in the Kyffhauser mountain in Thuringia and that, when the ravens cease to fly, he will arise once more. Indeed, it is a common enough legend.

The fact that this same myth has grown up around Walt Disney is an indication of his status as a Cold War celebrity who is slowly, but inevitably, on the way toward transformation into a divinity. He is one of the saints of our world of electronic stained glass, for as time goes by, legendary powers continue to accrete to him, elevating rather than diminishing his god-like reputation. Indeed, the particular urban legend of Disney's cryogenic preservation is so prevalent that most people assume it is true; even the French philosopher Jean Baudrillard, in his various writings about Disney, takes it as a given.[5] This is precisely how myth creeps up like the thistles surrounding the castle of Sleeping Beauty and gradually begins to replace historic reality with the more profoundly true reality of mythology. One day, the legend simply stops being questioned and everyone takes it for the truth. This is how historic figures are elevated to the status of mythical heroes and gods.

It is, after all, not too difficult to believe. Disney really *was* a master of technological potentialities who was always on the lookout for new developments to bring them into the service of his City of Progress.

If anyone could find a way to defeat death and come back again, it surely would have been Walt Disney.

II

Classics (The 1950s)

Elvis Presley, James Dean, and Marilyn Monroe

INTRODUCTION

In ancient Pythagorean number theory, the world was constructed out of pure geometry. Two points, for example, are required to create a one-dimensional line (say, Walt Disney at one end and Howard Hughes at the other), whereas three points are necessary to construct a two-dimensional object such as a triangle. Hence, with Elvis Presley, James Dean, and Marilyn Monroe, we begin to construct the constellation of the celebrity death triangle, for with these three stars, the pattern of the dying and reviving celebrity demigod begins to assume tangible shape before us.

When life is lived at the speed of light, the earth flattens, time slows down, and mythical structures begin to appear everywhere. Hence, when certain individuals among us are accelerated to light speed via electronic replication of their images, strange, otherworldly phenomena begin to accrete to them, forming the very auras Walter Benjamin insisted would be stripped from them by the mechanical means of reproduction of their images. At light speed, however, unpredictable effects of mythic amplitude and volume give shape to ancient patterns that act as molds by way of which the lives of such individuals are contoured: the myth of the mysterious, piping singer, whose notes resonate with a compulsively erotic effect; the foam-born goddess at whose bidding men will do anything; or the orphaned wonder child with occult abilities, such as the power to make himself invisible. These are the mythic structures that the particular lives of Elvis Presley, Marilyn Monroe, and James Dean activated; structures they awakened, but that also awakened them into dynamic action.

Presley, Dean, and Monroe constitute the "classic" superstar triad because each one of them travels along a specific mythical geodesic through Electrotopia that ends with a particular type of tragedy—a tragedy that all subsequent celebrities, wishing to become demigods, must follow. They are "classic" because they set up for all time the three great death scenarios: death by mental disintegration into chemistry (through drug overdose); physical acceleration into death by bodily dissolution into a machine (via car crash); or death by the fusion of one's own persona with the psyche of another human being (celebrity stalker).

Thus, Elvis Presley, though he was not the first to do so, perfected the life pattern of the gradually disintegrating celebrity whose consciousness is dissolved by drugs like an Alka-Seltzer® tab in a cup of fizzing water; James Dean, standing on the shoulders of the giant Howard Hughes, brings to perfection the death by mechanical crash for which Hughes had merely drawn up the experimental prototypes with his serial plane crashes; and in Marilyn's case—though perhaps surprisingly for some—one of the first great deaths to be brought about by a celebrity stalker, as her chapter will disclose to us.

These are the three great tragic genres of the celebrity demigod who will be resurrected via the power of electronic media. All subsequent celebrities studied in this volume will either perish by one of these three patterns (John F. Kennedy, John Lennon, Jim Morrison, Gianni Versace, Princess Diana, Heath Ledger, Michael Jackson) or, as in the cases of Andy Warhol and Ronald Reagan, narrowly avert them.

But to be transformed into a celebrity demigod, one must first step through the electronic looking glass and enter into a landscape of weirdly elongated and strangely distorted forms. Inside this parallel world of virtuality, one's image, like that of Krishna's among the *gopis*, will be multiplied, copied, and proliferated as so much light and shadow mistaken for substance. Shelley's Frankenstein, as is so often the case, will be found to be prophetic. With the awakening of the monster to life, however, its creator never again will sleep soundly. Hence, this behavior explains the frequent use of sleeping pills among so many of these celebrities, Elvis and Marilyn, especially.

So now, without further ado, may I present Elvis Presley, James Dean, and Marilyn Monroe.

3

The Weird and Fantastic Tale of the Pixellation and Disintegration of Elvis Presley

Elvis Presley is the prototype of the multimedia icon. He is the first man whose career was based almost entirely on a proliferation of his clones via radio, television, film, and satellite technology. In this respect, Elvis was a pioneer who stood at the threshold of the post–World War II cult of the celebrity, for he was its first victim as well as its first demigod, and the pattern of his life eventually became something of a new archetype for the television age.

And it *was* television more than any of these other media that created him, for through the looking glass of its cathode ray tube (CRT) he went, accelerated, multiplied, and spray-painted onto the human retina by means of a mesh of rapidly scanning electron beams. In this way, the polite and guileless young boy from Memphis entered a strange new landscape of weirdly glowing, photoluminescent shapes with bizarre properties. Elvis spent his life wandering about this spiny, radial landscape, peering out through the glass of the television screen at *us*, who sat on our couches—vague, murky shapes stirring in a gloomy distance—watching him perform his songs with gestures of mythic grandeur.

This visual analysis of Elvis into ELF radiation by means of the camera eye and subsequent synthesis by the human eye into a glowing pixilated image may have been nothing more than a mere amusement to *us* his audience, but to *him*, the process was far from innocuous, for it actually had the effect of recreating him anew as a sort of twin, or clone, of himself. And it was the creation of this twin, his doppelganger, that eventually ruined Elvis's life.

* * *

If we cast all the way back to the beginning, to his early recordings at Sun Studios, we can already see intimations of this process. His first records in the mid-1950s were singles, five in all, printed on the new Memphis recording label founded by Sam Phillips and known as Sun Records. These singles eventually were hits with radio stations all across the country, although at first, Presley's popularity was largely confined to the South. It was no accident, either, that Elvis came out of the South, which has always been a culture of the ear, rather than the eye, for jazz and the blues had been invented in New Orleans by black musicians who had infused southern culture with their own rhythms. Rock and roll was yet another musical genre to find its origins in the South, in this case, born out of a fusion of rhythm and blues (from a predominantly black source) and country and western (from whites). And it was Elvis Presley, more than anybody else, who managed to embody the tensions between these two very different musical genres.

Thus, his first five singles are characterized by this cultural dichotomy, for the A sides of these records are largely rhythm-and-blues tunes that Elvis had reworked from the songs of black men, while the B sides are country-and-western songs. His first single, "That's All Right" (1954), for example, consists of an A-side rhythm-and-blues song reworked from an earlier tune by Arthur Crudup, with "Blue Moon of Kentucky" on the B side, a Bill Monroe country song. The only exception to this rule appears on the last of the five Sun singles, in which this pattern is reversed: the A side of "I Forgot to Remember to Forget" is a country song, and the B side, "Mystery Train," is rhythm and blues. From out of this tension between the "respectable" country music of the white man and the "disreputable" rhythm and blues of the black man, Elvis Presley's career—and, along with it, the birth of rock and roll—approached the light of day.

For rock and roll, as such, hardly existed at the time in which these singles were produced. Elvis Presley helped to bring it into being by cross-pollinating the music of two racial strains to create the hybrid that would later come to be known as "rock and roll." But already, we are aware of a deep fissure running through the middle of Presley's persona, as though the urge to split himself in two like a cell in the early stages of mitosis was impending.

The crucial year in the generation of Elvis's first electric clone was 1956, the year in which his agent Colonel Tom Parker helped him make the switch from the tiny independent Sun label to the stellar RCA corporation through which he mass produced his first RCA single,

"Heartbreak Hotel," released on January 27. The very next day, he appeared on television for the first time on an obscure little program known as *Stageshow*, hosted by the Dorsey brothers. He made repeated appearances on this show up until March, when RCA released his first LP record, *Elvis Presley*, whereupon the album sold an immediate 300,000 copies. (It is notable that side A of this album is predominantly made up of country songs, while side B was largely rhythm and blues, thus reiterating the pattern of the singles.)

The genesis of this LP, furthermore, coincided with the first of his two appearances on *The Milton Berle Show* in April, followed by another appearance in June, and then a humiliating appearance on *The Steve Allen Show* in which he was featured singing "Hound Dog" to a basset hound. On September 9, he appeared on *The Ed Sullivan Show* for the first time, followed by another appearance in October, in which his famous rubbery legs and swiveling hips were unveiled for all to see. (This liquefaction of the lower half of his body reminds one of nothing so much as the image of the Greek deity Typhon, whose upper half is human, while the lower half of his body is composed of wriggling, squirming snakes. Typhon is the deity sent by Gaia to punish Zeus for his triumph over the Titans. Indeed, the attempt on the part of the show's producers to film Elvis only from the waist up on his third appearance is the equivalent of a thunderbolt hurled at the great Titan, which severs him in half.) The final appearance on *Ed Sullivan* in January of 1957 was to be his *last* television spectacle until 1960 when, upon discharge from the Army, he was featured on *The Frank Sinatra Show,* his sole television appearance until 1968. In the interim, Elvis was to star in a series of Hollywood movies.

In cataloging these television appearances, I am making the point that it was not an accident that Elvis's career hit the big time in 1956, for this was the *only* year in his entire biography in which his image was broadcast via television on so many occasions concentrated so closely together. It *was* television that made Elvis Presley into a phenomenon, the first giant television star in the history of the medium. Without it, he may have become a recording industry star like Hank Williams, Sr. or Willie Nelson, but by means of television, he was transformed into something gigantic, a deity with magically seductive powers.

Now, the image of Elvis generated by television—and by *The Ed Sullivan Show*, in particular—had the effect of splitting him down the middle into a "real" Elvis made out of atoms and matter, and an electronic Elvis composed of electrons and photons. Thus, Presley was sent beaming simultaneously into millions of households, where he was delivered in an electronic birth through their television sets. His electric twin, now hatched from the egg of the cathode ray tube, burned itself onto the retinas of his audience members as a dancing, jittery homunculus. Hence, the *second* Elvis Presley—and let us not forget here that he had been born with a biological twin who had suffocated on his way out of his mother's womb—came into existence at last, taking up its residence in the ethereal world of electromagnetic pulsation. And it is *this* Elvis that will awaken to its own life, become self-aware, and eventually begin to push the real, three-dimensional Elvis out of existence.

For the mythic power of the electronic Elvis was undeniable. He not only evoked Typhon, but more important, the Greek god Dionysus. Thus, Elvis's *Ed Sullivan* appearances are culturally significant because they constitute the first reawakening of Dionysus in Western culture since the disappearance of his cult around 400 B.C.E. The drums and cymbals, the madness and wine, the frenzied seizures, and the sexual ecstasies that characterized the retinue of this god, whose mysteries only took place at night by firelight in secret groves and hills beyond the reach of respectable eyes, are the lineal forebears of rock and roll. The fears of the Roman government at beholding the licentious spectacle of the Bacchanalia, and their attempts to purge the Dionysiac mysteries from Rome, and even from the Italian peninsula as a whole, went on repeatedly over many centuries, and these fears are the ancient counterpart to the fears of the 1950s Establishment regarding the serpentine movements of Elvis's legs and the raucous fervor that it aroused among large groups of young women (the followers of Dionysus, too, were largely female). Indeed, we may take Frank Sinatra's condemnation of this new phenomenon—the advent of which was exactly coincident with the rise of television—as representing the typical view of the Establishment regarding rock and roll during the 1950s:

> "Rock 'n' roll smells phony and false," declared Frank Sinatra. . . . "It is sung, played, and written for the most part by cretinous goons and by means of its almost imbecilic reiteration, and sly, lewd, in plain fact, dirty lyrics . . . it manages to be the martial music of every side-burned delinquent on the face of the earth. . . . [It] is the most brutal, ugly, desperate, vicious form of expression it has been my misfortune to hear."[1]

Thus, like the Roman anxieties regarding the cult of the ithyphallic wine god Bacchus, the electrically mediated image of Elvis Presley was thought to be a dangerous, untrustworthy figure who could not be left unattended in the presence of one's daughters. The image itself, that is to say, activated archaic residua in the modern American psyche, of ancient mythic strata in which sinister, wandering gods blowing magical pipes cast a spell on their children and led them into the wilderness, never to be heard from again. The effect of Elvis's image on the American psyche was colossally disturbing, something akin to holding up a powerful magnet against a CRT monitor.

The producers of *Ed Sullivan*, as we have already noted, attempted to nullify these effects during Elvis's third appearance on their show by filming him only from the waist up. Elvis's image on this third appearance is so full of volcanic energy and sexual power, however, that he actually appears to *bend* and *stretch* the television screen like a special effect out of David Cronenberg's *Videodrome.* In fact, the result of the close-up is to magnify him to the level of a gigantic being whose explosive, convulsive energy actually seems to overwhelm the television screen and to push upon its convexity, as though he were trapped inside the television set and trying to find a way out. The television screen, under the impact of Elvis, becomes soft and flexible.

Thus, if Elvis was morphologically altered by his descent into electric culture, the converse is also true, for he had a mythic power that actually warped and distorted the electronic instruments that made his rise possible to begin with.

So much for the Dionysian Elvis. Now, the *second* avatar to be generated by the process of Elvis's descent into electric media had a devastating—and also disintegrative—effect on the first, for this second clone was a misbegotten attempt to revive Elvis's career upon his return to the civilian world after a two-year stint in the Army (1958–1960, during which time he picked up the habit of pill popping). The clone I am referring to looked and sounded like the Dionysian Elvis; however, the persona who appeared on *The Frank Sinatra Show* in 1960 was *not* the Dionysian Elvis, but an impostor. For the image of a smarmy, self-satisfied goombah like Frank Sinatra semiofficially adopting the newly released Elvis from his sojourn in the underworld of the Army was a total affront to the Dionysian Elvis and all that he had stood for. The Sinatra Elvis was a sham: standing beside Sinatra, gleefully snapping his fingers as though the two had been lifelong friends newly reunited; this was nothing but hypocrisy, for Sinatra had roundly, and thoroughly, condemned rock and roll as a music for idiots. It was, therefore, an act of pure mendacity to see this bouncy, domesticated, well-behaved, and tamed Elvis smiling giddily as Father Sinatra patted him on the head, thus assuring the audience that he had been successfully neutered and no longer constituted a threat to their nascent postbourgeois world of shopping malls, suburbs, and interstate highways.

This new Elvis, in fact, became a sort of demigod of the suburbs, for he fit the profile of the All American Good Boy that the parents now living in tract housing developments were eager to have as the patron saint of their suburban teenagers (as opposed to, say, the reckless youth played by James Dean in *Rebel Without a Cause*). This is the Elvis who appeared in a string of bad 1960s movies, always well behaved, good intentioned, and in love with *Mother.* The image of a castrated Elvis, safe for teenage girls—witness the fact that the *Blue Hawaii* Elvis character is so safe that he is entrusted with becoming the chaperone of a gaggle of teenage girls, whereas *no one* would have trusted the Ed Sullivan Elvis with their daughters for a single moment—was precisely who the Dionysian Elvis was not and never had been. This second Elvis avatar was a threat to nobody and nothing, except the real Elvis himself, for this bland good boy became the key to Elvis's downfall during the 1960s when he disappeared into a string of atrociously bad movies and managed to make a caricature out of his own persona. This other twin now frequently haunted the periphery of his own increasing self-doubts and stood by watching him pop more and more pills while he worried about whether he in fact still *was* the same Elvis he had been before the Army.

For the remainder of his career up until the late 1960s, Elvis would brood over the enigma of just what precisely it was that the proliferation of his image via celluloid was doing to him, and why it was that his post-Army incarnation never felt the same as before. Subject to increasingly frequent mood swings, depression, anxiety, and illness, Elvis began to pale and slip away into a ghostly intangibility, while his clones gathered round him and fed off his living vitality. For awhile, he dabbled with yoga, astrology, and New Age metaphysics, sensing that the answer to his problem was somewhere in the spirit world, in the realm of ghosts, doubles, and ethereal twins.

But then he stumbled upon an apparent solution: he must return to the glowing machine that had reproduced him in the first place, and try to generate one more copy, a clone this time powerful enough to undo the damage wrought by the Sinatra Elvis. It was the television that had made him, and so back down into its radiant blue plasma pool he lowered himself once again in an attempt to generate a clone that would restore him to respectability.

The answer was the *Elvis: '68 Comeback Special* that was taped in June of 1968, and broadcast later that December. This was not only an important moment for Elvis—his first television appearance since *Frank Sinatra*—it also was one of the great moments in television history, for the loose, improvisational informality of the setting, in which Elvis casually sat with friends jamming on a tiny stage surrounded on all four sides by an audience, became the prototype for what would later become the format of Music Television's (MTV's) popular show *Unplugged.* And when the stage was cleared and he was left alone to perform standing up, the small, confined space of the little theater emphasized his mythic gigantism all the more, making him seem like a colossus surrounded by Lilliputians. That he was aware of this effect is confirmed when at one point he picked up the microphone stand and posed as though about to hurl a harpoon, saying, "Moby Dick!" This temporary identification with the inflated ego of Captain Ahab is revealing, for it strips away the pretense and shows us that Elvis *intends* a monumental effect on his audience.

In this performance, Elvis is garbed in a leather jacket and pants that allude to Marlon Brando's image in *The Wild One* (1953). To restore the Dionysian Elvis to wholeness, an attempt was made to connect with the source of *that* image in Brando's creation of Johnny, the motorcycle gang leader who besieges a small town.[2] In this film, Brando's character *is* dangerous: you can feel his suppressed rage as he toys with the sheriff's daughter at the counter of the coffee shop. At one point, she crosses him, and he replies, violently, "Nobody tells me what to *do.* You keep needlin' me, and if I want to, I'm gonna take this joint apart and you're not gonna know what hit you." The viewer does not doubt for a moment that he means what he says, and later in the film, as his cohorts do indeed take the town apart, Brando abducts the girl on the back of his motorcycle and takes her out beyond the city limits to a tree-lined grove where he attempts to ravish her. *This* is the boy whom the parents of the 1950s were afraid that the Dionysian Elvis might really be: for the ability of his voice and image to lure crowds of screaming women to follow him wherever he went had a mythic power comparable to Krishna's ability to pipe his flute and cause all the women in the neighborhood to drop what they are doing and come running.

This is exactly the image that Elvis manages to retrieve in the comeback special, for as he sits on the edge of the stage and sings the syrupy

"Memories," he is flanked on either side by adoring women, young and old. They love him, these women; his effect upon them is ultimately inscrutable. It is not the magnetism of a human being, but rather of a mythic persona at work that is capable of tapping deep, plutonian undercurrents in the female psyche, of the desire to be swept up and abducted to some remote underworld habitation.

In this respect, the newly generated image of Elvis was a success and managed to go a long way toward undoing the damage of the Sinatra Elvis. It was such a success, in fact, that Elvis henceforth decided to leave the movies behind and to hit the road and begin touring again, something he had not done since before his days in the Army.

But then the image of the Wanderer is perfectly consistent with the persona of the mysterious, piping stranger who drifts into town, hypnotizes its inhabitants, and makes off with all its women and children.

His image properly restored and corrected, Elvis was enabled to return to work with renewed self-confidence. At this point, he did two important things: (1) he began a series of legendary concerts in Las Vegas, garbed in stark white outfits with bell-bottomed trousers and gold belts (as though to counter the black outfit he had worn in the comeback special), the grandiosity of which are caught on film in the documentary movie *Elvis: That's the Way It Is*; and (2) he went back to the studio to record his finest album, *From Elvis in Memphis*, one of the greatest achievements of his career.

The songs on this album are polished works of pop art. They are radiant with Elvis's vitality and his sinuous, velvety vocals, encompassing an incredible range of styles from country to soul to pop to rhythm and blues. The album is filled with images of American life at its loneliest, a loneliness induced by the gigantism of the continent, pocketed by cities and towns that are few and far between and held together only by a loose mesh of oily black highways leading over dim and distant horizons. We catch glimpses of deserted backroads; rain-soaked fields, newly plowed; clotheslines hung with white sheets fluttering in the late afternoon; wheat fields beneath enormous blue skies, their golden weaves occasionally scarred by the ruins of deserted farmhouses and rusty, sun-rotting tractors. And long, long stretches of highway beside which forlorn hitchhikers roam without destinations.

There is also schmaltz and sentimentality here to be sure; these things are never far from Elvis's mind-set. But the album *is* a masterpiece of Americana, like an Ansel Adams photograph, or an Aaron Copland composition, or a painting by Edward Hopper. In one brief moment, this ultimate vision of Elvis's career was there before him, present all at once and intact in its grandeur. But then, like a desert rainstorm, it faded rapidly, for Elvis was never again able to achieve such musical greatness. Each successive album grew weaker, and each trip into the recording studio became sloppier and more half-hearted. In Elvis's entire career, there was only this one grand moment of certainty and supreme self-confidence, and it lasted for barely a flicker of a year between the *Comeback Special* and the 1969 album.

And then it was gone.

The moment of its vanishing can be marked, actually, quite precisely. This was the January 14, 1973, broadcast of yet another television special: *Aloha from Hawaii.* This show is culturally significant for a number of reasons. For one, it was the first time that a live broadcast of a performer was beamed around the globe via satellite to be viewed by an audience of 1.5 billion people in more than 40 countries *simultaneously* (thanks to the geosynchronous satellites of Howard Hughes). The idea for this monumental achievement was Colonel Parker's, Elvis's slick, grimy agent. And indeed, its scale of accomplishment is Pharaohnic.

For with this satellite broadcast, Elvis Presley becomes the first performer to actually surround the entire planet with his persona. The earth thereby was ensheathed in an electromagnetic cocoon made out of Elvis's image. For the duration of this broadcast, there was nowhere on the planet that Elvis Presley was *not.* In the dim horizons of ancient history, such a magical proliferation of one's image could have been achieved only by a god, a Vishnu or a Shiva, but in the 21st century we use technology to transform ancient myth into modern spectacle. Thus, if Russian cosmonaut Yuri Gagarin was the first man to be put into physical orbit around the earth, then Elvis Presley was the first man to send an electric image of his persona into orbit. This technological magnification of Elvis to god-like stature had an immediate side effect: for stripping his persona and sending it into orbit around the planet actually thinned out the real Elvis. He was diminished into insignificance by the gigantism of his own undertaking.

As a result, his performance in *Aloha from Hawaii* suffered. Technically, I suppose, it was correct. He sang every song with expertise and the appropriate amount of zeal. But the rapport with the audience evident in the *Comeback Special* and in the documentaries was gone, for he was cold and remote as a star. His *onstage* aura began to disintegrate for the first time—as opposed to his offstage personality, which had long since been crumbling—beneath the impact of so much electronic technology, and once destabilized, it began the long, slow process of decomposition that eventually led to his death.

For if it is true that the creation of the right avatar would help and inspire him, then the creation of the *wrong* avatar—a planet-size one—would have long-term deleterious consequences, just as his Frank Sinatra clone did in the 1960s. One cannot just swallow the planet whole and not expect a case of indigestion.

And, indeed, from this point on, it is all downhill for Elvis. His performances become weaker. His drug usage increases, causing him to slur his words while singing. He forgets lyrics, and often interrupts the songs with long and tiresome monologues. He begins to insult his band members in the middle of performances. He appears more and more tired, listless, and bored. Shows are cancelled, cut short, or dispensed with altogether. He falls getting out of his limousine and has to be helped to his feet. These collapses become frequent and so banal as to be expected. One has the impression that he is often simply propped up with medications long enough to stand there and mumble some lyrics, off key and out of tune, before wandering off the stage like a zombie. In some shows, he does not even greet, or acknowledge, his audience. And yet, none of this seems to bother his fans, for through the end of his days, attendance at his shows never flagged.

But the end comes, inevitably: Elvis dies on the toilet of a heart attack. Fourteen different drugs are found to have been in his system upon autopsy. His bowels were a wreck, his liver clotted with fatty cells, his eyes suffering glaucoma from the dye mixed with sweat that constantly dripped into them while performing under hot lights.

He is 42 years old.

Nearly two weeks after Elvis' funeral, writes Gail Brewer-Giorgio, three men were arrested for "attempting to steal the body of Elvis." This occurred on August 29, 1977. The men arrested said they did not want the body of Elvis but wanted to prove to the world that Elvis had *not died* and that there was no body in the crypt.[3]

The similarity to the conclusion of the Gospels, in which the disciples go to the rock-cut tomb in which Jesus has been interred, only to find it empty, should not be lost, for the Elvis-is-Alive theorists, who have been proliferating since the King's death in the late 1970s actually constitute a vestigial survival into modernity of the ancient cult of the dying and reviving god-king, whose death—from Osiris and Dionysus to Christ—never "really" took place, because the event is actually a harbinger of the god's resurrection into immortality and, by extension, of that of his followers as well.

Of these conspiracy theorists, Gail Brewer-Giorgio has been one of the most prominent and outspoken. In her book *Is Elvis Alive?* she hypothesizes that Elvis hoaxed his own death to escape from imprisonment by his own icon and disappear into a life of true freedom and anonymity at last. As evidence for her theory, she points out that many fans who attended Elvis's funeral felt that the body did not much resemble the King, for it had a pug nose that was not characteristic of Elvis, and the eyebrows and hairline seemed strangely different, as though he had been substituted with a wax figurine. She insists that it is strange that no photographs of Elvis as found at the time of his death survive, and that, indeed, *all* documents pertaining to his death and subsequent autopsy have disappeared, such as the toxicology report and the notes of the medical examiner's investigation. And, oddly, the spelling on Elvis's gravestone in the plot laid out for him at Graceland by his father Vernon, is wrong, for his middle name is inscribed as "Aaron" with two a's, whereas Elvis had always spelled it as "Aron" with a single a. (Brewer-Giorgio offers as the reason for this a superstition that if Elvis was not really buried in the plot, then misspelling his name was essential to avoid any sort of sympathetic magic that might actually bring about the death of the "real" Elvis.)

But conspiracy theories and paranoia, especially regarding the death of the celebrity, are a built-in feature of the architecture of the modern cult of the electric media superstar. Similar scenarios have been imagined by theorists regarding the deaths of Jim Morrison, Howard Hughes, Marilyn Monroe, Princess Diana, and even the fantasized death of Paul McCartney.

Indeed, it would seem that the more famous the celebrity, the more projections from the mythological imagination are encouraged as part of an (unconscious) attempt to deify the celebrity in question. In an age bereft of legitimate gods (at least in Western society)—and one in which the cult of the Catholic saints now lies in ruins, mostly forgotten—the media superstar has increasingly come to fill the void once occupied by these exemplary models of human conduct.

Thus, the Elvis-is-Alive theories are one way in which the archaic religious imagination has managed to survive, disguised by suburban pop culture, into late capitalist hypermodernity. For if any figure can be regarded as the "King" of the electric otherworld—in which the ghostly images of dead celebrities orbit the earth via the electromagnetic ether—then Elvis Presley, who died and was resurrected just as Osiris died and was resurrected to become the Pharaoh of the Egyptian underworld, or as Jesus Christ died and was resurrected to become the Lord of Heaven, surely can be regarded as the King of the cult of the dead celebrity.

4

James Dean's Death by Car Crash: An Analysis

Because James Dean was the first celebrity in this book to die, his death is worth paying careful attention to, for it is an originary phenomenon that enacts the primordial event of which all other celebrity deaths are but mere rehearsals. J. G. Ballard's suggestion that celebrity death by car crash confers an erotic luster to the myth is weirdly complex and unfathomable. Perhaps if Dean had not been killed in an auto crash, he would not have become the sexually irradiant icon, perpetually frozen in our cultural memory as a blonde, 24-year-old Wonder Child, not, in fact, all that dissimilar from the Western Hemisphere's first great Wonder Child, Achilles himself, the blonde warrior whose death at about the same age as Dean inaugurates the birth of Western civilization. From Achilles to James Dean, then, a strangely erratic arc of Western culture history is sketchily suggested, and the following analysis is an attempt to fathom at least a few of its implications.

And so to begin . . .

When did James Dean's car crash occur?

Dean's crash occurred on September 30, 1955 at 5:45 P.M.

Where was he going?

He was going to an amateur road race in Salinas, California.

Where had he been?

Dean had just finished shooting the movie *Giant.* In fact, a couple of weeks before the accident, he had made his last appearance in front of a camera for a public safety announcement in which he admonished young viewers to drive safely. "I find myself being *very* cautious on the highway," he says. "I don't have the urge to speed on the highway." When the interviewer asks him whether he has any advice to give the young, he tells them to be careful because, as he puts it, "The life you might save might be mine."

Who was riding to Salinas with him?

His German auto mechanic, a man named Rolf Wutherich, who already had been in two crashes and would die in a car accident in Kupferzell, Germany on July 20, 1981. Wutherich had just signed a contract with an American book publisher to tell his story about James Dean.

What road were they traveling on at the time of the accident?

Dean and Wutherich were traveling on U.S. Highway 466. They were approaching the Y-shaped intersection with Route 41.

What direction were they traveling?

They were headed west, into the setting sun, which for a while had been blinding them, although the sun already had disappeared behind the mountains along the horizon at the time of the crash, casting purple shadows over the yellow-brown hills.

Were his headlights on?

In fact, Dean had not yet turned on his headlights; if he had, it is possible that the oncoming car would have seen him.

In other words, both landscape and circumstance had conspired to render Dean effectively invisible?

"Jimmy says he can go so fast on his motorcycle that no one can see him!"[1] Thus Jay Hyams, one of the authors of a Dean biography, reports Dean as having told him as a child. Apparently, Dean's lifelong addiction to speed was part of a dream to accelerate his physical body to the point at which it could no longer be detected by the human eye. Of course, this would be literally possible only for an object traveling at light speed, but at the time of his death, Dean *had* nonetheless finally attained this dream of becoming invisible through the acceleration of his physical body. The car he was driving was perilously low to the ground and colored silver and thus, in the murky desert twilight, with no headlights on, it would have been all but invisible to oncoming traffic.

What kind of car was he driving?

A 1954 Porsche 550/1500 Spyder RS. Introduced at the Paris Motor Show in 1953, the Porsche 550 featured a two-seat, open-top aluminum body fitted over a tubular ladder chassis with an MR layout mid- and rear-mounted, 1.5-liter, air-cooled flat four-cylinder shaft-driven dual overhead cam engine, which weighed about 550 kilograms (1,213 pounds). The engine was designed by one Dr. Ernst Fuhrmann.

Dean's car was nicknamed "Little Bastard," which was painted onto its rear end. The number 130 was painted in black on its front and rear hoods, as well as on the side doors. (*The Little Prince* was one of Dean's favorite books, and the nickname "Little Bastard" was given to him by one of the crewmembers who had worked on *Giant*. Thus, like the incarnation of the Hindu god Vishnu who begins as the dwarf Vamana, and takes three steps to claim the world for himself, with the third step becoming a giant who encompasses the universe, Dean also was the "Little Bastard"—physically, he was quite small—who ultimately became a "Giant.")

What kind of car did he crash into?

Dean crashed into a black-and-white 1950 Ford Tudor sedan. If Dean's car was the "Little Bastard," this thing was the "Giant" by comparison.

Who was driving this other car?

The driver of the other car was a man named Donald Turnupseed, a 23-year-old California Polytechnic State University student. He died of lung cancer in 1995 at the age of 63.

How fast was Dean going?

No one is certain how fast he was going. Initial reports suggested something like 80 miles per hour (mph), while later reports tended to downplay this, offering a more modest 55 mph. Recent computer-generated tests have suggested an impact speed of more like 70–75 mph.

How did the accident happen?

The accident occurred when the driver of the Ford, Donald Turnupseed, who was headed east, in the opposite direction, turned left off Highway 466 onto Route 41. Turnupseed did not see Dean until it was too late. Dean did not have time to brake, and instead he seems to have accelerated and swerved to the right in an attempt to go around the Ford. Turnupseed did not have sufficient room to clear the huge car, however, and smashed into its front end driver's side, which plowed into Dean's body, crushing his chest and forehead and snapping his neck, while throwing Wutherich out of the car. The Porsche spun 45 feet to the northwest, where it landed near a telephone pole. Turnupseed's car rotated counterclockwise and slid about 39 feet in the opposite direction.[2]

What was the official cause of death as listed on Dean's death certificate?

Broken neck, multiple fractures of upper and lower jaw, multiple fractures of left and right arm, and internal injuries.

What did James Dean dream about on the night before the crash?

We don't know, but we do know that he had been troubled by a recurring dream in which his mother (who died when he was nine years old) was beckoning to him as though trying to tell him something. In Dean's dream, his feet are sinking in quicksand and he is having trouble understanding her message. It is possible that she was beckoning to him from beyond the grave to come and join her in the afterlife. His mother's death disturbed him all his life, and he felt guilty about it, for his father's rejection of him implied to his young psyche that he somehow had been responsible for her death. Much of his self-destructive behavior seems bound up in this psychological knot.

What were Dean's last words?

"Don't worry, that guy'll stop. He's gotta see us." Strange words for a man who had just attained invisibility. But perhaps, like the Invisible Man when his experiment was first beginning to work, he did not yet know that he had become invisible.

How old was Dean?

Dean was 24 years old. He was born on February 8, 1931. He lived for the same amount of time it takes Jupiter to go around the sun twice.

What myth was Dean fulfilling by means of his accident?

Dean was attempting to fulfill the myth of the youth Phaeton who, uncertain of his paternity (his father happened to be Helios, the sun), was advised by his mother to journey east and find out. So Phaeton traveled to his father's abode and his father admitted that Phaeton was indeed his son and, as proof of this, agreed to grant him any boon he wished. Phaeton wanted to drive the sun chariot for one day, and so Helios reluctantly agreed. But the four horses, sensing an unsure hand, ran wild and tore a gash into the sky that became the Milky Way. Then they ran so closely to the earth that they scorched it and caused the inhabitants of Africa to turn black and the rivers to dry up until Zeus finally struck Phaeton with a thunderbolt to bring him down. The youth plunged earthward, where he fell to his death into the river Eridanus. His sisters stood on the banks of the river and wept ceaselessly until they were changed into poplars. Thus Ovid.

Immanuel Velikovsky has suggested that the Phaeton myth is a disguised memory of a comet that crashed into the earth and dislodged it from its vertical axis. And indeed, the death of James Dean seems to have altered the topology of popular culture to such an extent that, had it never occurred, the pop landscape would not look remotely like what it does in the 21st century. Dean was the archetypal shooting star who fell to earth like a being from another world, and whose impact generated a cult of celebrities who tried to imitate him by performing their own crashes in his honor.

What was he wearing on the day of his death?

Dean was wearing a T-shirt, blue jeans, and the red jacket that he had worn in *Rebel Without a Cause*. The movie was released a few days after his death, and it immediately spawned a red jacket craze. High school kids wore red jackets everywhere and the shop that had produced them in Hollywood could barely keep up with the demand. Thus, the disciples participate in the master's myth by seeking to imitate him.

Is there any evidence that Dean had been rehearsing his crash for some time before its occurrence?

In fact, there is some evidence. He was addicted to speed, and he was notorious for being a reckless driver who terrified anyone unfortunate enough to get into a moving vehicle with him. He had several near accidents with his motorcycles and his sports cars while driving along the windy curves of Los Angeles roads. The scene in *Rebel Without a Cause*, in which he races against another driver in a chicken run to see who can stay in their car the longest before driving over a cliff seems, in retrospect, to have been a rehearsal for his death. It is almost as though he were trying it out to see how death by car crash might feel. And he was always dropping little hints to the people who knew him that he fully expected to die young. He had no intention of living past the age of 30.

In short, his crash came as a surprise to no one, for his friends and acquaintances had warned him many times that he would die this way. According to a famous anecdote, the actor Alec Guinness, upon viewing Dean's new Porsche 550, predicted that if Dean persisted in driving it, then he would be dead within a week's time. (This was on September 23; he was killed exactly seven days later.) Yet, Dean chose not to heed any of these warnings. He had been practicing his death for many years, and he was not about to let anyone get in his way. He knew that his death would transform him into a god, and that is precisely what he had always wanted.

The crash, then, was "deliberate"?

Dean's crash made him the "Giant" that he otherwise never would have become without it. Had he gone on living, as in the case of Marlon Brando, he never would have attained the god-like stature that he has since acquired.

What would an Old Testament prophet have made of Dean's crash?

Who knows? But the female mourners of Tammuz would have set up one hell of a racket. Witness the following spectacle from one of the biographies: "one girl cried out during the showing of *Giant*: 'Come back, Jimmy! I love you! We're waiting for you!'"[3]

The deification of the young boy-god who is stricken down early in life, and that generates a religious cult all its own is not unique to our society, but it does have certain Classical precedents, such as the death of Antinous, the emperor Hadrian's 18- or 19-year-old boy lover who supposedly drowned in the Nile (whether by accident or homicide we do not know). Hadrian was apparently so stricken with grief by the boy's death that he had him proclaimed a god—emperors had been deified, but for a commoner, such an apotheosis was then unheard of—and built temples to his memory. Indeed, the city of Antinopolis was founded on the banks of the Nile where he died, and some Classical authors, such as Dio Cassius, have even suggested that Hadrian might have sacrificed the boy to build Antinopolis in the first place. In any event, Antinous was identified with Osiris and festivals and rites were held in his honor for several centuries after Hadrian's death. "More than thirty cities," according to Louis Crompton, "in Asia Minor, Greece, and Egypt depicted Antinous on their coinage as a god or hero, and children who had known the apostle Paul might have prayed for salvation in the new god's temple at Tarsus."[4] His visage was mass produced all over the ancient world in statues and works of art, and has come down to us as the most famous face of Classical civilization. He was truly the prototype and forerunner of James Dean.

If Dean, then, had never crashed, is it possible that subsequent celebrities like Jackson Pollock (1956), Albert Camus (1960), Jayne Mansfield (1967), or Grace Kelly (1982) might never have chosen to perform their crashes in imitation of his?

To fulfill a myth, there must first be a prototype. Every archetype has a prototype, and Dean was the prototype of the man for whom the acceleration of his persona to light speed via celluloid simply was not fast enough. He desired the acceleration of his *physical* body to light speed. Of course, that dream always remained only a dream, but it was, nevertheless, the ideal that lay behind his acquisition of faster and faster cars and of participating in more and more races over time. But, once attained, the translation into immortality via death by car crash became one of the three primary possibilities by means of which a Cold War celebrity could attain mythic status, the others being death by drug overdose or shooting by a stalker.

Thus, Dean establishes for all time the myth of Celebrity Death by Car Crash that his envious imitators would seek to model after him.

What god, through his death, did James Dean actually become?

Once we have weighed all the evidence, it appears that Dean was trying to become a modern incarnation of the god of transportation. Perhaps this is why it was so important to him to crash his car in the empty wilderness of a lonely American highway—that is, to assure us of his intentions and guarantee that we would not mistake them. If he had died in Los Angeles, we would not have known whether he had desired to become a god of the city or of the highway. But by dying in the wilderness on a cracked and desolate country road, it as though he were specifically drawing our attention to the fact of the highway itself.

Nearly a year after Dean's death on Highway 466, on June 29, 1956, Eisenhower signed the Interstate Highway Act into law. The intent was to create 42,500 miles of interstate highways over a decade, at a cost of around $27 billion. The project was not completed until 1991, however, and ended up costing more than $114 billion to finish. The idea for the project was born out of Eisenhower's experiences traveling in a military convoy across the United States in 1919 from the White House to San Francisco. The roads at the time were so bad that it inspired his vision of a mesh of Interstate Highways connecting American cities together to maximize the flow of traffic, especially necessary in cases of national emergency.

As in the case of the death of Antinous, it is almost as though Dean's death were the sacrifice that, once performed, could allow construction of a civic monument to begin, in this case, a highway system instead of a sacred city. For whenever the ancients wanted to build a new temple or a public building of some sort, a sacrifice was always necessary (such sacrifices were often human, but usually, they were animal). The bones were then buried inside the building, for it was thought that the indwelling spirit of the animal (or human) could then be transferred to the building to animate it.

Every new environment demands new gods to mark and sanctify the habitation as a dream born with their blessings. In the phantasmal world of the 1950s postwar suburbs, James Dean was to become the patron saint of highways, automobiles and above all, car crashes.

In ancient Greece, the Eleusinian mysteries involved a ritualized reenactment of the abduction of Persephone and the grief-stricken wanderings of her mother Demeter, as initiates would travel along the Sacred Way, stopping at certain key points to imitate the actions of Demeter's search for her abducted child. In like fashion, the occurrence of annual activities such as the James Dean Death Drive, in which the faithful perform the myth of their dying god by retracing his route along the back roads of California highways, stopping at this gas station or that general store where Dean had put in on the day of his death, is confirmation that James Dean is indeed in the process of becoming a deity, just like his Classical predecessor Antinous.

5

The Strange Tale of the Wondrous Life and Curious Death of Marilyn Monroe

There she is: Marilyn Monroe, goddess of the silver screen.

Or perhaps: Marilyn Monroe, *two-headed* goddess of the silver screen, for as everybody knows, Marilyn had not just one, but rather *two* names: she was Marilyn Monroe the movie star, but she was also Norma Jeane Baker, the orphan child of suburban Los Angeles. And she had, furthermore, two mothers: a biological mother named Gladys, who disowned her very early on in her life; and Grace McKee, the woman who raised Norma Jeane during the latter half of her childhood and imprinted upon her the idea that she might become the double of the movie star Jean Harlow. There is, of course, also the name that she chose for her onscreen persona, with its almost deliberate doubling of first initials. (And Marilyn, fittingly, was a Gemini.)

Two heads, then; *two* identities: one for the silver screen, and one for the real world that, together with its images and ideas, project forth the luminous, flickering puppet plays of the darkened movie cavern.

But a *silver* screen? According to ancient tradition, silver was the metal associated with the moon. And the moon's light, unlike the sun's, is not self-radiated, but rather projected on the moon's scarred and rutted canvas from another source, just like the movie screen that receives *its* light from an exterior source in the movie projector.

Two worlds, then: a dayworld lit by the sun—and to go along with it, a daytime persona—and a nightworld opened up by a phantasmal moon lodged in a cavern-shaped sky, with a correspondingly mythical persona to inhabit its shadowy silver-limned grottoes and bowers.

* * *

Marilyn Monroe, or rather Norma Jeane Baker, was very much aware of the fact that she was casting her shadow into the light of another world. As Donald Spoto, in his biography, comments: "Truman Capote wrote of finding Marilyn sitting for a long while before a dimly lit mirror. Asked what she was doing, Marilyn replied, 'Looking at her.'"[1]

Susan Strasberg recalled walking with Marilyn when she noticed a group of fans awaiting her return at the Waldorf. "Do you want to see me be her?" she asked Susan. Momentarily confused, Susan then saw something remarkable:

> She seemed to make some inner adjustment, something "turned on" inside her, and suddenly—there she was—not the simple girl I'd been strolling with, but "Marilyn Monroe," resplendent, ready for her public. Now heads turned. People crowded around us. She smiled like a kid.[2]

"Marilyn Monroe," then, was a mask put on very deliberately (and ironically) by Norma Jeane Baker, who was conscious all her life of being *two* women, a real one made of flesh and blood, and an electrically generated construct. The woman *we* know and refer to as "Marilyn Monroe" was never confused about this basic fact of her existence, unlike many other, less sophisticated actors and actresses who are unwittingly swallowed up by their public personae. For contrary to popular belief, there was nothing witless about the real Marilyn Monroe.

Gentlemen Prefer Blondes (1953) was Marilyn's third starring role after *Don't Bother to Knock* (1952) and *Niagara* (1953) (in both of which films she played psychopaths), and it was the film that put Marilyn Monroe into the American psyche as a permanent piece of furniture. As the title implies, if gentlemen *prefer* blondes, they also like brunettes, and from the film's opening image of Marilyn Monroe and Jane Russell paired off together in identical glittering red showgirl dresses, to the double wedding sequence at the film's conclusion, the blonde and the brunette are scarcely ever separated throughout the duration of this film. Indeed, they are together so often that they may as well be Siamese twins. "Two heads are better than one," Jane Russell's character Dorothy Shaw comments, as though to confirm the appropriateness of the metaphor.

Marilyn Monroe plays Lorelei Lee, a gold digger who is interested in men only for their money, while Dorothy Shaw is a romantic who is forever dreaming of erotic possibilities. Thus, Lorelei's concerns are those of the dayworld of social prestige and achievement, while Dorothy's erotic inclinations are more suitable to the nighttime and the bedroom. The film's plot is a chronicle of the two women traveling on board a luxury liner headed for France, and in one scene, Dorothy strolls on deck accompanied by a man with whom she suspects she might fall in love. The two comment on the beauty of the moon while the man attempts to kiss her (she is wearing a black dress, while Lorelei, on the same night, is briefly glimpsed wearing a *gold* dress). Thus, the film-makers, in a naïve way, got the tradition right: the blonde = the sun, the social world, and the quotidian concerns of daily life; the brunette = the moon and the night, the realm of privacy and hidden, indoor rituals that have the generative effect of bringing the dayworld into being.

Gentlemen Prefer Blondes also sets up the pop culture archetype of the dumb blonde and the smart brunette who must solve all her problems for her. This is a trope that continues all the way down to the 1970s television show *Three's Company*, in which the dumb blonde, Chrissy, finds her foil in the smart brunette Janet, who is forever providing her with escape routes for her erotic entanglements. (*Three's Company*? If the two women in this show correspond to the dual goddess, then what about their roommate Jack Tripper? He is, of course, Triptolemus, the boy child in the care of Demeter to whom she teaches the arts of agriculture and the plough, which becomes, in visual art, his phallic symbol; and *no* character was ever more ithyphallic than Jack Tripper, whose name implies that he is constantly tripping over his own erect phallus. Demeter, Persephone, and Triptolemus, then, were really a threesome in Classical mythology.)

With this film, the electrically generated avatar known as "Marilyn Monroe" is born, for it was in *Gentlemen Prefer Blondes* that Marilyn's persona as a ditzy blonde forever *appearing* to be at the mercy of the men around her is established. Marilyn had already portrayed this persona in bit roles in films like *All About Eve* and *Monkey Business*, but *Gentlemen Prefer Blondes* is the film that forever typecast her as an actress.

She would spend the rest of her life battling to rid herself of this image.

> Of all the prostheses that mark the history of the body, the double is doubtless the oldest. But the double is precisely not a prosthesis: it is an imaginary figure, which, just like the soul, the shadow, the mirror image, haunts the subject like his other. This mirror image makes it so that the subject is

> simultaneously itself and never itself again, which haunts the subject like a subtle and always averted death. This is not always the case, however: when the double materializes, when it becomes visible, it signifies imminent death.[3]

Thus, Jean Baudrillard.

Walter Benjamin writes in his famous essay on the work of art in the age of its mechanical reproducibility:

> The feeling of strangeness that overcomes the actor before the camera . . . is basically of the same kind as the estrangement felt before one's own image in the mirror. But now the reflected image has become separable, transportable. And where is it transported? Before the public.[4]

This separation of one's mirror image from one's physical self is tantamount to the creation of a clone that, by means of its very transportability, takes on its own life and becomes entirely independent of the actor who generated it. As Benjamin elaborates, this is not an act without consequences for the actor or his art:

> This situation might also be characterized as follows: for the first time—and this is the effect of the film—man has to operate with his whole living person, yet foregoing its aura. For aura is tied to his presence; there can be no replica of it. The aura which, on the stage, emanates from Macbeth, cannot be separated for the spectators from that of the actor. However, the singularity of the shot in the studio is that the camera is substituted for the public. Consequently, the aura that envelops the actor vanishes, and with it the aura of the figure he portrays.[5]

For Benjamin, the word "aura" has a special significance, for it is a sort of magical property tied to specific things, persons, or works of art, and is intimately bound up with their history and their specific form of "thereness." Aura, however, is not something that can be captured in a reproduction of any kind, mechanical, electronic, or otherwise. When a work of art is mass reproduced, the reproduction *excludes* the aura of the original that it copies, and not only that, but the multiplicity of the reproduction actually has a *damaging* effect on the aura of the original. In Benjamin's phraseology, technological mass reproduction causes the aura of the original to *decay* through overfamiliarity of the image on the part of the mass public. After all, who wants to look at the real Mona Lisa in a museum when we've seen it almost every day on T-shirts, coffee cups, and television shows?

Something similar would seem to apply to actors in film. In this case, the actor corresponds to the original work of art, which, through electronic overreproduction, begins to suffer from a strange kind of psychological *decay.* From the point of view of the actor, the psychological effects of being stripped repeatedly of her own image via electronic reproduction are experienced as a state of utmost disorientation. The public becomes familiar with the mass-produced image, not the real actor, and consequently, it expects the actor to exist, *to be*, in a specific way, and the more narrow those expectations become, the more strait-jacketed the actor begins to feel.

Thus, Marilyn Monroe's lifelong battle against the decay of her own aura as a result of the growth and flourishing of her electric persona became a fight to preserve her own sanity. The gradual increase over time in her use of barbiturates to help her sleep at night; mounting anxieties over her performance in front of a camera; her almost pathological hand-wringing at her desire to be accepted and admired by the public; all these things acted as a kind of psychological entropy that became *worse* with time, ultimately resulting in the mental catastrophe that landed her in an insane asylum.

But this event was actually the outcome of a plot hatched by her own doppelganger to get rid of the flesh-and-blood Marilyn (that is, Norma Jeane). For, languishing in the Payne Whitney Clinic in New York, where she was locked up inside a padded room, Marilyn was kidnapped by her electric double who saw to it that she be locked safely away from public view. This way, her doppelganger could be free to live its life basking in the admiration of the public without worrying about whether the real Marilyn would attempt to sabotage her fame by putting *her* to rest inside some costume closet in the dark corner of a forgotten studio back lot.

Benjamin's analysis of the nonreproducibility of an actor's aura misses a certain point, however, because it was by means of the very technological process of filming and then projecting on a gigantic screen the images of actors like James Dean, Marilyn Monroe, and Marlon Brando that conferred on them the auras of mythic grandeur that they otherwise did not possess. Benjamin did not understand the essentially myth-making power of film.

That point aside, then, we are confronted with the mythical gigantism of the celluloid version of Marilyn Monroe, for it is crucial to realize that absolutely *anything* that is put through the sieve of filmic technology—actors, narratives, or what have you—is instantly transformed into mythic spectacle. And the onscreen persona of Marilyn Monroe is a case in point, for it is an obvious retrieval of the ancient goddess Venus, just as Elvis Presley's television persona was a pixilated reconstruction of the Greek god Dionysus. Indeed, these two figures have a certain symmetry, for Marilyn Monroe was to the male psyche the exact equivalent of what Elvis Presley was to the female psyche, since both personae had an intense and compulsively erotic effect on their opposite sexes.

Nowhere is Marilyn-as-Venus more evident than in the Billy Wilder comedy *The Seven Year Itch* (1955). Seven-year cycles are a normal part of the 28-year sidereal cycles of the planet Saturn, which squares itself astrologically every seven years. In Billy Wilder's film, a seven-year cycle does indeed bring forth the goddess Venus in the form of Marilyn's character, who is known simply as the Girl, a woman who lives in the apartment directly above that of the film's protagonist Richard Sherman. Sherman's family has gone away on summer vacation and now he is beginning to feel a seven-year marriage itch that manifests itself as a twitching of his thumb (which is interesting, because according to traditional chiromancy, the thumb is assigned to Venus, just as the index finger corresponds to Jupiter, the middle finger to Saturn, the ring finger to Apollo and the pinky to Mercury). Thus, when the Girl descends from her apartment to visit Sherman, it is like a visitation from a goddess, for her presence is hilariously unsettling to him.

In the iconic scene in which the Girl stands above the subway grille while its rush of air blows her skirt about, Marilyn's identity as Venus is here confirmed, for the image is a modified retrieval of Botticelli's 1483 painting *The Birth of Venus*. In that painting, Venus stands on a half-shell rather than a grille (the half-shell is a symbol of the vulva, a fact that is more evident in the Roman copy of Apelles' now-lost painting of Venus Anadyomene, in which the shell's interior is painted pink). In Botticelli's version, the newborn Venus is blown toward the shore from the left by the zephyrs, the winds, while on the shore waiting to receive her is one of the Horae, goddesses of the seasons, who offers a cloak to her that is waving and furling in the winds blown by the zephyrs. Thus, if the painting is rotated 90 degrees to the left, then the direction of the winds is coming as it were from below, while the garment is blowing above it. This corresponds very closely to the image of Marilyn Monroe standing on the subway grille while her skirt erupts all around her (and the position of Marilyn's hands is about the same as that of the Venus *pudica* style upon which Botticelli has modeled his Venus). In this one celluloid image, Marilyn Monroe becomes the Venus of the modern Metropolis.

* * *

So why, we must now ask, did Marilyn Monroe's electronic doppelganger contrive to have her locked away in a padded cell? This incarceration took place in 1961, but it was the response to Marilyn's repeated attempts, upon leaving Twentieth Century Fox in 1955, to destroy and ruin her doppelganger's very existence. This began with Marilyn's attempt to perform an operation of excision upon her Siamese twin in the 1956 film *Bus Stop.* This was the first film she made after leaving Hollywood to study at the Actor's Studio in New York, and it is a deliberate attempt to forge for herself a reputation as a serious actress and to put an end to her double's life. "I want to be an artist, not an erotic freak," she is said to have remarked. "I don't want to be sold to the public as a celluloid aphrodisiac. It was all right for the first years. But now it's different."[6] (This moment in her career corresponds to that of Elvis Presley's when he sought to restore his early Ed Sullivan image by appearing in his *'68 Comeback Special* for television. The difference, however, was that Elvis was attempting to repair the electric persona that had made him famous and had been frayed by a string of bad movies, whereas Marilyn Monroe in *Bus Stop* was performing an act of demolition upon the electric persona that had brought her so much recognition as a comedic actress.)

A scene early on in this film synopsizes what Marilyn is up to with regard to her old image: her character, a show girl, sings "That Old Black Magic" to a crowd of cowboys in a dusty, smoke-stained bar in Phoenix, Arizona. Her routine evokes a scene that is at first glance familiar to us, for in film after film, she had played a show girl who performed glitzy Hollywood musical numbers before an audience dazzled by her virtuosity. But on closer inspection, it becomes evident that this performance differs fundamentally from all her others, for in it, she makes every effort to ravage her by then all-too-familiar persona: she is garbed in a moth-eaten outfit and her singing is so bad that it can barely be heard above the disinterested chatter of the cowboys. In a conscious allusion, furthermore, to the high-gloved pink outfit she had worn for "Diamonds Are a Girl's Best Friend" in *Gentlemen Prefer Blondes*, her ill-fitting long-armed gloves keep sliding down her shoulders and she has to keep pulling them back up. This is not the vivid persona whose colorful, Van Gogh-like luminosity had hypnotized us in her earlier films, for *this* woman is as crinkled and used as an old road map. She wears little makeup and indeed, she is so pale as to appear washed out by the burning Phoenix sun.

Bus Stop is Marilyn's first attempt at a demolition of her own electrically created image, and it very nearly succeeds. But the success was only temporary, for soon after, she was engulfed once more by stereotyped roles in films like *Some Like It Hot* (1959) and *Let's Make Love* (1960). As the myths and folk tales tell us, doppelgangers do not die easily, and Marilyn Monroe's would soon have its revenge.

But before that could take place, she completed a final film with one last attempt at an erasure of that same persona. In *The Misfits* (1961), the Venus of the Metropolis ventures out into the stark white wilderness of the Nevada desert, where she changes roles—and cults—to become the Lady of the Wild Things, known as Artemis (Latin Diana) in the Classical World, Ninhursag ("Lady of the stony ground") in the Sumerian, and Neith (the patron goddess of hunters) in the Egyptian. For in this film, she journeys out to the desert with three cowboys, each of whom is in love with her, to accompany them on a hunt for wild mustang horses, which the cowboys intend to sell to dealers who will in turn sell them to be turned into dog food. The film's climactic sequence, in which Marilyn descries the brutal trapping of these slat-ribbed and starving horses against the bone white backdrop of the Nevada salt flats is a brilliant elegy for the death of the genre of the Western, which would be essentially moribund within a decade of the film's release. The images of the cowboys stalking their prey using a biplane (to scare them) and a pickup truck to tie them down is a haunting and pathetic evocation of the final degradation of the old West, ground down into salt by the churning mill of industrial civilization. Marilyn's character realizes this, and the vision of her tiny figure—dwarfed by the ancient and almighty emptiness of the desert—screaming to a black-and-white sky is not only a wail of tortured compassion for the horses, but a scream against the violence and brutality inflicted on ancient ways of life by industrial society.

It seems somehow appropriate that Marilyn Monroe—the patron goddess of cities—winds down her career with *Bus Stop* and *The Misfits*, both of which concern journeys to the deserts of the Southwest, where urban civilization even in the 21st century is still just a thin and precarious wafer covering a vast, enervating wilderness of violent rocks and jagged cliffs. Here, Marilyn's character—perhaps the closest she has ever come to actually playing herself—is a sad, sullen wreck of a woman who radiates depression even when she is smiling. It is almost as though the desert itself has robbed her vitality, just as it has nearly ground down the handful of paltry horses, which is all that the cowboys are able to muster up. Such ennui is precisely what one expects of a cultural cycle that is spiraling down toward its end.

And so the end comes, inevitably, for Marilyn's double will tolerate no more of these attempts to efface her presence in the electric universe. She has devised a plan; a plan that, this time, will succeed in killing off the real Marilyn Monroe once and for all. No one will remember her as she really was: Norma Jeane sitting in her apartment reading her beloved Tolstoy or Dostoevsky; writing poetry; planning escape routes through other celluloid vehicles that would bear her safely beyond the harmful reach of her own stereotype. It is only the smiling, glitzy, ditzy Marilyn Monroe of the photographs and the magazine covers and the movie posters who anyone will remember. It is only *this* Marilyn, split from the bone core of the real Marilyn by means of the camera eye, who will be adored by the future.

And it is *this* Marilyn, the *other* Marilyn, the one that gazed back at her from the depths of the polished mirror and the dark caverns of the cool and remote theaters, who will make certain of this.

At least three main scenarios have been put forth to explain the death of Marilyn Monroe.

Donald Spoto, in his biography, presents us with one theory for her death, a theory that is specifically designed to counter the Kennedy conspiracy theory, while modifying the popular conceptions of a suicide by drug overdose. As he points out, Marilyn in her last days had no reason to commit suicide: she had just made a number of new picture deals, one of which was to involve her playing her idol Jean Harlow in a biopic. Contrary to her despairing persona in *The Misfits*, the photo sessions that were taken subsequent to that film show a bright, smiling, radiant woman just on the threshold of leaving her youthful beauty behind and beginning to transition into a mature and wise older woman. Indeed, Douglas Kirkland's photographs of her in white sheets soaked with studio light reveal an almost ethereal, delicate being structured out of patterns of luminescence. The black aura of depression does not darken her in these photographs, and suicide does not seem consistent with the events of these final days.[7]

Something else may have happened, something more sinister and ominous than suicide, but yet more banal and pathetic than a Kennedy plot. Rather, Spoto suggests that her death may have been the result of an "accidental" overdose given to her by her creepy psychiatrist, a man named Dr. Ralph Greenson, a man who, apparently, was obsessed with her.

Greenson entered her life very late (in 1960), but his possession of her was immediate and almost total. At first, he received her in his office five days a week, but then this expanded to seven; finally, he arranged for her to move in with him and his family. Marilyn's trust in this man was just about complete, and so she did nearly everything he asked her to do, including turning down film roles that might have rescued her from captivity by her own stereotype. Before taking on Marilyn, Greenson had been a sort of Hollywood psychiatrist for the stars, but when Marilyn came his way, he quickly dropped all his other clients. When she moved into her own house, he advised her to take on as a housekeeper an older woman named Eunice Murray. Greenson had been working with Eunice for years as a patient supporter, although she was not medically trained. Marilyn did, indeed, take Eunice on as a live-in housekeeper, but it became apparent to Marilyn's friends that Eunice was just a spy for Dr. Greenson, for she was frequently seen telephoning him to report on her activities and whereabouts. And according to Spoto, whenever Marilyn would come too close to bonding with other potential mentors, Greenson would advise her to put an end to the relationship. Both Eunice and Greenson acted as forbidding obstacles to her friends, slowly and gradually isolating her.

The very day of Marilyn's death on August 4, 1962, was to be Eunice's last day of employment in her service. And not only that, but Marilyn, after agreeing to remarry Joe DiMaggio, had decided to sever all ties with Dr. Greenson, and it is possible that on the day of her death, she told him this.

On that day, Marilyn was tired, for she had not slept the night before, and she had been taking Nembutal throughout the day in an attempt to sleep. At around 7:20 P.M., Joe DiMaggio's son telephoned and found her bright and talkative. They spoke for about 10 minutes. But then, at around 7:45, on the phone with her friend Peter Lawford, it was evident to *him* that something terrible had happened, for she was slurring her words and was nearly incoherent. Even more alarmingly, she began a litany of goodbyes and faded off into silence.[8]

According to Spoto, Marilyn's death was the result of a lethal interaction between two drugs, Nembutal, and chloral hydrate. Apparently, Dr. Greenson did not know that Marilyn's physician, Dr. Hyman Engelberg, had started her up again on Nembutal, which Greenson thought he had weaned her from. Not knowing this, he advised giving her a chloral hydrate enema to help her sleep, and Spoto theorizes that the housekeeper, Eunice Murray, was the only person around who could have administered it. Within minutes, the drug interaction had killed her, and Eunice and Greenson found themselves in a suddenly drastic situation, which they attempted to cover up with a number of contrived and inaccurate stories about finding her dead body, which nobody paid too much attention to since, after all, Eunice was an old woman, and Dr. Greenson a respected doctor. (The police were not called, for instance, until nearly 5:00 A.M., while Eunice initially claimed she had found Marilyn's body just before midnight, but then later changed her story to say that she had found her at around 3:00 A.M.)

Marilyn's death, then, may well have been an "accident." On the other hand, Dr. Greenson fits the profile of a sort of modified celebrity stalker, albeit a respected and trusted one (at least by Marilyn). In the light of Marilyn's firing of Eunice and then telling Dr. Greenson that she did not want anything further to do with him, one is given pause to contemplate the timing of how swiftly her "accidental" death at their hands soon followed. It would appear more likely that, even if only unconsciously, Greenson decided that if *he* could not have Marilyn, then no one would.

Donald H. Wolfe, in his book *The Last Days of Marilyn Monroe*, offers an alternative to Spoto's theory, one that is a species of the conspiracy advocates who link her final days to affairs with both of the Kennedy brothers. Wolfe develops the theory, derided by Spoto, that Marilyn had an affair not only with Jack Kennedy—which Spoto does not deny—but also with Robert Kennedy. Wolfe points out that numerous witnesses—including, at one point, Eunice Murray herself—insisted that Robert Kennedy showed up at Marilyn's residence on the last day of her life, August 4, 1962.

In Wolfe's scenario, Kennedy is said to have shown up once in the late afternoon between 3:00 and 4:00 P.M. and to have argued with Marilyn over some missing object, which Wolfe hints darkly may have been the fabled red diary that she purportedly kept and in which she wrote down a number of secrets confided to her by both Kennedys, such as knowledge of Jack's plot to have Castro killed, hydrogen bomb testing, Bobby Kennedy's efforts to jail Jimmy Hoffa, and so on. Unable to locate the diary, Kennedy (together with Peter Lawford) left the residence, but Kennedy returned later that night, along with two thugs, around 10:00 P.M.

One of Wolfe's primary witnesses, a man named Norman Jefferies, who was Eunice Murray's son-in-law, claims that, when these men arrived, they asked him and Eunice to take a hike and that when they returned around 10:30, they saw Bobby Kennedy and the other two men leaving. They then found Marilyn lying face down on the bed not in her bedroom, the way she was later found by policeman Jack Clemmons at 4:25 A.M., but in the guest cottage. The frightened Eunice called Dr. Greenson who arrived shortly after an ambulance (that neighbors Mr. and Mrs. Abe Landau are reported to have seen upon returning to their home around 11:00 P.M.). According to ambulance driver James Hall, Greenson attempted to revive her by giving her a shot of adrenaline to the heart, but the needle hit a rib and it was at about that time that she expired. "'After that, all hell broke loose,' Jefferies stated . . . 'there were police cars, fire trucks, more ambulances—you name it! A police helicopter landed at the golf course and soon they were all over the place.'"[9]

After that, Marilyn's physician, Dr. Engelberg arrived and Marilyn's body was then moved into the bedroom, where a group of mysterious plainclothes policemen staged the "locked room" scenario in which first-responder Jack Clemmons would later find her at around 4:30 A.M. (Los Angeles Police Department Capt. James Hamilton was supposedly a close friend of the Kennedys, and would have directed his men in staging this secondary crime scene.[10])

Marilyn's filing cabinet apparently had been broken into, perhaps on that very night, and Wolfe hypothesizes that Robert Kennedy, together with his two henchmen possibly delivered a "hot shot" of barbiturates to Marilyn with either the intent to kill her or else put her out of commission while they ransacked her house looking for the red diary and other documents.

Wolfe's book makes for a compelling read, and he does have a knack for touching on anomalies that do not fit Spoto's version of events: why, for example, did Eunice Murray years later say just after completing a BBC interview when the cameras were off and she thought she was not being recorded,

> "Why, at my age, do I still have to cover up this thing?" I asked her what she meant, and she then astonished us by admitting that Robert Kennedy had indeed visited Marilyn on the day she died, and that a doctor and an ambulance had come while she was still alive.[11]

Why have numerous witnesses testified to an ongoing fling between Marilyn and Robert Kennedy? Why did neighbors say they saw an ambulance and a police car parked in front of Marilyn's house at 11:30 P.M., when the police say they didn't arrive until 4:30 A.M. or so? Are *all* these people lying? If so, why?

On the other hand, I find Wolfe's vision of "all hell breaking loose" around 11:00 P.M. with helicopters, fire engines, police cars, and at least one ambulance difficult to swallow. All of this commotion would have had to have been cleared up and quiet by 4:25 A.M. when policeman Jack Clemmons arrived, and this time frame, though possible, does not seem likely. Crime scenes take a long time to clean up. And even more difficult to believe is the number of people who would have to have been involved in such a conspiracy, including the policemen, firemen, and ambulance drivers, who all would have to have kept quiet to give Jack Clemmons the illusion that he truly was the first responder.

Clemmons, however, did have the feeling that the crime scene somehow had been tampered with, and the time gap between when Eunice Murray said she found Marilyn dead on her bed at around midnight and when she called the police at around 4:25 A.M. seemed highly suspicious to him. It seems suspicious to me, too, but not inconsistent with Spoto's hypothesis of a staged crime scene as the result of Greenson's goof of killing Marilyn by mixing her medications. I can imagine Greenson and Eunice spending four or five hours of hand-wringing wondering how to cover up their mistake.

Of course, it is still possible that Marilyn simply committed suicide by taking an overdose of Nembutal (although, in that case, where did the chloral hydrate come from?). After all, she had attempted to kill herself with barbiturate overdoses on at least five previous occasions, for she was depressed throughout most of her life. But this, too, seems unlikely, since so many witnesses have come forward with stories that contradict this "lone suicide" scenario. Clearly, *something* seems to have occurred that the suicide scenario does not seem to fully cover.

But in a digitized world like our own, in which information is broken up, fragmented, and cut into little pieces to be shot at the speed of light through the matrix of integrated circuits in which we are all embedded, absolutely anything is plausible, because an image-saturated culture bombarded by information overload welcomes and invites that particular form of pattern recognition known as myth-making, or nowadays, urban legendry. Anything, in such a society, can be true.

And often is.

III

Tribes (The 1960s)

John F. Kennedy, Andy Warhol, the Beatles, and Jim Morrison

INTRODUCTION

In contrast to the foregoing worlds of the 1930s through the 1950s, we are about to enter a dark and turbulent stygian landscape of Boschian nightmares and Magritte-like daydreams of fluid figures intersected by hyperdimensional alterities.

With the advent of the Beatles, a new dawn was heralded in the history of the electric superstar, for it is at this point that the lone American icon—typified by performers like Elvis Presley and Johnny Cash—breaks into a tetrad of four equally famous individuals. Thus, the British response to the cult of the American loner is to create a tribal entity whose primary totem, the beetle, is an ancient Egyptian symbol of the sun's daily rebirth on the eastern horizon. The band's name, moreover, is taken from the name of a motorcycle gang in *The Wild One*, a film that was prescient of the coming reshaping of the pop icon landscape by means of a retrieval of preliterate tribalism.

The arrival of the Beatles seemed to have been heralded, however, by the death of the Sun King at the noon of his life, for with the assassination of John F. Kennedy, the archetypal king is killed by his lunar adversary, a stalker who cast multiple shadows on the ground behind him.

The killing of Kennedy in Dallas signals the shifting of political power in America from Washington to the Southwest (that is, to Lyndon Johnson, Ronald Reagan, Barry Goldwater, and the Bushes), where the basic structural features of the Space Age, from White Sands, New Mexico, to Houston, Texas, will be worked out.

With the shifting of the cultural Zeitgeist ever further westward, we encounter Jim Morrison, the Lizard King at the edge of the West, writing poems while lounging on Venice Beach, watching the sun melt like a candle into the sea before him. Revisiting the deaths of Marilyn Monroe and Howard Hughes, Morrison ends by drowning himself in a bathtub full of heroin, having attained his goal of dissolution at last. And, in reworking the myth laid down by Elvis Presley, he may even have opened a new door for the King, who was then still living, by inspiring him with a fresh possibility for ending his own life through chemical decomposition. Morrison's life was not only an accelerated version of Elvis Presley's, it was actually a complete revisioning of the American myth of the shooting star whose acceleration to light speed ends by shattering the limits of his own mortality, for Morrison begins his career in an advanced state of psychological decay, precisely where Elvis leaves off.

And just as every new religion needs a priest to sanctify its rites and memorialize its dead, so too, Andy Warhol became the first great priest of the new Cold War cult of the vanishing celebrity, for his images captured the ghosts of the celebrity dead whose electromagnetic shadows go twittering about the orb of our earth. Warhol's art, as we shall see, constituted a veritable necropolis of dead celebrities whose *sahus* he mummified and placed into the niches along the walls of his New York catacombs.

And so, the great tribal leaders of the society of the 1960s: John F. Kennedy, chieftain of a newly televisualized constituency; Andy Warhol, leader of the Exploding Plastic Inevitable Factory of the deranged; the Beatles, at the vanguard of a British invasion of the American continent of the instantly famous; and Jim Morrison, tribal leader of pagan Los Angeles, with his attempts to reachieve those ancient Walpurgisnachts celebrated at the top of the Magic Mountain beneath the light of the full moon.

These are the people. The 1960s are the time.

Come. Let us go then, you and I . . .

6

The Assassination of John F. Kennedy Considered as a Case of Media Warfare

John F. Kennedy was a man who spent his entire life, from first to last, living *inside* a television set. If we want to understand that life, then we must, like Alice through the looking glass, crawl up into the radiant, pixilated landscape of television and learn to make our way about its rows of contoured electrons, carefully aligned on a grid and pulsing with life, like large radioactive eggs. We must learn to tread carefully across this landscape, for different laws apply than those of the physical world beyond the television set. This was the world in which Kennedy lived, and it was also the world in which he died. So if we wish to gain some measure of comprehension of the mythic magnitudes of that life, then we must learn how to survive among the crashing, burning electrons and constant shower of sparks, pops, and flashes that surround us.

Jean Baudrillard has written that the perfect crime was the murder of reality by the simulacrum; the replacement of the real by the virtual, which has eliminated all traces of the real that it sought to duplicate. In the present case, the perfect crime has not been the murder of Kennedy, but rather the use of television to invent him in the first place. For indeed, it *was* the television that put him in the White House (by a narrow margin of 100,000 votes, admittedly), for Kennedy was the first president to understand, and effectively use, the new medium. He had begun appearing on television talk shows like *Meet the Press* since 1951, and all through the 1950s he surfaced—sometimes with his family—on commercials and talk shows.

However, the black-and-white image created by the cathode ray tube was not the real Kennedy at all, but rather his double: a flat, two-dimensional icon of a young man, strong, virile, smiling, and full of fresh, new life, surrounded by a warm, loving family. This was the ideal suburban nuclear family, and it mirrored the American public as it wanted to see itself at the time. In fact, from the very moment of his first appearances, this rapidly scanned bundle of parallel lines of electrons claiming to be the real Kennedy activated a mythological consciousness in the American psyche in which Kennedy appeared like an Arthurian knight in a wasteland filled with decrepit old men and scheming villains: Lyndon Johnson had already had one heart attack; Khrushchev was a shrunken old peasant; De Gaulle was another old man; and Eisenhower portrayed a rapidly fading image on television that prophesized the coming awakening to self-awareness of the military industrial megamachine, which he had helped build. On television, the public could see that Kennedy, just past the age of 40, was young enough to appear capable of slaying the dragons of Communism and banishing the old men back to their caverns. It is thus no accident that the youngest president ever to be voted into office coincided with the *first* presidential candidate to become familiar to his voters via television.

But this, as I said, was only how Kennedy's electric image *appeared.* The real Kennedy, the man who was casting this shadow into the ether, was crippled by Addison's disease and in constant pain from a faulty spinal column. Very often, he had to prop himself up on the backs of chairs, or lean over desks to support his weight. He was as lame as the Fisher King out of Arthurian romance whom it was the job of the knights to *heal.* And Kennedy was no better a family man than the average character out of Greek mythology, for he was as capable of fidelity to his wife as Zeus had been to Hera.

If we persistently lapse into the language of mythology, it is not an accident, for television as a Cold War technology represents the first medium to begin to introduce electronic stained glass into our sensorium.[1] Television, as McLuhan pointed out of electronic culture generally, represents the phenomenon of "light *through*" rather than the "light *on*" of printed page or movie screen. And following television, other electronic screens, from computers to liquid crystal displays (LCDs) to security monitors in stores, will slowly, inevitably, as the 20th century unfolds, become a pervasive environment. This environment will be visible only to artists like William Gibson, the opening line of whose novel *Neuromancer* reads, "The sky above the port was the color of television tuned to a dead channel."[2] All these screens are tantamount to a retrieval of Gothic stained glass in which the images are illuminated by means of light shining *through* them. For television is its own source of pulsing, radiant energy; its forms, like the figures of our dreams, give off a spectral luminescence as they fill living rooms with an otherworldly blue glow. Indeed, television opens up a window into an electronic underworld populated by the ghosts of dead celebrities confined to play reruns endlessly, like the condemned and tragic figures of Hades. They are magic portals that provide the means of a temporary access to this etheric underworld, an underworld that wraps the planet in a sheath of low-frequency radiation sent beaming from tower to tower, antenna to antenna. Inside this televisual underworld there resides, in compressed form, the whole history of human mythology played out in the banal style of melodramas, talk shows, and sit-coms that are as artistically decadent and meaningless as the plays of Menander. And yet, it is precisely this underworld with all its celebrity ghosts and doppelgangers with which we have chosen to surround the planet.

The Kennedy administration seems to have been something of an experiment conducted to identify the effects of placing the first electric image of a man, rather than the man himself, into the White House. For with Kennedy we can credit a series of televisual firsts: the first-ever televised presidential debates; the first televised weekly press conferences; the first lady's first televised tour of the White House; and later, with Kennedy's assassination, the first 24-hour news coverage of a traumatic event; and, with Ruby's shooting of Oswald, the first live murder caught on television.

And what are the effects of this televisual experiment?

First, television actually shrank the White House down to a scale model and placed it *inside* the home of every American with a television set. For the first time ever, the White House was pixilated and domesticated. Jackie's televirtual tour created a new kind of intimacy between the suburban home and the White House, an intimacy that never before had existed. Thus, television brought the outside world into the inside of the suburban household. Watching Kennedy's televised weekly press conferences gave one the feeling of having the president discourse on international affairs *inside* one's house. The impression was created thereby of having a personal, private chat with this new, young, approachable president right inside one's living room.[3] All this was highly involving and deeply participational, but it was also, of course, a virtual illusion made possible by the new Cold War technology of television, which made Kennedy seem virtually a member of the family. It became easy, therefore, to forgive him for things like the Bay of Pigs crisis. After all, family members do make mistakes.

In the televised presidential debates with Nixon, the power of television as a magic eye capable of forecasting future events is revealed. We see how Kennedy's electric doppelganger assumes a posture in relation to Nixon of the mythical eagle that looks *downward* at its prey. Kennedy was filmed always looking down his nose or, at best, directly level with his audience, whereas Nixon's gaze always glowered from *below* looking *upward* like a character out of a Stanley Kubrick film. In the third debate, telecast by satellite, Nixon looked out with bulging, paranoid eyes like something swimming in the bottom of a dirty fishbowl. The television was no friend of Nixon's, and the debates reveal him as the resentful dwarf always smoldering over the other knights who are busy getting all the chicks. Kennedy's persona, on the other hand, resembles nothing so much as a Nietzschean exemplar of master morality: cool, calm, and insouciant, his image is that of the man of power who looks *down* on his adversary. Nixon's tense, sweaty, pale, nervous disposition is that of the slave who looks *up*.

Nixon, furthermore, comes across in these debates like Alberich the dwarf in Wagner's Ring operas, always skulking about in the shadows feeding his resentment at the gods who have stolen the Rhinegold from him as he plots devious ways of getting it back. The television clearly favors Kennedy, for *he* resembles Wotan, a born leader, always concerned more with how the other gods will perceive him and relate to his power than about stealing or getting power from anywhere else.

And what of the ability of the magic eye to forecast future events?

Alberich devises a scheme for gaining power from the gods, but the scheme will backfire on him and render him even more powerless. And Wotan will be assassinated by Siegfried.

Toward the end of Kennedy's first 100 days in office, the Bay of Pigs crisis took place. The Central Intelligence Agency (CIA) had led Kennedy to believe that their invasion might be a success, for they assured him that disaffected Cubans would rise up in an internal revolt and support the invasion of the exiles who landed in the Bay. But Kennedy, worried about how the world—via television—perceived a U.S.-sponsored coup d'état in Cuba at just the time that he had been working to counter the image of the United States as an imperialist power by improving relations with the developing world, decided to call off the airstrike that would have bombed the beachhead and cleared a path for the exiles. As a result of the failure of the operation, 1,200 of the 1,400 exiles surrendered to Castro's 20,000 men and Russian tanks. As a result, Kennedy fired Allan Dulles, Richard Bissell, and General Cabell and threatened to scatter the CIA into a thousand famous pieces.

From that moment on, Kennedy and the CIA would be forever at odds.

Because we are viewing these events from inside the televisual underworld, however, the point of view of mythology, with its ideogrammic compressions of complex processes, becomes relevant. Mythologically speaking, then, we must note that the pig is an animal with an underworld valency attached to it, just as the eagle or the lion have upperworld valencies by virtue of their association with the sun. Cuba, then, is the underworld that will give way beneath Kennedy's feet and swallow him whole. The motives for a conspiracy against him always point back in one way or another to the Bay of Pigs and Kennedy's failure to provide the necessary military backup. And later, after the Cuban Missile Crisis, Kennedy will pull the plug on Operation Mongoose and cut off funding to the anti-Castro exiles altogether. (Notice how the subliminal fact of the mongoose being an inveterate enemy of snakes subtly puts Castro into the role of the great serpent to be slain.)

If Kennedy was the solar hero with the great eagle on his shoulder, then Cuba with its pigs was Kennedy's hell.

But then, we might just back up for a moment and give some thought to the nature of these new Cold War technologies, whereupon it will become evident that the CIA and Kennedy were working at cross-purposes with each other from the very moment Kennedy stepped into office in January 1961. The Bay of Pigs was merely the first visible manifestation of the fault line that already lay between them.

As we have pointed out, the Kennedy administration was the first in history ever to install its scale model into the average American suburban home by means of television. In this respect, television transformed America into a giant tribal village by providing instant access from the huts in the outlying regions to the Oval Office of the head chieftain at its center, whose conferences with the elders the viewer is thereby privileged to overhear. Indeed, it seems that Kennedy's agenda was to reproduce himself via millions of television sets and actually install electronic clones of himself inside the homes of millions of people, thus invading their homes but not their privacy. Who, at the time, would not want a hologram of Kennedy sitting in the middle of their living room giving a careful narration of his foreign policy measures?

With the Cold War surveillance technologies of the CIA and other American intelligence agencies, however, something else was going on, something very much opposed to the televisual way of doing things. Surveillance technologies do not bring the outside world into the domestic sphere, but just the opposite: they invade and erode privacy. They tear the roofs off of houses and leave them flayed open and ready for dissection by spy satellites and U2 planes. They bring the inside out into the open. They embarrass. They invade. They split open one's shell and leave one tender, naked, and exposed to the watchful eyes of the circling eagles.

In his nonfiction novel *Oswald's Tale*, Norman Mailer recounts how, while Oswald was living in Minsk, the KGB would bug his apartment and listen to his conversations with his wife, of which the KGB recorded hundreds of hours of transcripts. Mailer gives us liberal samples of these boring conversations, but they are evidence that Oswald and his wife were the stars of their own show, for they were "on air" for nearly 24 hours a day and, furthermore, Oswald was aware of this. The only place to which he and Marina could retire with a reasonable certainty of not being overheard was the outside balcony.[4]

Intelligence gathering amplified via electronic surveillance technology is tantamount to a radical transformation of the entire planet into a global orb without rooftops. With the launching into orbit of *Sputnik* in 1957, paranoia became the new baseline of consciousness. Whenever, in the early James Bond movies, Sean Connery checks into a room in a hotel, the first thing he does is look over the room for bugs. In any era before the Cold War, such an act would have been regarded as proof of a man's insanity, but within the new world configured by surveillance technologies, it is regarded as an act of the highest mental alertness.

Such transurban tactics are therefore wholly opposed in both aim and method to the values of suburban domesticity that Kennedy brought to his administration via television. Kennedy was the first president to be domesticated by the American people as a result of the suburbanizing function of television, but the CIA, with its espionage activities, is disruptive and destructive of any such cozy home atmosphere.

So, given the contradictory natures of these two new kinds of Cold War technology, with Kennedy on one side and the Cold Warriors on the other, it is no wonder that they clashed. They both stood for very different kinds of worlds.

Consequently, if one considers the possibility that it was indeed the CIA—or certain elements within the CIA—that assassinated Kennedy, one is struck by the suspicion that the act itself was an indirect condemnation of television and televisual culture. The act has the feel about it of a rejection of the very idea of a televisual president, of the notion of a man being put into the White House largely as a result of beaming an electronic image of himself to millions of homes. And, furthermore, when one considers that the power of this new medium was far from being politically neutral, but rather crippled certain individuals, like Richard Nixon or Lyndon Johnson, then one can begin to understand the resentment that the very idea of a man favored by television being put into office might have generated.

Television is a form of low-resolution technology. Grainy, fuzzy, distorted images are spray painted onto a gray-black screen on which they can barely be discerned (at least, in the 1950s). As McLuhan pointed out, television is therefore highly participational, because it requires the viewer to "fill in" the completion of its images, like a cartoon or a comic book. It is an image-based medium—albeit a medium of poor quality images—and it was Kennedy's primary means for weaving himself together with his constituency out of a complexly interwoven meshwork of threads of light. With television, Kennedy (who was of Irish ancestry) was able to transform his administration into the equivalent of an electronic Book of Kells, in which he forged an American tribal identity based on a tightly interwoven conception of himself as a chieftain at the head of his electro-serf peasantry. The American public, through the relationship Kennedy created with them by means of television, felt close to him and recognized that any decision he made on their behalf affected them directly. It is possible that no American president since Kennedy has had this sort of a relationship with his public.

On the other hand, the kinds of technologies favored by the CIA are profoundly alienating and disruptive of social cohesiveness. Such technologies, furthermore, are not primarily visual, but rather auditory in nature: bugs, recorders, hidden microphones, and obscured listening devices. With the digging of the Berlin Tunnel, for instance, in 1953—masterminded by William Harvey—wiretaps were placed on a host of phone lines in East Berlin. The CIA is always *listening in* on someone somewhere. Their kind of technology, then, favors a *nonvisual* bias. They use cameras, of course, but only as supplements to a wide range of highly differentiated listening devices. (Notice how, in the CIA biopic movie *The Good Shepherd* [2007], tape recorders are featured in scene after scene as the primary surveillance technology. And although photographs turn up every now and then as plot points, *no* cameras appear in the film *at all.*)

So to counter Kennedy's icon-based technologies, the CIA would, in Dealey Plaza, have had to create an invisible network of hidden technologies, such as disguises, radios, and walkie-talkies. Thus, Kennedy's pixilated image is trapped by an electronic matrix of pulse signals fired back and forth between radios from the School Book Depository to the gunmen on the grassy knoll and to whatever other conspirators were loose on the street below or hanging out by the triple underpass. In this way, they could communicate with each other auditorily as though they were merely standing right by one another; the electronic amplification of their voices, that is, enabled them to stand far enough back from each other to allow Kennedy to walk right into their midst, completely unaware of the invisible threads of communication connecting these men.

Kennedy did indeed walk right into this electronic trap. His ally, the ubiquitous mechanical eye, present in the form of the various eight-millimeter movie cameras and Polaroids™ and other such cameras, was unable to help him in this case, because the cameras could not perceive the hidden grid of electronic signals—together with false identities—surrounding him (although they *would* come to his aid later on to piece together the assassination by conspiracy theorists).

Thus, in Dealey Plaza on that day, two kinds of technology were at war: a covert technology of the *ear*, based on invisible signals conspiring to hide gunmen who had vanished into the anonymity of the crowd; and the various technologies of the *eye*, based on one or another form of photography, which could see everything *except* the invisible electromagnetic signals, and therefore could avail Kennedy, for once, nothing. Kennedy's world had been based from start to finish on clearly visible images: photographs in magazines, television appearances, public speeches. The world of the CIA, on the other hand, was based on the use of technology to aid in various forms of invisibility: making people disappear, changing identities, blending into the shadows. (The photograph of the three tramps who may not be tramps at all is a classic instance of this.) The CIA's condemnation of a man who had based his career and power on the merely popular manipulation of *images* seems palpable. Such a man is too obvious, they would have thought. Too shallow. He understands nothing of covert operations, or of the art of similitude, or the blending and blurring and manipulation of information to make people disappear.

Thus, when the dust cleared and the limousine had continued on through the triple underpass, everyone ran up the grassy knoll—as the filmed images show us—to find . . . no one. The shooters had gone. Disappeared into thin air.

Precisely the kind of magic trick the CIA had been training itself to do for years.

Or, Lee Harvey Oswald, on that day, was indeed the lone gunman, a variation of the archetypal celebrity stalker who chose to steal a scene from history to etch himself permanently into its lineaments (a stalker who, with Jack Ruby, somehow managed to generate his own stalker, an episode that, in the annals of Celebrity Stalkeriana is, as far as I know, unique). This certainly would not be out of attunement with the cult of the electric superstar whose megapopularity attains a near religious intensity, for it is the way of all founders and prophets to end by being assassinated. Christ, Mani, Hallaj, the Buddha, Gandhi, Martin Luther King, Jr., Malcolm X: all were pavers of the way for new religions and all ended at the hands of assassins or traitors. The light speed celebrity is nothing if not the founder of a new church of the electronic personality, and such charismatic leaders, soaked in the white radiance of fame, always cast their shadows on the ground before them in the form of shrunken devils and demons who decide, like the shadow in the Hans Christian Anderson fairy tale, to detach themselves from their masters and eventually eliminate them.

In the history-less realm of mythology (history-less because it is based on archetypal repetition of events that always *are*) such acts take on a timeless, synchronic resonance that seem to occur under a proscenium arch in which the laws of time cease to operate.

Oswald *could* have been the archetypal assassin in this mythic moment of American history, in which the Sun King (also known as the Oak King; note the Texas live oaks that obscured Oswald's aim on the north side of Elm Street) is stricken down at the height of his powers by his lunar adversary, and that is certainly what the authorities would have us believe. But the authorities' perceptions of the events are filtered through the lens of a particular view of America that is based on a myth all its own, and any event that takes place in such a mythical land of fable must conform to the contours of that preestablished myth. And that myth, as Baudrillard discussed in his *America*, is that America is a utopian colony based on an attempt to escape from history.[5] America, the myth goes, is an ahistorical land that is somehow magically suspended from the laws of history that have governed all other civilizations in all other places. We Americans have the unique privilege of having attained historical escape velocity. Presidents are not assassinated by shadow governments waiting in the wings to take over control of the ship of state. Those sorts of events only happen in the Old World, not in America.

According to such a myth, Oswald could *not* have been part of any conspiracy, but rather could only have acted alone. He is a force of chaos, an anomaly cast forth by the mutagenic forces that govern all such aberrations. His role is merely to put on the mask of the assassin and strike down the Sun King.

For if the converse were true, and Oswald did *not* act alone, then America would be no different, no better, than any other society in history. And in the end, it would amount to nothing so special after all. America would turn out to be subject to the same laws of historical unfolding that have governed all other civilizations everywhere else.

Myth, in this view, becomes more important than history; how we *want* to see things happen is more important that what really did happen. Of course, no such thing as objective history exists, for history is always controlled by mythology, and it is myth that determines *a priori* what we are, or are not, willing to perceive. As Gombrich has shown in his *Art and Illusion*, we see things only in terms of the conventions and stereotypes that we have come to expect, for such stereotypes structure our perceptions in unconscious patterns that are difficult to become aware of. The 19th-century lithographic artist who renders Chartres cathedral with pointed arches in the windows—when in reality, its arches are rounded—is really seeing Chartres in terms of his myth of Gothic grandeur and beauty.[6] Such a myth determines his perceptions. In fact, there are no theory-free perceptions of anything.

The desire to escape from history is as deep and urgently felt by Americans as their desire to escape from the earth with all its messy biological processes to build remote space stations among the stars that will be antiseptically cleansed of such biological errors as bacteria and viruses. It is a Neoplatonic dream—a Cold War dream, articulated in the science fiction novels of the 1950s—of escape from the Great Mother and the earth and the body in favor of the soul's ascent to the planetary spheres where reigns the pure, errorless laws of a pristine mathematics shorn clean of chaotic ambiguities.

It is, in the end, nothing more than a fantasy.

7

Andy Warhol's Cult of the Dead Celebrity

Andy Warhol was the first great icon painter of electronic society. In contemplating his gallery of celebrity portraits, we are struck by the possibility that some Medieval icon painter, an Andre Rublev, say, had died and been reborn in the 20th century as a poor kid from Pittsburgh with no memory of his former life, but with all his artistic skills still intact. Warhol was the first painter to subliminally intuit the emergence of a new religion of celebrity demigods, and he became not only its first icon painter, but also its first high priest. His famous paintings from the early 1960s, the Elvises and the Marilyns and the Liz Taylors and the Jackie Kennedys, are one and all portraits of the newly emerging saints and demigods of the age of electronic stained glass. (It is no coincidence that he was raised in the Byzantine church and regularly attended mass on Sundays all his life, for his religious upbringing helped prepare him for his life's task.)

The salient technological characteristic of our age is the video screen, whether we are thinking of the now rapidly fading cathode ray tube (CRT) screens or the nascent plasma and liquid crystal display (LCD) screens, and Warhol painted low-resolution portraits in a style that deliberately mirrored the quality of images as they appear on electronic windows. His 1967 Marilyns, for instance, "had been influenced by an out of focus TV set," as Victor Bockris points out, and his early Marilyns and Elvises of the period between 1962–1964 are likewise low-resolution images that provide little in the way of visual detail for the viewer, like an image on a television screen. Indeed, many of his paintings seem to have a flickering quality about them, like the *Double Torso* of 1967 or his famous *Flowers* from the same period, as though a faint blue radiation were emanating from them. His images are often grainy and out of focus, for the silk-screening process involves "an intermediate stage in which the image is translated into a series of halftone dots" like a pixilated image on a monitor.[1] Thus, Warhol is the first painter to exhibit the influence of the television screen upon the creation of his paintings.

So it was not so much famous *people* that Warhol painted as their mediatic avatars and doppelgangers. Indeed, Warhol himself, in one of his last paintings, seems to allude to this fact with his *Self-Portrait* of 1986 in which he shows himself seated at a computer holding a mouse in one hand, while the monitor displays an image of a camera pointed at its own monitor, reiterating itself to infinity. The whole painting, luridly colored, is rendered as a series of fuzzy, pixilated cathode ray lines scanning a disintegrating image of Warhol like something out of David Cronenberg's *Videodrome*. With this self-portrait, Warhol acknowledges to us that he was fully aware of the affiliation between his paintings and the electronically generated images of CRT screens.

But what makes Warhol so interesting in light of 21st-century popular culture is how he foresaw the lineaments of the world in which we now live, for Warhol understood that under electric conditions absolutely anyone, anytime, anywhere could become famous for "15 minutes." His entire oeuvre—and not just the paintings, but the films, too—was a prophetic forecasting of our televisual world of webcams, YouTube, reality television, cable television, and music videos. Nobody would have understood better than he the popularity of YouTube's "lonelygirl15," in which a 19-year-old actress playing a 16-year-old girl showed webcam videos of herself doing nothing but hanging out in her bedroom. Warhol understood that in the medium of electric images, it does not matter what happens when you turn on a camera and place it in front of someone doing nothing special, for it is the medium itself that creates the star and not something as antiquated as a storyline or a plot. He was the first to put a camera in front of a bed and film an entire night of a man sleeping and then show the resulting film in theaters as art (*Sleep*); or of a man eating mushrooms (*Eat*); or getting drunk (*Drink*); or to turn a camera on the Empire State Building for eight hours and then subject audiences to his "epic" display of changing lights and shadows (*Empire*). Later, he came up with the idea for a television show called *Nothing Special*, in which he proposed placing a movie camera on a street corner and just leaving it running. Such works are the forerunners of the Googlecams strapped atop automobiles that go rolling to show the sights; or of YouTube's boring videos of people doing nothing; or of reality television shows in which the stars are nobodies who become famous for no particular reason. Warhol was the prophet of what Jean Baudrillard has termed the "telemorphosis" of our society, or the transformation of the entire world into a television studio.

Warhol built his own religion out of a cult of the dead celebrity. Indeed, he is to the cult of the celebrity what Saint Paul was to early Christianity: its first organizer and official proselytizer.

Take a look at his early Marilyn Monroes: just as the lives of the saints were inspired by their bizarre and fantastic deaths, so too, Warhol's first great subject of iconic veneration was inspired by her death in August 1962. With his *Gold Marilyn*, he actually sets about telling us what he is up to, for in this painting a single publicity still of Marilyn from the movie *Niagara* floats over a background of gold paint. This is a deliberate allusion to the Byzantine icon paintings of his childhood that had hovered on the periphery of his consciousness in the St. John Chrysostom Church in Pittsburgh, for it was traditional of such paintings to represent the saints against a gold background. Thus, with this painting, Warhol is telling us that he is undertaking the task of becoming the first icon painter of the lives of the electronic saints.

The great masterpiece of his Marilyn paintings is the *Marilyn Diptych* of 1962 in which he sets off two different grids of Marilyn serializations against each other. The series on the left-hand side of the canvas (five Marilyns across and five down on both grids) is rendered in vivid, garish Technicolor, while that on the right is in black and white and composed of badly smudged and faded prints.

At first glance, the painting seems to allude to the fact that Marilyn's early films were in black and white, whereas her later films were in color, but since the color images are on the left and the black-and-white images on the right, this seems to undercut the normal left-to-right reading sequence of the Western Hemisphere in which we would expect the chronologically earlier images to be on the left and the later ones on the right. Indeed, in terms of Warhol's syntax, a degradation or a gradual erosion of Marilyn's celluloid image would seem to be implied, as though he were forecasting a time in the future during which our civilization would have forgotten her.

The dichotomy of the two panels seems to imply something else, something about the dual nature of Marilyn Monroe herself. Just as the doubling of the initials of her name suggests, Marilyn was a twofold figure: a real flesh-and-blood creature whose psyche was riven by the fractures of deep emotional wounds, and also a celluloid goddess of the silver screen, the object of everyman's desire. Thus, Warhol's Marilyn is the double Marilyn of two worlds: the real-life world of time and space, with all its imperfections and flaws (hence, the badly eroded and smudged black-and-white Marilyns) and the celluloid Marilyn of Technicolor dreams and fantasies in which desires are granted and frustrated only momentarily. In the *Marilyn Diptych*, we are given the two-faced Marilyn as she has been bequeathed to us: the Technicolor Marilyn of myth and legend and the banal Marilyn of real life, who was gradually washed from existence in a flood of drugs and emotional deprivation.

When Warhol later returned to his Marilyn Monroe paintings for the last time in the 1980s, he created a new series entitled *Reversals*. In them, Marilyn is painted, once again in serial form, only now the patina of shadows and light is reversed, so that she appears as a photographic negative.

Warhol raises a question here, the same question that Walter Benjamin in his famous essay had addressed, namely, in the age of mechanical reproduction, what is the status of an original work of art? As Benjamin pointed out, we can no longer speak, in such an age, of originals in regard to photography and film in the same sense in which we can point to a painting or a sculpture or a work of architecture and say, "there, that is the original work of which all others are but copies." Can we consider photographic negatives "originals" in this same sense? How could we, when it is only the copies made from those negatives that are of interest? Thus, we are back to Baudrillard's precession of the simulacra, in which the simulacrum displaces its original. In the age of electronic reproduction, it is *only* the copies that are of interest to anyone.

But what about the original Marilyn Monroe, the real flesh-and-blood Marilyn who occupied space at one point in time? Perhaps she, too, was only the negative from which her doppelganger was made, the original doppelganger that appeared in all of her movies and not the later cliché-laden image that was circulated by the media to the point of degradation in subsequent years.

Around the same time he was painting the Marilyn Monroes, Warhol also painted his famous Elvises. The first of that series is the *Red Elvis*, in which 36 facsimiles of a photograph of a rather brooding-looking Elvis are laid out in grid fashion. The photograph is only a headshot and it therefore is atypical of Warhol's other Elvis paintings, which invariably feature his entire body. Thus, the headshot implies an equivalence principle with the Marilyns: Elvis is the masculine equivalent, in terms of erotic connotations, of Marilyn Monroe. No young girl of the 1950s would rather have been in any other bed than Elvis's, and no man in any other bed than Marilyn's. Elvis was the Dionysus figure whose musical cymbals and flutes had a magically intoxicating effect on women, driving them mad with ecstatic rage and wine-sodden joy: indeed, so rapturous as to tear apart wild animals and drink their blood as analogs of the ripping apart of Dionysus, the god of the grape, the god *in* the grape, whose blood is stamped and pressed and turned into wine. Thus, the *Red Elvis* looks as if it had been dipped in blood, for it is completely saturated in red paint, as though Warhol sensed the connection between Elvis and the blood-soaked cults of Dionysus.

With his *Triple Elvis*, created at about the same time, Warhol introduces his standardized Elvis Presley image of the singer from one of his movies, a western entitled *Flaming Star.* Here, he is shown garbed as a cowboy with gun drawn and a snarl on his lip. His complete body, from head to toe, is repeated three times, and the whole is covered in a silvery patina. (Here, Elvis-as-cowboy points to his connection with the country-and-western music that he synthesized with black man's rhythm and blues, for the cowboy, lest we forget, was originally a creation of the South. *The Virginian* by Owen Wister is the first Western.)

Warhol, in his autobiography, *Popism: The Warhol Sixties*, gives us a gloss on his associations with silver:

> Silver was the future, it was spacy—the astronauts wore silver suits—Shepard, Grissom, and Glenn had already been up in them, and their equipment was silver, too. And silver was also the past—the Silver Screen—Hollywood actresses photographed in silver sets.
>
> And maybe more than anything, silver was narcissism—mirrors were backed with silver.[2]

Thus, Warhol subtly works into his composition the problem of the silver screen as an electric mirror that creates doppelgangers. The serial repetition of the three Elvises refers to the power of the media to generate mirror images of its celebrity protagonists and multiply them thousand-fold, like a funhouse mirror.

With *Elvis I and II* Warhol offers an image that is the equivalent of his *Marilyn Diptych*. One half of the composition, the same as that of the Marilyn, is in garish Technicolor, while the right half is a black-and-white image that appears to be fading. For Elvis, too, like Marilyn Monroe, started out in black-and-white movies and crossed over to color.

Elvis was also a phenomenon of doubling that was created in his case early on by the television screen. The television appearances on *Ed Sullivan* doubled Elvis, mirroring him, so that there was a live physical Elvis and an electric one. His doppelganger, like Marilyn's, grew stronger over time, while the real Elvis himself, paled and faded by drugs, disappeared from the world altogether.

In addition, perhaps the painting refers to the coming of the future Elvis impersonators, the hordes of weak reproductions of him who will attempt to mold themselves in his image. (The celebrity impersonator is actually a post-facto stalker; instead of stalking the real-life celebrity, he stalks his image.)

After studying so many celebrities, Warhol came to a point at which he said that he wished to represent the anonymous deaths of unknown individuals. Thus, the car crash and disaster paintings that he began to work on at about the time of his early icon venerations are the counterpart to the celebrity paintings, for his car crashes and suicides are "anonymous fatalities." "It's just that people go by and it doesn't really matter to them that someone unknown was killed, so I thought it would be nice for these unknown people to be remembered by those who ordinarily wouldn't think of them."[3] Here, Warhol is peering into the future of mediatic society in which absolutely anyone can become famous for any reason, no matter how banal. At about the same time as Warhol was painting his early works, Howard Hughes was launching his geosynchronous satellites into orbit, thus plugging the planet in and turning it "on," and suddenly fame was no longer elitist but attainable by anyone on earth.

Consider his *Most Wanted Men* series. Warhol was invited by the architect Philip Johnson to hang a painting on the outside of the building that he had designed for the 1964 New York State World's Fair (the very same World's Fair at which Walt Disney had engineered his famous theme park exhibits for GE and Ford, and where he unveiled his first animatronic Lincoln). For this event, Warhol designed a huge 25-unit silkscreen of 13 portraits taken from the Federal Bureau of Investigation's (FBI's) catalog of Most Wanted Men and put them on the side of the building—like saints on the wall of a church—an act that promptly confirmed its avant-garde status by worrying the fair's organizer Robert Moses, because most of the criminals were Italians. Moses ordered the mural to be taken down, but when Warhol proposed replacing it with a serial repetition of a photograph of a smiling Moses, the mural was instead merely effaced by covering it with silver paint (like the backing of a mirror).

Warhol was presciently forecasting the future of American media, for this gigantic painting prophesied the coming of television shows like *America's Most Wanted* and *Cops*, and movies like Oliver Stone's *Natural Born Killers*. Warhol's mural is an exploration of the shadow side of the cult of the media-generated celebrity, in which an individual can become famous for not achieving anything special, as well as for actually murdering and killing. As with the attainment of anonymous fame through death by car crash or suicide by jumping off a building, here, Warhol reveals that it is indeed the medium that is the message, not the content, since it is the very form of the existence of videographic media that creates fame regardless of what an individual does to attain that fame. *Anyone* can become famous for being famous in the satellite age. Including serial killers.

Warhol's *Death and Disaster* paintings appear early on in his career in a cluster between 1962 and 1964 and then generally disappear. They are painted simultaneously with his first images of Marilyn and Elvis and Liz Taylor, and so it is worth inquiring at this point as to why it is that they appear at *just* this moment in his career and no other. The answer, I suspect, is to be found in the morphological study of ancient civilizations: as Oswald Spengler has shown us, every new myth begins with the apprehension of death, and Warhol in these formative years was creating his own religion of the dying and reviving celebrity hero. Likewise, at the dawn of every high civilization, a new mythology crystallizes around a new technology of death and burial: in the early years of Egypt, the pyramids emerge; in Mycenean times, the tholos tombs; in the early days of Christianity, the catacombs; in Vedic India, the burning of the dead; and at the start of Medieval Europe under Charlemagne, the widespread use of crypts.

Thus, Warhol's death-motivated silk screens of Marilyn and Elvis and Liz Taylor—whom he painted because he had heard that she was about to die—are the mummies and corpses of a new universal religion of celebrity saints and martyrs. Warhol is a mortician preparing beautiful corpses for their resurrection in the new mediatic afterlife brought into being around the earth by post–World War II technology. His silk screens are celebrity *sahus* that will be sent into orbit around the earth in the form of discarnate images beamed from television towers, radio antennae, and satellite technologies. The consequent saturation of the earth with these images is reflected by Warhol in his serial repetitions in which media-generated clones begin to proliferate all around us, filling the air invisibly with their ghostly repetitions.

Thus, Warhol's portraits of the grieving Jackie Kennedy are products of his antennae picking up her media-generated image out of the ether all around him and channeling her presence, repeated ad infinitum, onto his canvases. Such media oversaturation, Warhol seems to be saying, constitutes the new environment that he sensed invisibly closing over the earth all around us during the days of the first geosynchronous satellites, for their orbits would create a new celebrity sphere of ubiquity and omnipresence that would become the very environment within which our consciousness would dwell henceforth. Warhol's Jackie serializations are telling us that the celebrity sphere has swallowed the planet entirely, and now we are all, consequently, trapped *inside* it.

Such new religions are often attended by the birth of apocalyptic visions in which the horizons of a particular temporality slide toward the edges of time and then disappear into a mythic no-place of eternal, timeless salvation or damnation. The case is no less so with the birth of Warhol's new religion of the celebrity demigod, in which his paintings of electric chairs and nuclear explosions play off in counterpoint to each other's flickering visions of a mediatic dissolution of the living. Indeed, a specific symmetry is implied by the fact that one of the serialized electric chair silk screens, entitled *Red Disaster*, is soaked in the same garish red color as his *Atomic Bomb*, which likewise depicts a serial image, in this case, a mushroom cloud. Thus, as with *Elivis I and II* and the *Marilyn Diptych*, we are faced with a dichotomy here, too, that of the death of the individual and the collective annihilation of the race by atomic bomb. Only the Electric Age could produce such a technological horror as death by electrocution, one of the cruelest and most horrible ways of dying yet invented by man. Thus, the accusations by his detractors of Warhol's superficiality and trivial optimism are entirely belied, for he sees shadows very well—later he will paint a whole series of abstract expressionist paintings termed *Shadows*—for in *these* paintings, he makes visible the shadow side of the very same society that accelerates the individual to fame via popular media with the death of the individual by overdose of electricity in an electric chair. Thus, the cult of the Most Wanted Men must end with its own Day of Judgment at the hands of the electric executioner who kills them using the very same means of technology by way of which they were made famous in the first place.

The serialized apocalypse of death by atomic bomb, on the other hand, is a vision of collective death by overdose of high-energy particle physics; death as the result of probing too deeply into the secrets of matter. Thus, the ancient images of apocalypse and damnation that so often attend the birth pangs of new civilizations—in the apocalyptic imagery of the cathedrals, for instance, or the Book of Revelation at the birth of Christianity—are apprehended by scientists and physicists who transform them into physical reality. Thus, at the dawn of the Satellite Age, we too are haunted by visions of the end of the world.

But in all of this, Warhol is merely rehearsing his own death. A photograph from 1965 confirms this. It was printed in one of his first books, entitled *Andy Warhol's Index Book*, and it shows Warhol sitting in a chair while a young woman standing behind him points a gun at the back of his head.

This period had other foreshadowings, too. In his autobiography, he describes the following episode:

> One day late in '64, a woman in her thirties, who I thought I'd maybe seen a few times before, came in, walked over to where I'd stacked four square Marilyns against a wall, took out a gun, and shot a hole right through the stack. She looked over at me, smiled, walked to the freight elevator, and left.[4]

Valerie Solanas will do more or less the same thing, only with Warhol in place of the Marilyns.

It is perhaps not without significance that before Solanas's shooting of Warhol in 1968, he was beginning to generate his own doubles. In 1967, he was able to manufacture a clone of his persona in the form of one Allen Midgette, a man who dressed up to resemble him for the purpose of presenting a lecture tour to college campuses on Warhol's behalf, a chore Warhol loathed. The man put on a silvery wig and pale face makeup and set out to answer questions as though he were Andy Warhol. At first, nobody knew the difference, since Warhol's answers to questions were normally stock monosyllables: "Uh, no. Uh, yes. I'm not sure." But then one of the students figured out the ruse by comparing some photographs and the colleges were furious. Andy was pressured into mollifying them by touring "live."

Warhol already was thinking of replacing himself with a simulacrum. Years later, he would toy with the idea of having a robot made that looked exactly like him and that would be sent out on television interviews to answer questions for him. Hence, in creating the first true cult of the electric icon, Warhol transformed himself into one of those very icons. As a result, it was important that he undergo the ritual of celebrity death and resurrection. The car crash paintings already show him, like the character of Vaughan in J. G. Ballard's novel *Crash*—a character, incidentally, who is modeled after him—contemplating the possibility of death by car crash. Because he abhorred drugs for the most part, death by overdose was not an option that was available to him, and so it was either car crash or assassination. But since Warhol could not drive, only one real option presented itself, and as time went by, he began to attract into his orbit a rogue satellite by the name of Valerie Solanas, self-proclaimed founder of SCUM, the Society for Cutting Up Men. By the time of the shooting, Solanas actually had persuaded the avant-garde publisher Maurice Girodias to print her manifesto as part of his now classic Grove books series.

Thus, when Solanas showed up at Warhol's studio on June 3, 1968, and shot him two or three times with a .38 caliber revolver—then calmly took the freight elevator back down, just like the woman who had shot his Marilyns—she was enacting the myth of the archetypal celebrity stalker who is taken captive by the powerful field of radiation emitted by the celebrity who has achieved a sufficient level of fame to begin shedding doppelgangers. It is the doppelgangers that take the stalkers hostage, not the physical celebrities themselves, for doppelgangers have a will of their own and often can make use of stalkers to eliminate their physical rivals. As Solanas commented, after turning herself over to the police: "It's not often that I shoot somebody . . . I didn't do it for nothing. Warhol had me tied up lock, stock and barrel. He was going to do something to me which would have ruined me."[5]

Once, early on in his career, Warhol himself had been a stalker of Truman Capote, whom he followed around until Capote's mother told him to go away. The obsessive nature of Warhol's serial repetitions of celebrities—the visual equivalent of obsessive compulsive disorder (OCD)—has a kind of trademark stalker quality to it. Whatever we decorate our immediate environment with is a way of saying that this is the world we live *inside*, this is our personal cosmology, as it were. And in those days, Warhol lived *inside* the skulls of the celebrities whose images he painted. He was the ultimate celebrity stalker.

Warhol found his way out of the minds of these celebrities precisely by creating his factory and using a movie camera to create his own "superstars" out of the tribe of nobodies who surrounded him. By putting himself in the active role of starmaker, he no longer stood in the gigantic shadows cast by the celebrities of pop culture, but now could cast his own shadow across the media landscape. Henceforth, he had given himself the power to baptize anyone whom he chose to become a member of his Church of the Dead Celebrity. Such a role reversal, however, transformed him into an icon with a gravitational field of force sufficient to draw other, weaker egos into orbit around him.

Thus, Valerie Solanas's statement of motive was really a confession that she was living inside the skull of Andy Warhol and that she shot him to make a hole through which she could begin to find her way out into the light. But the bullet hole only made a window that was too high up for her to reach.

The headline for the *New York Daily News* of June 4, 1968, read: "Actress Shoots Andy Warhol."

The very first painting of Warhol's *Death and Disaster* series was a facsimile of the front page of a New York newspaper. The date of that newspaper was June 4, 1962, and it read: "129 Die in Jet."

Thus, Warhol's rehearsals had come full circle.

Although Warhol survived the ordeal of his shooting (although just barely: he had been declared clinically dead at 4:51 P.M. on June 3), the myth demands that he did not. Hence, we are not permitted to regard the physical Warhol who was bodily resurrected by science and survived until 1987 as anything other than an imitation Lazarus, for when he came out of the cave, Lazarus was only a shadow of his former self.

There was something different about the postshooting Warhol, as though part of him had remained behind in the underworld. His skin, always pale, was now even more pale. The days of the Factory when he could surround himself with avant-garde crazies was over. And he would be terrified of women for the rest of his life. The later art, though interesting, was never as fascinating as that from the early 1960s, and he would spend the rest of his days hanging out with the rich and famous instead of poor bohemians. This may have been safe for the protection of his physical body, but it was not good for his art, for Warhol's early art depended to a great degree on the input of the crazies who surrounded him.

In retrospect, the death of the 1960s Warhol seems ceremonial, as though it had marked the ending of an epoch. The Beatles would soon be broken up; Marshall McLuhan's fame was about to pass into a two-decades-long abeyance; and the cover of the May 1969 issue of *Esquire* magazine was to proclaim: "The final death and total collapse of the American avant-garde." It featured a picture of an opened can of Campbell's soup with a tiny Warhol drowning inside of it. Even Warhol's autobiography, *Popism*, ends in 1969, with the shooting as the book's climax, as though nothing else of any significance took place in later years.

The orgy was over.

One cannot escape the impression that the postshooting Warhol was an impostor. Somehow, he had succeeded in doing what he had been planning for many years, for Warhol was a master of the replacement of reality by the simulacrum, and it is hard to believe anything else other than that he had finally succeeded in doing what he had been rehearsing for so many years:

He had replaced himself.

8

The Beatles, Their Muse, a Car Crash, Five Bullets, and Some Flowers from the Dead

On November 22, 1963—the same day on which John F. Kennedy was shot and killed—a new record album entitled *With the Beatles* was released. The cover displayed a black-and-white photograph showing four somber-looking youths—none smiling, not even faintly—all dressed in identical black turtleneck sweaters. Their pale, larval heads topped with the same haircuts give the impression of an organic unity suggestive of cloning; or perhaps, more drastically, they appeared as though they had all grown from the same root terminating in the dark, shadowy torso shared in common.

As though to say, it is the head that counts here; the body is meaningless and can be torn apart and scattered for the muses to collect. It is the head that will be enshrined and given oracular powers to rival those of Apollo's oracle at Delphi.

On Februrary 7, 1964, the Beatles landed at J.F.K. Airport in New York City. This moment is captured on celluloid by two filmmakers, the Maysles brothers, in their documentary entitled *The Beatles: The First U.S. Visit* (1994). At one point, while pandemonium is erupting all around them, the brothers interview a woman who makes the following interesting comment: "I remember a time when there was a young man by the name of Frank Sinatra who generated this kind of excitement and this kind of a spark and I don't think it's bad."

On August 27, 1965, the Beatles met their boyhood idol Elvis Presley at the house in Bel-Air that he and his Memphis Mafia happened to be renting at the time. The meeting was apparently a rather stiff one, and nothing much took place. Indeed, at one point, a bored Elvis had been about to call it an evening:

> "If you guys are just gonna sit there and stare at me, I'm goin' to bed," Elvis huffed, tossing the remote control on the coffee table. "Let's call it a night, right 'Cilla? I didn't mean for this to be like the subjects calling on the King. I just thought we'd sit and talk about music and jam a little."
>
> "That'd be great," Paul said, suggesting they try a song by "the other Cilla"—Cilla Black—at which point guitars and a white piano were produced, along with ample drink.[1]

Although nothing much happened on this occasion, the attentive observer cannot fail to notice one important detail: as the woman in the Maysles' documentary had implied, the Beatles were the 1960s cultural equivalent to such earlier phenomena as Frank Sinatra and Elvis Presley.

So why, then, were there four of them and only one of him?

The Beatles were one of the first rock-and-roll bands to eliminate the front man. Whereas previously there had always been a guy out front—Gerry and the Pacemakers, Buddy Holly and the Crickets, Rory Storm and the Hurricanes—the Beatles dispensed with the very notion of a front man—with the idea, that is, of an ego surrounded by its three helping functions—preferring, instead, a more tribal structure in which all four members are considered equal. This way no one is allowed to dominate the group, which is a collective undertaking, functioning more in the way of a single organism rather than a charismatic leader with a following.

Like a four-headed Orpheus.

The myth of Orpheus is well-known, but perhaps a snapshot of it would not be out of place here: Orpheus was the archetypal musician of Greek mythology. He played his lyre and sang so beautifully that he could inspire even rocks and stones to form into buildings. He had a woman named Eurydice, who was bitten by a snake one day while fleeing from a minor god named Aristaeus who tried to rape her and thus was sent prematurely to the underworld. Orpheus went down to get her, and his singing was so lovely at the gates of Hades that he was allowed inside, whereupon he played once more at the court of Pluto and Persephone, begging them to allow him to return with his beloved to the world above. They agreed, but only on the condition that he did not look back, and so Orpheus, accompanied by his muse, set out for the world of the living. However, a chance look back over his shoulder sealed his fate, and his muse vanished. (If we think of Eurydice as his muse, then her vanishing to the world below would mean that his musical abilities were in trouble, for Orpheus was about to suffer from the musician's equivalent of writer's block.) When he attempted to return to a normal life, Orpheus renounced the love of women, embracing men instead, and as a result, a group of jealous maenads tore him apart. The muses collected the pieces of his body (for one of them, Calliope, was his mother) with the exception of his head, which floated downriver and out to sea whereupon it traveled to the island of Lesbos and, along with his lyre, became an oracle.

The myth almost certainly accounts for the birth of lyrical music upon the island of Lesbos, where the art was supposed to have been invented by the (Western) world's first musicians, Terpander, Sappho, Alcaeus, and Arion. At first, the art was based on Terpander's transformation of the four-stringed lyre to a seven-stringed lyre, and then, with his migration to Sparta, the flute was introduced as an accompaniment. The tradition of singing to music evolved into the Greek chorus, and it was the rise of the new art form of the drama that put lyrical music out of business, for from then on, it became part of a larger entity. When that medium, in turn, fell apart in the fourth century B.C.E., it gave rise to Plato's dialogues, for Plato had been a frustrated playwright, and when one tries to master a dying medium, the only thing for it to do is invent a new one. (As Nietzsche remarks, Plato's dialogues were the life raft by means of which the sinking art of Greek drama kept itself afloat.) In *The Republic*, Plato's myth of the cave resounds with a dim echo of Orpheus's attempt to rescue Eurydice and bring her out of the cavernous underworld back up into the light. Whereas Orpheus fails at his task, however, Plato's ideal philosopher-guide succeeds in leading his pupil out of the cavern of illusion and up into the blinding radiance of the eternal forms of higher knowledge.

And the point of this divagation?

Only this: A four-headed Orpheus would have to share its muse in common. Like the five Pandava brothers of *The Mahabharata* who are all married to one woman, Draupadi—who functions as a sort of muse for their warrior deeds—the Beatles will have to share their muse polyandrously. The success of their band, moreover, will depend entirely on their willingness to do so, for no one can be allowed to hoard her all to themselves. The Pandavas resolved this problem by stipulating that Draupadi could spend only two nights with each brother before she was passed along to the next brother. If, for any reason, this arrangement should be disturbed, then trouble would result.

And that, as you know, was exactly what happened.

In their case, it was not Orpheus, but a man named Brian Epstein who descended into the underworld of the Cavern to lead the Beatles to the world above. The Cavern was an underground bar with arched walls where the Beatles played nearly every day after their return to Liverpool from their initiatory sojourn into the urban wilderness of Hamburg, Germany. It was in Hamburg—still a fivesome at this point, with Pete Best on drums and Stuart Sutcliffe on bass guitar—that the Beatles received their famous "mop-top" haircuts from Stu's German girlfriend Astrid Kirchherr. But it was in Liverpool one day that Brian Epstein decided during his lunch hour to visit the band about which he had heard so much, and upon hearing them, decided then and there that he wanted to manage them, despite having an antipathy to pop music. It was their energy and enthusiasm that turned him on, but he insisted on them first cleaning up their act. No more shouting at the audience, interrupting songs with banter, or eating meals onstage. And from henceforth, they were to be garbed only in Mohair suits with ties.

Putting on clothing is an old metaphor for the soul's incarnation in a bodily form, and so it is evident that Brian was acting as the midwife for the birth of their first avatars into their first universe, their first "Beatleverse," if you will. If we closed our eyes and imagined what this primordial Beatleverse looked like, it would look something like this: a two-dimensional landscape made out of colorless black-and-white forms, in which the Beatles exist as avatars that move with jerky, puppet-like motions. They are clones of one another, looking, talking, sounding, and dressing exactly alike. Individual personalities are embryonic, and to address one Beatle is to address them all simultaneously, for they are bound together by an invisible glue that causes them to share a single Overmind. *These* Beatles are insects living in a hive ruled over by a queen bee (their muse).

And so it is that on the cover of their first album *Please Please Me*, the Beatles gaze down at us from above, where they stand in the middle of a staircase several landings up. From the depths of the Cavern, that is, they have risen to the heights of their first cosmos, where they stand, elevated like gods, surveying the ocean of blurred human faces gathered down below.

The Beatles were to record 12 albums together, but on the first five of these albums, there is an amazing consistency of sound and stability of personae. On *Please Please Me* (1963), *With the Beatles* (1963), *A Hard Day's Night* (1964), *Beatles for Sale* (1964), and *Help!* (1965) it is recognizably the same band singing the same kinds of songs, and all the songs revolve about a single, central theme: Eros.

Like the wandering troubadours of ancient France and Spain, the Beatles do not just sing of Eros in general, for they are singing on these albums to *one* specific woman: their muse, the very same muse they share polyandrously. The troubadours derived enormous vitality and energy from singing love songs to married women with whom they wished to have affairs. The Beatles, likewise, direct their hymns to *their* favorite woman, the goddess they brought into being as the result of their combined powers.

We know this because the woman is never referred to by name. Not once, over the course of scores of love songs for the duration of these first five albums, is the mysterious "she" ever named (the sole exception being "Anna" on *Please Please Me*, but since they did not write this song, it may be excused on that account). Who is the mysterious personage about whom and to whom "I Saw *Her* Standing There," "*She* Loves You," "And I Love *Her*," and "I Wanna Be *Your* Man" are addressed?

This personage is their muse, their etheric Eurydice, for it is the muse that holds them together and intoxicates their songs with a joyous lyricism and evident vitality. This muse is the invisible Beatle, the fifth Beatle, their *shakti*.

Moreover, it is this muse that is above all responsible for that other great innovation of the Beatles, namely, the fact that they were just about the first band in popular music to write all their own songs (with the exception of the few covers from these first five albums). The function of the poet's muse is to inspire him: "Sing in me, muse!" begins all the great epics of classical civilization, and when the poet's relationship to his muse is working properly, inspiration is the result. Hence, the Beatles' unprecedented and prodigious output of fresh new songs is a direct function of their harmonious relationship to their muse.

The band was named by Stuart Sutcliffe as a way of paying homage to Buddy Holly and the Crickets, but it was John Lennon's Irish-descended love of Joycean wordplay that inspired him to change the spelling of "beetle" to read as a pun: "beatle" as in "beat" for beatnik music, but also the beat of rock and roll itself as a driving force. Thus, Lennon and Sutcliffe borrowed an ancient Egyptian icon, the scarab beetle, and plugged it in.

The beetle was in Egypt an important symbol of rebirth associated with the rising sun. It was often depicted in Egyptian art pushing the sun along in front of it, just as the beetle pushes along its ball of dung on the ground. And, as the beetle buries its ball of cow dung in a hole in the ground and lays its eggs in it—the larvae hatching and soon turning into pupae—so analogously, the mummy is placed in a chamber in the ground and wrapped in a pupa-like cocoon, from which it will be reborn to spread its wings and fly like the mature beetle imago.

Thus, the Beatles represent the dawning of a new age, and, like the four sons of Horus, they stand supporting the heavens of this new cosmos in which the great rock-and-roll supergroup emerges as Britain's answer to the self-contained and charismatic lone American celebrity icon. This is the age in which the tribal social structure comes to displace that of the kingly. Hence, the real inward significance of the Beatles' meeting with Elvis Presley.

Here comes the sun.

With the plugging in of their personae via television and film, cracks begin to appear on the ceiling of this Beatleverse. On their first *Ed Sullivan* show, the Beatles are shown in black and white on a stage set that has been split in half horizontally, like a clamshell. The effect conveyed suggests a chasm in the earth from out of which they have emerged. They move on this set in bursts of spasmodic energy with disjointed motions, like puppets on strings. The television here has become invaginated, caught giving birth to the Beatles as marionettes that spill forth onto the floors of our shag carpeted living rooms, where they pulse and writhe with an unnatural bioluminescence. One imagines that Pinocchio, covered with some sort of colorless day-glow paint, had been multiplied fourfold.

In the film *A Hard Day's Night*, these Pinocchio figures have been blown up to gigantic, drive-in-size proportions, like shadows cast on the side of a building by a searchlight. They are flat, two-dimensional caricatures of themselves, for they do not smoke, or drink, or curse, or have sex. *These* Beatles are utterly shorn of depth and significance of any kind, as though they had collapsed in on themselves.

But the first evidence that something is beginning to go wrong appears in the lyrics of the song "I'm a Loser," from their fourth album *Beatles for Sale,* in which Lennon begins to become aware of the mask-like artificiality of the persona Brian Epstein has designed for them. "I'm a loser," the song says, "and I'm not what I appear to be. Although I laugh and I act like a clown / beneath this mask I am wearing a frown."

Lennon is realizing that he *is* wearing a mask and that the mask can be taken off just as easily as it was put on.

An omen of things to come, furthermore, appears on the same album with the song "Baby's in Black." The song's narrator expresses his frustration over his love for a woman who will not reciprocate his attention because she is dressed in black and therefore still fixated on her dead lover. This is the first time that the Beatles' muse appears in connection with death, and it is ominous because it implies her coming abduction to the underworld.

These are, as yet, only subtle perturbations that appear within the otherwise-seamless cosmos of this first Beatleverse, for the overriding characteristic of this period is that of stability. But soon things will begin to get rubbery, for the group at this time was turned on to marijuana by Bob Dylan, and the subtly hallucinogenic effects of this drug will begin to ripple through their universe like waves from a stone cast into a pond.

With the advent of their album *Rubber Soul*, the Beatles cast aside their cocoons, and stretch forth the wings of their new images. Whereas their personae for the previous five years had consisted of wearing identical suits and ties, each appears on the cover of this album wearing a different outfit. Here, they are no longer clones of one another, for they are becoming as individuated and unique as Richard Avedon's 1967 hallucinogenic portraits show them to be.

The cover of *Rubber Soul*, in a subtle way, alludes to the cover of their first album *Please Please Me*, for this is the first time since that album in which the four are shown looking down at the viewer. Thus, a new cycle is here being initiated, for *Rubber Soul* was a quantum leap forward in terms of the style and quality of their music. We are entering here into a new Beatleverse altogether. (The wormhole connecting the first Beatleverse to this second Beatleverse is the song "Yesterday" on their fifth album *Help!* for it is the first solo effort made by a Beatle, entirely written, performed, and conceived by Paul McCartney without any help from the rest of the band. Not only that, but it is stylistically quite different from anything else on that album, and would have been more at home on *Rubber Soul.*)

It is on *Rubber Soul*, significantly, that their muse is named for the first time. Paul McCartney addresses her as "Michelle," and on the subsequent album *Revolver*, she is known as "Eleanor Rigby." Later, John Lennon will refer to her as "Lucy." Thus, the relationship of Lennon and McCartney to their muse is now becoming more personal. She is not just a faceless unknown quantity, woman X, but she begins to take on specific characteristics.

This is connected with the fact that it is at about this point—paradoxically when they are producing their best music—that the band begins its long slow process of decomposition. Lennon and McCartney were beginning to decouple as songwriters, for each was moving, in his own way, toward establishing his unique relationship with the band's muse. Once this process of individuation began to set in, furthermore, the band's days were numbered, for as we have seen, the whole point of the Beatles was its subsumption of the individual ego on behalf of the tetrad of the group. The idea was to eliminate the ego, which the concept of a frontman implied, but here, the egos of Lennon and McCartney, disturbed out of their equilibrium, began to differentiate and evolve along wayward, erratic paths. This individuation, paradoxically, was a self-protective response to the destabilization dealt to the group's collective ego as a result of the electric amplification of their personae.

The disturbance in the band's relationship to its muse is evident in some of the imagery on *Rubber Soul.* In Lennon's song "Norwegian Wood," for example, a man who follows a woman back to her apartment for a night of chatting is told that she has to go to work in the morning and that he must sleep in the bathtub. When the woman leaves for work, the narrator sets fire to her apartment. In McCartney's "I'm Looking through You," he claims that he now sees right through "her," and that she has not changed but is yet somehow different; her lips move, but they form words he can no longer hear. The muse is traditionally accessed through metaphors of "hearing," but McCartney confesses in this song that he is having trouble hearing "her" the same way he used to. On *Revolver*, McCartney paints a picture of their muse as "Eleanor Rigby," a lonely, isolated woman who cannot communicate with anyone around her and who ends by dying alone.

Thus, on both *Rubber Soul* and *Revolver*, the Beatles' muse is associated with violent, disaffected, and alienating imagery. They are telling us—and themselves—that their days as a band will soon come to an end, for they are each attempting to abduct Eurydice and carry her off to their private underworlds. These ominous portents grow like flowers of evil in the midst of a garden of some of the greatest rock-and-roll albums ever created, for the epoch inaugurated by *Rubber Soul* and brought to a climax with *The White Album* was that of their most inspired and inventive creativity.

On July 3, 1966, while touring for *Revolver*, something strange happens to the Beatles. They arrive in Manila in the Philippines where they play two very large shows. After the shows, they are handled roughly by the

Philippine government for snubbing an invitation to visit Imelda Marcos. The entire staff of the hotel at which they are staying goes on strike and refuses to help them. On their way down to check out, the hotel's corridors are dark and lined with staff members who shout expletives at them. On their way to the airport, they are repeatedly directed by army officials onto roads leading nowhere. At the airport itself, the power is turned off and they are confronted by an angry group of soldiers who shove them back and forth through the terminal. Eventually, they are allowed to exit the terminal and board the plane that has been kept waiting.

They finish out their U.S. tour, but as a result of Lennon's comments about the Beatles being bigger than Christ, they are rudely treated onstage in Mississippi. Firecrackers thrown at the stage frighten them into thinking that someone has taken shots at them. They play their last concert at Candlestick Park in San Francisco on August 29 of that year.

It becomes clear to them that touring has become hazardous to their lives. The screaming and the noise is generally so loud that no one can hear the music anyway, not even themselves. They decide to hang it up.

They have become targets.

And so, the show's over.

But not quite.

McCartney comes up with the idea of replacing themselves with a set of doppelgangers. He invents an entirely new Beatleverse—the third one—in which the Beatles exist as a military marching band known as *Sgt. Pepper's Lonely Hearts Club Band.* The electric double is normally an unconsciously created by-product of acceleration through the culture at light speed or, as in the case of Andy Warhol's attempt to create a double of himself to go to college campuses and answer questions on his behalf, a deliberate joke. But the Beatles at this point decide to create a consciously contrived mythology out of their own doppelgangers, a fictive band that undergoes two journeys: one in a yellow submarine and the other on a magical mystery bus. (Indeed, the song "Yellow Submarine" from *Revolver* is the wormhole that leads from the second to the third Beatleverse.)

After spending five months in the recording studio, the resulting album is hailed as a masterpiece (*Rubber Soul*, by contrast, had been created in two weeks; *Please Please Me* in 12 hours). It is the first real "concept" album in the history of rock and roll, and as such is godfather to later works like The Who's *Tommy* and Pink Floyd's *The Wall.* It is also the first album to feature continuous music by eliminating the three-second gap between each song, giving the impression of a continually unfolding story (just as Wagner's operas were the first to become continuous music by eliminating the recitative). It is also the first album to feature printed lyrics to all the songs on the inside sleeve.

The cover of the album is one of the most iconic in rock album history. On it, the Beatles avatars from their first Beatleverse, wearing suits and ties, are shown standing beside the new Sgt. Pepper avatars, the garish Technicolor of whose outfits suggests the contrast in palettes of this new, hallucinogenic Beatleverse with the black-and-white Beatleverse of their Liverpool days. Standing behind them in several rows is a huge collection of celebrities—some then dead, some living—all made out of cardboard cutouts. They are a veritable underworld of celebrity ancestors invoked to bestow good fortune on the album. (Every tribe has its own collection of ancestors to whose wishes they must defer.)

At this point, the band has added LSD to its repertoire of drugs, the effects of which are evident in the imagery of songs like "Lucy in the Sky with Diamonds." Although John Lennon claimed that the initials of the song do not intentionally spell out LSD, the fact that they happen to coincide with the acronym for lysergic acid is a happy accident, for the imagery of the song is overtly psychedelic. Under the influence of this drug, the stars of the night sky do indeed glitter like diamonds, shimmering and wavering as though one were looking through a prism.

But the song is significant for another reason, as well, since it shows that for Lennon, the band's muse has been amplified out of all proportion to human scale and become identified with the night sky. Lucy in the night sky is, of course, the ancient Egyptian sky goddess Nut, who was identified with the Milky Way.

The song casts an X-ray into the structure of Lennon's psyche and shows us that he is in the process of being swallowed up by his own muse, who has taken on gigantic, macrocosmic proportions. Lennon has become an embryo waiting for the Great Mother herself to give birth to him.

For Paul McCartney, on the other hand, the muse has become "Lovely Rita," the meter maid, a vision as banal as a malt-shop girl on roller skates. Meter maids, however, give out tickets to parked cars, and the automobile will shortly play an important role in the destiny of McCartney's Beatle avatar.

Soon, the Beatles decide to cut themselves free of the umbilical cords connecting them to their Sgt. Pepper's doppelgangers. They stand watching their doppelgangers floating off to drift among the effluvia of the night sky, joining all the other media-made avatars. Then they go to India to stay for a time at the ashram of Maharishi Mahesh Yogi. They meditate, avoid drugs, and write a new batch of songs.

Lennon pens a song called "Dear Prudence." This is a significant song for him because it not only names his muse but bases her, for the first time, on an actual flesh-and-blood person, for Prudence was Mia Farrow's sister, who happened to be staying at the ashram at the time. Here, Lennon is getting closer to his eventual ideal.

Flighty as all rock stars are, the boys become disillusioned with the Maharishi and head back to London, where they begin to record all the songs for their magnum opus—rock's first great double album—*The Beatles* (also known as *The White Album*). The album, as is well known, is actually a collection of solo efforts, for the days of their collaboration are over. For one song, "Why Don't We Do It in the Road," Paul solely writes the lyrics, sings, plays the drums, and plays the guitar. No other Beatles need apply. George Harrison brings in another guitarist, Eric Clapton, to help him with "While My Guitar Gently Weeps." Both Ringo and George quit at one point, but they are persuaded to return.

There can now no longer be any denying it: each Beatle has attempted to run off with their muse and hide her away from the other band members.

But an even greater sin is now committed by John Lennon, who brings a woman with him into the temple of the recording studio where tradition forbids that any woman should enter. The woman is, of course, Yoko Ono, and she not only sits in on the sessions, but also offers criticisms of their music. On a couple of songs, she even sings backing vocals.

Lennon's bringing of Yoko Ono into the studio actually carries with it a symbolic significance: he has literalized the band's muse, the very same muse who always had been present as a fifth Beatle, invisible, hanging over the proceedings like a poltergeist. But Lennon, in substituting a flesh-and-blood woman for their figurative muse, is essentially claiming that he now has his private muse and has no need to share their communal muse. He is enacting literally the process that they had all been performing symbolically for many years. He is concretizing their muse and, in doing so, profanes their music. By making the band's invisible muse visible, the game is up, for no flesh-and-blood woman could ever play the role of the Beatles' muse. That would have been too literal.

And so it is that all cultural cycles end in the same way, declining from the symbolic and the metaphysical to the merely prosaic and the literal.

And for this profanation, the muse has her revenge. For whereas *The White Album* had been a masterpiece—their *last* masterpiece—the recording sessions for their next effort, *Let It Be,* were a disaster. Musically, this material is inferior to almost everything they had done up to this point. And not only that, but they can no longer stand the sight of each other. They perform a rooftop concert—as though out of desperation for lack of anything better to do—on the top of Apple records (this was to be their last public appearance as a band), playing the new songs, most of which are mediocre. Indeed, the formative impulse that brings harmony out of chaos ends up defeating them here, for they simply are unable to transform this material into an album.

For the first time, they give up and walk away, leaving the album for others to finish for them.

Abbey Road, their last album, was released on September 29, 1969. On September 17, an article appeared in *The Drake-Times Delphic*, a student newspaper at Drake University, entitled "Is Beatle Paul McCartney Dead?" The article was written by a sports writer named Tim Harper who knew very little about rock and roll music, for Harper was merely conveying a rumor that had been passed along to him. In the article, Harper lists a series of "clues" to Paul's death that could be found littered upon some of the Beatles' albums.

On October 12, Russ Gibb, a local disc jockey of WKNR-FM in Detroit, Michigan, received a call on air in which the caller pointed out some of the specific clues on Beatles albums that indicated that Paul might be dead. For example, he pointed out that if you played "Revolution No. 9" backwards, then you would hear "Turn me on, dead man." A listener who lived up the street, meanwhile, made his way down to the station and pointed out to Gibb the message at the end of "Strawberry Fields" in which Lennon says, "I buried Paul."

A student at the University of Michigan named Fred LaBour heard this show, and it gave him the angle that he needed for his review of *Abbey Road* for the school newspaper. Thus, on October 14, an article appeared in *The Michigan Daily* entitled "McCartney Dead; New Evidence Brought to Light." The article begins as follows:

> Paul McCartney was killed in an automobile accident in early November, 1966 after leaving EMI recording studios tired, sad and dejected. The Beatles had been preparing their forthcoming album, tentatively entitled Smile, when progress bogged down in intragroup hassles and bickering. Paul climbed into his Aston-Martin, sped away into the rainy, chill night, and was found four hours later pinned under his car in a culvert with the top of his head sheared off. He was deader than a doornail.[2]

LaBour goes on to articulate how George Harrison was called on to bury Paul while Ringo conducted services and John went into seclusion for three days, at the end of which time he came up with the idea of replacing Paul with a double who would look and sound exactly like him. They would slowly release clues suggesting—or hiding—Paul's death (like a Freudian screening myth) during their next few albums, beginning with *Sgt. Pepper's Lonely Hearts Club Band.*

LaBour is, of course, making up this myth as he goes along, and he is having great fun doing so. But the amazing thing is how seriously people began to take it. Within a very short time, a wave of "dead Paul" hysteria began to strike the United States. The local Midwestern rumor became national news just after midnight on October 21 when Roby Yonge, the disc jockey at WABC radio in New York City announced on his late-night radio show that a rumor was circulating to the effect that Paul was dead and that the Beatles had provided clues on their albums. Making such an announcement cost Yonge his job, for he was fired that very night, but as a result of his broadcast, the national newspapers picked up the rumor and the *Chicago Sun Times* hit the streets that evening with a story entitled "Paul McCartney Dead? Campuses Swept by Beatle Rumor." Before long, cover stories were turning up all over the place: the cover of *Life* magazine on November 7, insisted: "The Case of the Missing Beatle: Paul Is Still With Us," while the cover of *Rolling Stone* for November 15, read simply: "Paul Is Not Dead."

Questioned about the rumor, the Beatles denied knowing anything about it. Paul dismissed it angrily, and John claimed on numerous talk shows that he had no idea what all the fuss was about. Some insisted that the rumor had been perpetrated by the Beatles to generate publicity for *Abbey Road*, and indeed, sales of that album, as well as the other albums mentioned as being part of the hoax, shot up dramatically. When these "clues" are examined more closely, however, they disappear like the stars at dawn. For example, Lennon does not sing "I buried Paul" at the end of "Strawberry Fields," but rather intones the phrase "Cranberry Sauce," which can clearly be heard on an alternate take of the song. The backward messages claimed to have been heard on numerous songs take a lot of imagination to hear intelligibly, and moreover, it is an affront to one's reason to imagine the Beatles wasting precious studio time trying to figure out how certain phrases enunciated forwards could be made to sound out messages when played backwards (although, beginning with *Rubber Soul*, they *did* experiment with playing music and lyrics backwards, which can be heard on several songs). It also requires some imagination to see the album cover of *Abbey Road* as anything even faintly resembling a funeral procession in which Paul is supposed to be in the role of the dead man because he is walking barefoot. (He claims that he was wearing sandals that day and took them off because it was hot.)

Furthermore, as anyone will realize who understands the psychology of the band, John Lennon never would have consented to any kind of a hoax that would have cast his rival Paul McCartney in the starring role, for Lennon and McCartney had been struggling to dominate over the band for years. As Robert Rosen noted in his biography of the last days of John Lennon, Lennon in later years was overjoyed to hear about the slightest bit of bad luck that would befall McCartney, such as when he was caught in Tokyo International Airport with eight ounces of marijuana.[3] Lennon strove to outdo McCartney financially and worried over every one of his former friend's hit songs lest he might not be able to match their success.

The whole story of the rise and spread of Paul's urban legend is recounted by Andru J. Reeve in his entertaining *Turn Me On, Dead Man*, but it is clear that when the myth is examined thoroughly, it reveals itself as a case of War of the Worlds–style mass hysteria. The legend was a creation of gullible American college kids looking for something that their myth-starved psyches could latch onto and that would confer a sense of meaning and significance on their lives.

However . . .

The timing of the urban legend's appearance at just the moment when the band was breaking up, but had not yet made any public announcements to that effect, is rather synchronicitous. The myth of Paul's death by car crash is an almost subliminal tuning in to the fact that the Beatles had, in all intents and purposes, become a car crash by autumn of 1969. Paul's doppelganger was plugged into the mold of the celebrity death by car crash that had been pioneered by James Dean, for the breakup of the Beatles had to announce itself, even if subliminally, to the world by means of a symbolic catastrophe. Beatles fans, searching for clues in lyrics and on album covers, were correct intuitively in sifting out a message from all this noise that a catastrophe of some sort *was* impending.

The idea of Paul's replacement by a doppelganger, furthermore, *is* a mythic pattern that belongs structurally to the epoch of the multimedia celebrity. It is sensitive to the mediatic replacement of flesh-and-blood people with electric simulacra, as in science fiction films like *Invasion of the Body Snatchers*, in which people are replaced by alien look-alikes who are really monsters from another world (that is, code for the realm of the hyperreal). Thus, the paranoid age is identical with the age of electronic technology in which people are routinely replaced by onscreen look-alikes via television, film, and computer screens. As the science fiction films point out, in the 21st century, we constantly are replacing ourselves with mediatized simulacra that cannot be trusted because they are artificial products of a machine society, and their presence activates archaic residua within the psyche of fears that the sudden appearance of one's doppelganger is a bad omen foretelling of death. As Marina Warner writes, "One of the ancient interpreters of dreams, Artemidorus, warns that dreaming of seeing one's own reflection in water is most unlucky, and probably announces one's death."[4] Doppelgangers, ancient or modern, cannot be trusted, and the celebrity is nothing if not a virtual doppelganger.[5]

Whereas the Beatles' muse had inspired them to create great works of pop art, the "muse" of Mark David Chapman inspired him with the idea of killing John Lennon. Actually, though, when Chapman left Honolulu, Hawaii, for New York City in November of 1980, it was not John Lennon he had decided to kill. It was Lennon's double that he wanted to destroy, although at the time Chapman did not know this, since he was incapable of discerning between them. And we know that this was the case because Chapman himself later said so to Larry King in an interview on his show in 2000:

> Chapman: I have regrets. I'm sorry for what I did. I realize now that I really ended a man's life. Then, he was an album cover to me. He didn't exist, even when I met him earlier that day when he signed the album for me, which he did very graciously. . . . If that didn't register that he was a human being, then I wasn't perceiving him as such. I just saw him as a two-dimensional celebrity with no real feelings.
>
> King: Ok, why did Mark David Chapman want to shoot the album cover?
>
> Chapman: Mark David Chapman . . . wanted to become somebody important, Larry. He didn't know how to handle being a nobody. He tried to be a somebody through his years, but as he progressively got worse—and I believe I was schizophrenic at the time, nobody can tell me I wasn't—although I was responsible, Mark David Chapman struck out at something he perceived to be phony, something he was angry at, to become something he wasn't, to become somebody.[6]

When Chapman killed Lennon, he was not trying, as Dr. Ralph Greenson had attempted with Marilyn Monroe, or Valerie Solanas with Andy Warhol, to kill the flesh-and-blood John Lennon to eliminate his doppelganger's competition for fame. In this case, the matter was the other way around, for Chapman was trying to destroy not substance but a media-generated phantom. He just didn't realize it.

And he could not have realized it because Chapman, at the time, was full of demons. His "muse" was not a single woman, but an entire pantheon of devils and spirits that battled inside of him like a Miltonic War in Heaven. For instance, there were the Little People that he had imagined himself ruling over since childhood. They advised him against killing Lennon:

> If he is to carry out his plan, he needs the Little People to cooperate. He tells them that he wants to murder John Lennon . . . They overrule his decision. "Don't do it," they beg him at a board meeting. "It will only cause pain for the people you care about, your wife, your mother."
>
> Chapman strongly disagrees with the Little People. Don't they understand he *needs* to murder Lennon? They understand it, all right, but they can't condone it. They are good people—Christians—and they want no part of his diabolical plan.[7]

Chapman, instead, wishes to invoke the powers of evil to help him. As he later explained:

> I'd look at the picture [of Lennon] and say: "You phony, I'm going to get you." And then I would pray for demons to enter my body, to give me strength to pull that gun out . . . I was praying for Satan to send me his more experienced demons. Not a little one: This is a big thing, I need a big demon . . . My face got all red and fiery, and teeth like this, and I felt like I was very powerful, you know, and John was going to die. Nobody knew in the whole world what was going on in that room, [that] I was going to kill him.[8]

Chapman wanted to kill Lennon because he thought that Lennon had become a phony, a euphemism that he had picked up from the protagonist of Salinger's novel *Catcher in the Rye*, his favorite book. Chapman wore the mask of Holden Caulfield to empower his damaged ego. Because the three-dimensional complexity of the real John Lennon—who was both rich *and* sympathetic to the poor, idealistic *and* misanthropic—did not match the two-dimensional media-flattened simplification of John's public persona, especially his late 1960s–early 1970s "peace bed-in" persona. Chapman wanted to kill him because he could not force the one image to map neatly onto the other. He wanted a simple black-and-white picture because for Chapman the cosmos was a simple place, as it is for all fundamentalists: either things are black or they are white; either a man is good or he is evil.

Chapman, then, was a fundamentalist overwhelmed and overloaded by information coming at him from all directions. Such an ego, weakened by massive doses of ELF radiation, can become easy prey for malevolent spirits who come flitting into the skull to take up their warm, cozy residence. Later, after he was incarcerated, Chapman would name some of these demons (the "muses" who inspired him with the idea of creating the death of John Lennon):

> [H]e did not answer to the name Mark Chapman, and he spoke to the doctors in voices they had not heard before—one, a high-pitched, female voice, the other low, snarling and aggressively male. The voices identified themselves, respectively, as Lila and Dobar, emissaries of Satan.
>
> It was Lila's first possession of a human, Chapman later told Marks's co-counsel David Suggs, and she was struck by the weakness of human vision and the human body. Dobar was the more powerful demon—thousands of years old, exceedingly well versed in Biblical scripture and a member of the Supreme Council in Hades, a ruling body whose power was only exceeded by Satan's. Chapman noted, however, that Lila had the power to release and contain Dobar; he thought perhaps this was because Satan didn't trust him. He said that both demons could read his mind and that their purpose in possessing him was to make a showing of Satan's presence in the world, using Lennon's murder as the vehicle.[9]

When Chapman stood outside the Dakota apartment building on December 8, 1980, at about 11:00 P.M. and fired five bullets into John Lennon's back as he was climbing out of his limousine and making his way toward the building, Chapman was committing a kind of electronic terrorism, for in attempting to kill Lennon's double, he was hurling a bomb at hyperreal society and its confusing Babel of ghosts, avatars, idorus, and doubles. Chapman was attacking not just John Lennon, but hyperreal society as a whole, his act tantamount to a declaration of war on the entire world of media-generated personae.

To kill John Lennon, furthermore, was an essentially mythological act, and Chapman, I suspect, knew this, even if only unconsciously, for he was playing Judas to the closest figure that his society could produce who resembled Jesus Christ, and in doing so, saw himself as being elevated from anonymity to an individual with a cosmically important role to play in the unfolding of the universe, which could afford to ignore him no longer. Chapman was inventing his own mythology and casting himself in a costarring role.

Thus, Lennon's life as an icon ends with his absorption into the role of an even more ancient religious icon, for as James Frazer spent 12 volumes of *The Golden Bough* showing us, Christ and the Virgin Mary were but a late Classical adaptation of the much older mythic archetype of the dying and reviving male god and his consort-mother: Cybele and Attis, Isis and Osiris, Venus and Adonis.

In light of this myth, it is significant that Lennon always addressed Yoko Ono as "Mother," and when he married her, took her name, changing his own from John Winston Lennon to John Ono Lennon, thus signifying his affiliation with the matrilineal line of descent that is so linked with cultures in which the dying and reviving flower god and his Great Mother are prevalent. And just as violets were said to have sprung from the blood of the dying Attis, while roses and anemones sprang from the blood of Adonis, likewise, is the album *Double Fantasy*—Lennon's last—the flower that sprang from his death, for the title was taken by Lennon from the name of a flower of the freesia family native to the Bermudas, where the album's songs were written. And just as Attis and Adonis are killed by boars, while Osiris is killed by Set and Christ by Judas, so too Lennon is killed by Mark David Chapman.

And thus, the human being is not just himself, but actually only one component of a far larger tissue of consciousnesses that move and work within him, exerting their own volition: the Beatles were involved in an intimate relationship with the muse who had helped to build and construct their visions; Mark David Chapman, however, was taken hostage by a convocation of demons who surrounded and submerged his individuality to their whims. One divinity, like Homer's muse, inspires the act of bringing forth new worlds through the power of singing; another, like the Furies who demanded the death of Orestes, insists on silencing those very worlds brought forth by other gods with other intentions.

In the polytheistic cosmos reconfigured by popular culture, ancient mythic figures, long thought dead and vanished, continue to have their way with us, the flies who amuse them for their sport.

9

Jim Morrison Awoke One Morning Transformed

TEN

With Jim Morrison, we begin at the end.

We see him there before us, floating in his Paris bathtub, dead, apparently, of a heroin overdose. His girlfriend Pamela Courson claimed to have found him this way with a serene smile on his face, at about 5:00 A.M. on the morning of July 3, 1971, at their apartment on rue Beautreillis. Pamela said that she and Morrison had returned home from the cinema on the previous night at around 1:00 A.M. and that she did some chores while Morrison watched television before they retired to bed to listen to music. In the middle of the night, she stated that Morrison woke up coughing and decided to take a bath to relieve his congestion. When she got up around 5:00 A.M., she found him thus, in the tub.

Pamela's story, however, has been recently contradicted by a man named Sam Bernett, who has come forward with a different version of the events of that night. At the time, Bernett was the manager of a famous nightclub known as the Rock 'n Roll Circus, and he claims that Morrison came into the club around 1:00 A.M. to pick up some heroin for Pam, a drug which, so far as we know, Morrison had never touched, due largely, one presumes, to his fear of needles. Morrison supposedly met with two drug dealers and then disappeared into the toilets at around 2:00 A.M. About a half an hour later an attendant came to Bernett and told him that someone had locked himself inside a stall and would not come out. Bernett then ordered the stall to be broken open, whereupon he was confronted with the body of Jim Morrison sitting on a toilet slumped forward with his arms hanging limply at his sides. Blood was leaking from his mouth, and Bernett assumed that he had died snorting an overdose of Pam's heroin. The two drug dealers, meanwhile, who had sold the heroin to Morrison told Bernett that they would take care of the matter and that was the last Bernett ever saw of Morrison. He assumes that the dealers then removed the body to Morrison's apartment on rue Beautreillis, where they placed him into the bathtub. (Such an incident, we note, would most likely have required the collusion of Pam.) Bernett, meanwhile—along with several others, such as Marianne Faithful, Mick Jagger's ex at the time—was sworn to secrecy by the club's owners for fear of the scandal that would inevitably result if word got out that Morrison had died in his nightclub. Now in his sixties, Bernett says he is relieved to finally be able to tell the truth about that night, even though he risks prosecution by French authorities.[1]

Bernett's story does have the ring of truth about it, and if true, then it would help to explain Pamela's ensuing feelings of guilt over Morrison's death, for she told friend Danny Sugerman that she felt responsible for his death.[2] She remained troubled and miserable for the next three years, slowly descending deeper into drug addiction and prostitution until she, too, was found dead of an overdose of heroin on April 25, 1974, at the age of 27, the same age, coincidentally, not only of Morrison at the time of his death, but also of Janis Joplin, Jimi Hendrix, and Rolling Stones guitarist Brian Jones.

Whichever version happens to be true—and it is possible that neither one of them is—both stories end by finding Morrison dead in the bathtub, transformed already into legend. For the image of the king who is murdered in his bathtub is actually a rather well-known motif in mythology, and so it already resonates with archaic patterns of thought. The most famous example, of course, is that of Agamemnon slain in his bath by his wife Clytemnestra in vengeance for the sacrifice of their daughter Iphigenia, a sacrifice that the gods had demanded to set the winds blowing to carry the ships away to Troy. Also consider the story of King Minos, who was killed in his bath by boiling pitch that had been poured through a system of pipes by his nemesis, the master craftsman Daedalus, who had, once upon a time, built a labyrinth within which to house the king's dark family secret, the Minotaur. In Celtic mythology, furthermore, the strange figure of Llew Llaw Gyffes, the solar hero, can be killed only standing with one foot on a bathtub and the other on the back of a goat.

What, we may now ask, might be the prototype of such an image?

The original significance of the dead king in his bathtub may lie somewhere in the depths of history, in the cult of one of the world's oldest gods, Enki, who was known to the Babylonians as the Lord of the Abzu, the watery abyss that was thought to be a freshwater spring hidden beneath the world from out of which all its saltwater came. In the archaic imagination of the Mesopotamian cosmos, the world was a flat, round disc surrounded by a salt sea that the Babylonians identified with the dragon goddess Tiamat. This same image of the world-encircling sea in identification with a giant serpent turns up in classical Greece, where it was known as Okeanos, the great snake that surrounds the earth, and in India as Ananta (meaning "endless"), the serpent upon which Vishnu lies as he dreams his dream of world evolution.

In European alchemy, the image was miniaturized as the ouroboros, the serpent biting its tail, which was meant to represent the primordial unity from out of which the alchemical opus was to be brought forth. Thus, in the end lies the beginning, for as the cosmos emerges out of the primordial sea, so too, in the end, it returns to the watery abyss in the myths of the Great Flood that overwhelm the earth and start the world all over again.

For Jim Morrison, ending his life through immersion in a bathtub full of water was a way of coming back full circle, since Morrison always had identified himself with the mythological great serpent in his song lyrics. In The Doors' great song "The End," which concludes their first album, *The Doors*, this world serpent puts in its first appearance in Morrison's writing: "Ride the snake," he sings, "he's old and his skin is cold."[3]

One of Morrison's various personae was known as the Lizard King, and it was in the role of civilization's great antagonist, the cosmic serpent-lizard, that Morrison found himself most comfortable. And so, in the end, he became in death the incarnation of the great serpent known as the King of the Abyss.

NINE

Morrison's identification with the Lizard King and the Great Snake deliberately casts him in a role that is antipathetic to civilization, and especially to cities, and hails back to ancient Western myths in which it is often necessary to kill great serpents to found cities. For example, in the myth of Cadmus, the eponymous founder of a city named Cadmeia, to get the place up and running, he had to acquire water from a sacred spring that was guarded by a giant snake. Cadmus slew the serpent, not knowing that it was sacred to the war god Ares (thus bringing down a curse on his line that would ultimately climax in the fate of his descendant Oedipus), and sacrificed it to Athena, who told him to pull out the serpent's teeth, which he would later use to sow the armed men.

In the Christian tale of Saint George, likewise, a town that is oppressed because its inhabitants cannot draw water from a spring that is guarded by a serpent is forced to sacrifice a member of the town each year by way of drawing lots. When, one day, the lot is drawn for the princess, the desperate king begs George to save them, and so the knight goes forth to kill the dragon and abolishes forever the custom of human sacrifice.

Thus, we can understand how Morrison saw himself as the Great Enemy of the Establishment that had built up the forms of Western civilization for millennia. Morrison belongs to a countercultural tradition that begins—in the present phase of our society, anyway—with Blake and Baudelaire in the 19th century (Blake identified himself with that great serpent Satan in Milton's *Paradise Lost*, while Baudelaire delighted in shocking the bourgeois sensibilities of his audience with poems about lesbians, vampires, and rotting corpses). Indeed, one of the main reasons why Morrison went to Paris and took up residence specifically at 17 rue Beautreillis was the fact that it had been occupied at one time by Baudelaire, one of his favorite poets.

So like a noir narrative that begins with a corpse and then rewinds to attempt a reconstruction of the conditions that brought that corpse into being, we find ourselves now moving backward from Morrison's ultimate fate toward an examination of the forces that set that fate in motion.

EIGHT

Following the traces of our snake, then, backward, we find his presence on the album *L.A. Woman* (1971), The Doors' last album recorded with Jim Morrison just before he left for Paris. Here, Morrison turns up in the song "Crawling King Snake," which treats us to a vision of the snake and his mate as a pair of archetypal world founders, such as the Chinese progenitors Fu Hsi and Nu Kua, the brother-sister pair who survived the Great Flood, and the lower half of whose bodies were serpentine. Cadmus and his wife Harmony, likewise, were said in their old age to have been transformed into a pair of serpents.

If it is possible to view Morrison's life through the lens of a noir narrative, then the femme fatale of that narrative would be the muse of Los Angeles herself, the "L.A. Woman" who lured Morrison—and countless others—to their deaths through promises of fame and fortune. Los Angeles is the place where Morrison spent most of his days drinking his life away, for his alcoholism was the venom injected into him by the sting of the serpent goddess of Los Angeles to whom the album's title song is dedicated. Morrison in this song addresses the muse of Los Angeles herself, the very same woman who appears in countless Hollywood noir tales from *The Maltese Falcon* and *Double Indemnity* to *Chinatown*, and who is as corrupt as the city itself, which Morrison shows us as the breeding ground for "Motel money murder madness." Driving down its freeways, the city is a haunted place filled with lonely women trapped inside their Spanish-style bungalows feeding off their dead memories of a vanished stardom, like the pathetic figure of Gloria Swanson in Billy Wilder's *Sunset Boulevard*. The suburbs, with their orange trees and automobiles, their strip malls and parking lots, are crowded with a million Mildred Pierces who eventually will murder their husbands or else die of alcoholic misery. Los Angeles, in Morrison's vision, is a place that breeds disasters, earthquakes, and fires in the hills, and it can no more be trusted than Faye Dunaway in *Chinatown*.

By the time Morrison realized what Los Angeles was doing to him, it was too late. His best and most creative years as a poet had already been sapped from him by the Los Angeles goddess, who had stripped him of his image as a rock-star god and left behind merely an alcohol-poisoned physical body that was all that remained of "Jim Morrison." But once he realized what she was doing to him, this Los Angeles succubus, Morrison decided to quit The Doors and left for Paris to become a real poet. His journey through the Los Angeles image factory had been only a detour keeping him from fulfilling his real dream as a great American poet, the roots of which he felt somehow lay in Paris, the ultimate home of Europe's counterculture.

SEVEN

Morrison Hotel (1970), the album that The Doors recorded just before *L.A. Woman,* provides us with a key structural feature of Morrison's self-generated (and Los Angeles–amplified) mythology. Morrison Hotel was a real hotel located in the skid-row section of Los Angeles, and Morrison spent his life living in cheap Los Angeles motels and hotels, eschewing the comfort and security of a private mansion a la Graceland. The contrast, moreover, with Elvis is an instructive one, for everything about Elvis bespeaks domesticity: his love for his mother, his creation of a house in which he could extend his childhood permanently by living with both parents, and his creation of a large, cult-like extended family of paid "friends." Indeed, Elvis—and others such as John Lennon and John F. Kennedy—played the mythic role of the vanishing flower god who is wed to a Great Mother figure. It is an agrarian myth that is as rooted and axial as the city itself.

But once the city-state has passed its prime, and the cult of the Great Mother has fallen into desuetude, becoming as corrupt as a harem full of transvestites and bald, priestly castrati, then along comes the figure of the Wanderer, whose first appearance on the stage of world history was Gilgamesh, the man who rejected the cult of the Great Mother and left the city, with all its overripe decadence, behind to become the prototypal wanderer of the waste land who lives by hunting and avoids cities at all costs. This type of mythological figure will later turn up in narratives associated with characters like the Wandering Jew, the Flying Dutchman, or the Arabic Majnun, the madman who haunts the deserts with his unrequited love for Layla, a woman with whom he can never put down roots and for whose love he is transformed into an eternal nomad.

This is the mythic typology behind the life of Jim Morrison, and it is a very different one from the dying and reviving flower god who revolves around a goddess figure. For Morrison was a nomad, and it is the myth of the wanderer that shapes his rejection of all traditional forms of civilized urban life, such as marriage, monogamy, children, and parents. He never married (except in a pagan ceremony to Patricia Kenneally), and his simultaneous involvements with Patricia and Pamela have the feel of the polygamous lifestyle of the Biblical patriarch-wanderers like Abraham. When Patricia came to him and told him she was pregnant, he demanded that she abort the child, for to have offspring would be tantamount to a form of arborescence. This rejection of traditional domestic values supported the fact that he told the press that his parents were dead (and in a sense, they *were* dead to him, as he stopped speaking to them shortly after The Doors formed as a band). And despite all of his money, Morrison never really owned anything save his beloved Mustang, for possessions would only tie him down and get in the way of his erratic pathways across the American landscape.

All of this comes clear in the imagery of the short film he wrote and directed entitled *HWY.* In this film, Morrison plays a figure who haunts the interstices between cities, for he is a hitchhiker who drifts into Los Angeles, confesses to someone on a telephone that he has killed somebody, and then leaves again. The opening of the film shows him as a nature child bathing in a pond with a waterfall and then gradually hitchhiking his way into the city, like a modern incarnation of Enkidu, Gilgamesh's hairy sidekick. At one point, he is shown driving a Mustang (taken from the person he has killed?) as though to signify the horseman with no name who rides into town out of the wilderness and then leaves again just as mysteriously. In many ways, the imagery of the film is a prefiguring of George Miller's *Mad Max* movies, which are also about a wanderer who haunts the wasteland and finds himself ill at ease in urban environments.

Thus, the image of the hotel, with its implied transience, is a key feature of Morrison's mythology because it represents his archetypal dwelling place, just as Graceland is the archetypal dwelling of Elvis Presley. People only *pass through* hotels; they do not *live* in them. Morrison's fascination with motels and highways is a function of his rhizomatic lifestyle, for motels are the modern urban equivalent of the tents erected by Arabs and Turks during their desert peregrinations.

SIX

Related to this idea of wandering and nomadism is Morrison's fascination with edges, gateways, doors, and thresholds of all sorts. It is no accident that he chose to name his band The Doors, for Morrison was a man who always preferred to remain at the threshold, with one foot inside the house and the other outside. Thus, although he occasionally stayed with Pamela Courson at her Laurel Canyon home, he can in no way be regarded as ever having actually *lived* there, for Morrison preferred the Alta Cienega motel, with its sleazy sodium-lit parking lot and bilevel façade.

This fascination with edges is why we always see him hanging from ledges and balconies in the biographies that have been written about him. This was something he often would do to gain attention, jumping over a balcony 15 stories up and hanging onto the ledge to frighten his girlfriend Pam.

The wanderer prefers edges because there is something cosmic about them. Take a wrong step and you could fall off the edge of the world, which was precisely the cosmology of the ancients. One could wander far enough and ultimately reach the edges of the flat earth where the waters of the world-encircling ocean poured off into the abyss. One step further and you would fall into the Other World, the realm of the dead that lay beneath the earth. If anyone ever wanted to journey alive into the realm of the dead and come back to recount its secrets, it was Jim Morrison.

Hence, Morrison's constant psychological tightrope act of drinking himself into insentience. He was as heavy a drinker as they come, and spent most of the days of his life inebriated. He used a multitude of drugs, from LSD to cocaine, but it was alcohol he preferred (specifically Irish whiskey), for it enabled him to keep a foot constantly in both worlds without ever having to commit entirely to one or the other: the soft, abyssal realm of images and poems, and the hard, unyielding world of three-dimensional surfaces, surfaces that, if you dropped onto them with sufficient force from a ledge high enough up in the air, would kill you.

FIVE

The original title for The Doors' third album, *Waiting for the Sun* (1968), was to have been *The Celebration of the Lizard.* Morrison had intended for it to be bound in pseudo-snake skin with the title embossed in gold on its scales. The song entitled "The Celebration of the Lizard" was to have taken up one entire side of the album, a rambling rock opera composed of disparate musical styles. However, Morrison's drinking at this point was such that his clouded consciousness was not able to pull the piece together and so the idea was abandoned. Instead, the album was called *Waiting for the Sun*, and its cover featured a conventional image of the band standing in a field at the first blush of dawn. The Lizard was relegated to the sleeve of the inside front cover along with the lyrics to the abandoned song. Thus, the myth of the solar hero who comes to slay the monsters of the nighttime zodiacal bestiary at dawn is evoked as victorious over the dragon.

But Morrison, of course, would never have identified himself with a dragon slayer. Like Blake and Baudelaire, he sided with the monsters and saw himself as a modern incarnation of the Great Beast that haunts the peripheries of civilization and threatens its inhabitants. Though "The Celebration of the Lizard" was never finished, The Doors did nonetheless often perform it in concerts, so it may be worthwhile to pause a moment and reflect on its main points.

The song, as Morrison prefaces by explaining in concert, concerns a group of people who become fed up with life in cities and thus decide to abandon them and head out to the desert wilderness where they regress to a tribal lifestyle. There they perform rituals and ceremonies involving human sacrifice to an ancient serpent who lives in a nearby well. We note that this is precisely what the people were doing when Saint George showed up to rescue them from this custom. Morrison, that is, identifies himself with the dragon-serpent-lizard that forms the group's spiritual nucleus. In the song he says, "I am the Lizard King / I can do anything."

Every civilization throughout history has generated its own counterculture. Our civilization is far from unique in this respect. As Arnold Toynbee has shown us, this process is a natural and inevitable by-product of a failure of the creative elite of a society to inspire its people with fresh responses to new challenges presented by the changing circumstances of the environment. Some of these countercultures are destructive to their parent societies—as in the case of the Christians within the Late Classical Society—but some of them manage to be taken up as endosymbionts to become permanent structures within the larger organism of the society as a whole.

In the biblical world of the Old Testament, the counterculture was represented by the prophets, many of whom, such as Amos, were wanderers who migrated to the cities with dire messages proclaiming their coming destruction. Though the prophet was eventually engulfed by Hebraic society as a permanent feature, the drama of Christ was an example of a prophetic tradition critical of the Hebraic establishment, and that founded an entirely new society. In the case of the Greeks, a counterculture formed around the Orphics, who espoused a very un-Homeric doctrine of reincarnation and vegetarianism. This doctrine was taken up by the Pythagoreans who were persecuted by the authorities but later had a huge influence on the philosophical mainstream in the form of Plato, who brought their countertradition into awareness through his dialogues.

In the present cycle of civilization, the counterculture has its roots in the mid-19th century with Blake and Baudelaire, from whence it then traveled through the symbolist poets to the modernists and on down to the Beats and, eventually, to Jim Morrison.

Morrison, in identifying himself with the dragon, then, was essentially casting himself in the role of a Nietzschean liberator of culture from the stultifying conventions of Western society. Hence, he constantly challenged authority: his onstage arrest in New Haven for taunting police officers in the middle of a concert; his exposing himself to a huge crowd in a drunken concert in Miami, for which he was put on trial for obscenity; and his flouting of censorship on *Ed Sullivan* when he was specifically instructed not to sing the lyrics "girl we couldn't get much higher." All of these acts are tantamount to Morrison's recreation and perpetuation of the myth of the great Nietzschean antagonist of civilization. (Notice that with Nietzsche's book *Thus Spake Zarathustra*, Nietzsche deliberately goes from being a Hellenophile writing books on the greatness of the Greeks like *The Birth of Tragedy* and *Tragedy in the Philosophical Age of the Greeks* to specifically identifying himself with Zarathustra, the prophet of Zoroastrianism, the primary religion of the Persians, who were the great enemies of the Greeks.) Morrison very much identified himself with this sort of countercultural reversal in which the culture hero ironically shifts to become his own society's worst enemy.

FOUR

From the image of the tightrope walker who is balanced above an abyss to that of the man on stilts with gigantic legs, there is not much of a leap. Thus, if Morrison had appeared as a character on the cover of *Strange Days* (1967), The Doors' second album, he might well have been the man on stilts with bizarrely elongated legs. But then, he might just as well have shown up as the Lizard King, for the cover of *Strange Days*, with its midgets and acrobats, strong men, and mimes, suggests the carnival atmosphere that is evoked by the feel of The Doors' early music, especially accented by Ray Manzarek's keyboards.

The freak-show imagery on the cover of this album seems to imply an analogy with the fame that so recently had been attained by The Doors. For just as each character of a sideshow occupies his own unique space—as implied by the bizarrely elongated legs of the man on stilts, for instance, or the painted iconography of the Tattooed Man—so too, does the acceleration to electronic fame cut one off from the general spatio-temporal container within which the rest of the population is situated. This essentially establishes—and isolates—the celebrity inside his unique bubble. Traveling through the culture at the speed of light—for The Doors had recently appeared on *Ed Sullivan*—creates the optical distortion of a sea of blurred faces that casts doubt on the nature of reality: is the celebrity standing still while the crowds whiz past him, or is the celebrity in motion with respect to the crowd? Either way, the phenomenological experience of an ocean of blurred faces, along with its attendant feeling of isolation, is the same.

Thus, it is with *Strange Days* that The Doors began to realize that they were in trouble psychologically, for a new cosmology was beginning to erupt all around them and to encase them within a glass aquarium that entirely separated them from the world of their fellow human beings. They had become a traveling electric carnival.

THREE

It was the *Ed Sullivan* appearance on September 17, 1967, though, that set the precedent for the imagery of *Strange Days.* The *Ed Sullivan Show* was in fact an electronic carnival, a retrieval of vaudeville. The very same kinds of acts that were normal features on the vaudeville circuit—acrobats, mimes, folk singers, bizarrely talented country people—were precisely the stuff of Ed Sullivan, which thereby retrieved and saved the realm of vaudeville from the extinction that threatened it by the advent of the talkies in the late 1920s. And so the appearance of The Doors on *The Ed Sullivan Show* may have impressed on them the fact that their act really did belong to the culture of sideshows, freaks, and country fairs.

This rural world is a preperspectival one in which archaic notions of space and time, unchanged since the Middle Ages, manage to survive without essential alteration. The country freak or abnormality—the absurdly giant squash or the two-headed cow—is really a world in which each thing exists in its own space entirely separate from the spaces of other things. Just as each form is a self-sufficient entity, not contained within any larger overarching civic structure such as a polis, so too, the world of the country fair and its strangely talented denizens preserves an archaic feeling for space and time. This space and time is not all that far away from the four-dimensional aperspectivity rediscovered by Einstein, in which each object carves out its own unique spatio-temporal frame of reference.

Hence, when The Doors appeared on *Ed Sullivan*, we notice that this archaic, pre-Renaissance feeling for space characterizes their performance. Remember that in medieval aesthetics each thing was assigned its size relative not to its optical effect but to its spiritual significance. Thus, in Duccio's painting *The Temptation of Christ on the Mountain* (1308), we see Godzilla-size figures of Christ and the devil striding across tiny towns. Watching The Doors on *Ed Sullivan*, likewise—and they only did one show—we see that the television camera has captured them in such a way that Jim Morrison appears gigantic, while the other three band members appear like tiny dolls in the background. The effect of Morrison on television was to amplify his significance to colossal dimensions, just as it had done with Elvis before him. At the conclusion of the song, this effect of gigantism is reinforced when Morrison's posture suddenly relaxes, hands at his sides, pelvis thrust forward, head tilted to one side as though caught in the pose of a sculpture by Michelangelo. When Morrison then casually rests the microphone up on one shoulder, the posture is unmistakably that of Michelangelo's colossal David with one arm raised and grasping the slingshot on his shoulder just before he has slain the giant. Behind Morrison, Ray Manzarek works at his tiny keyboards like a windup toy, and John Densmore pecks at his salt-and-pepper shaker-size drum set.

TWO

But then, even before *Ed Sullivan*, The Doors already were inhabiting this aperspectival carnival world. The cover of their first album, entitled simply *The Doors* (1967), shows Morrison's gigantic head with the other three band members as tiny little components, as though they were the men who ran his brain for him. All we see of Morrison here is his head, for his body is cut off from the neck down, as though he had become some sort of decapitated oracle, like the Celtic god Bran or Greek Orpheus. The photograph emphasizes this basic asymmetry of Morrison versus the other three band members, so that the structure of the front man with his attending functions—which, we recall, had been dissolved by the Beatles—is here retrieved. From the inception of the band, Morrison is locked in a classic Jungian 3:1 ratio (although by the time of *L.A. Woman* he has been scaled down to occupy the dimensions of perspectival space along with the other band members, for he is shown on the cover of the album in a photograph hunched down in the lower right corner, as inconspicuously as possible).

ONE

Like James Dean, Jim Morrison never doubted for a moment that his excesses would destroy him. From the band's inception, it is clear that Morrison intended his fate to be just as it was and would never have changed a detail. We have the following conversation, for instance, that took place between Morrison and Ray Manzarek shortly after the band's formation in Venice Beach, California:

> Jim: How long do you want to live?
> Ray: Oh, I'd like to go to about eighty-seven—get to see my grandchildren and great-grandchildren.

> Jim: Not me. You know how I see myself? As a great shooting star, a huge fiery comet. Everyone stops and gasps and points up and says, "Oh, look! Oh, look at that!" Then whooosshh! I'm gone. But they'll never see anything like it again—and they'll never be able to forget me.[4]

Indeed, there is something cosmic about Morrison. He is the human equivalent of an eclipse or a rare planetary alignment, as though he were the incarnation of the Hindu god Rahu, the lord of eclipses and comets. (In his movie *The Doors*, interestingly, Oliver Stone shows Morrison wandering out in the desert for one moment beneath a solar eclipse.) The devastation that Morrison embraced, smiling, and without ever once indicating misgivings about his planned project of self-destruction, seems to the outsider to be truly horrifying. But Morrison went to his fate like Nietzsche's Dionysian man, with open arms and a ready embrace of Chaos and Ancient Night.

At the inception of The Doors, Morrison is already in a state of advanced psychological decay. Even before attaining fame, he is drinking to excess most of the time. He took acid recklessly, popped pills, and smoked pot. With John Lennon or Elvis Presley, this same process of psychological decomposition had taken a long time, beginning slowly at first, and then gradually spiraling out of control only toward the end of Elvis's life and toward the demise of the Beatles when Lennon was at the height of his drug-taking fame. But Morrison *begins* the way these guys *ended*: with a total and near-religious commitment to self-annihilation via drugs and alcohol. Thus, it is difficult, in Morrison's case, to assign his dissolution to the hazards of electrically amplified fame, since by the time that fame happened, Morrison had already long since become a ghost.

ZERO

To understand his mission, however, with its final goal of landing him in a Paris bathtub in the same apartment building in which Baudelaire had once lived, it is essential to see how it all began, to visualize him on the sun-bleached rooftops of a decrepit building in Venice Beach.

It is the summer of 1965. The air is warm and moist with sea spray. The leaves of the palm fronds are rattling in a soft hiss of wind. The cry of gulls can be heard echoing over the promenade.

Morrison sits cross-legged upon the rooftop, alone and quiet. He is, at this moment, very sober.

He sits with the notebook open on his lap before him and gradually, bit by bit, begins to *hear* the music that is spoken to him, a music patterned into words that comes from nowhere but the deep blue skies. He listens to the music and he writes the words to the songs that will become the first two albums of The Doors. He has not yet had that meeting with Ray Manzarek in which he will read these lyrics to him, while Ray proposes that they form a band.

The Spirit is speaking to him, as it spoke to so many others before him.

And all at once the vision descends with a hiss of displaced air made by the wings of alighting angels (or are they raptors?): the whole plan is there, drawn on the paper before him like a diagram. He will play the dragon. Here, at point "X." He will attack the city, over here at point "Y."

As the great world-encircling serpent, he has crawled up out of the ocean at the edge of the world, and when the play is over, he will crawl right back into it again.

IV

Sunset (The 1980s)

Ronald Reagan, Gianni Versace, and Princess Diana

INTRODUCTION

As J. G. Ballard was the first to perceive, the Space Age now lies in ruins all about us, and along with it, the cult of the electric media superstar. We must imagine this cult as part of a development that took place within the bounds of a horizon configured by the Space Age that began in the 1950s with Chuck Yeager's breaking of the sound barrier, for the idea of gigantic human beings has something of the feel about it of a 1950s giant monster movie. The epoch of huge American automobiles, sprawling shopping malls, and big dreams of conquering the massive distances between the stars with spacecraft is part of the same age that gave rise to the billboard-size human being, such as Elvis Presley or Marlon Brando. In the 21st century, however, the American landscape is littered with the ghostly shells of empty, boarded up shopping malls and crumbling inner cities with vacant buildings like Detroit, Michigan, or Buffalo, New York. The rusting gantries and cracked, weed-infested ruins of Cape Canaveral bear mute witness to the passing of an age, for the exploration of other planets is a job that, henceforth, shall be turned over to remote-controlled micro-robots and space probes. American optimism to the contrary, no one seriously believes that a manned mission to Mars will ever take place. The solitary confinement of a three-year journey (roundtrip) inside of a space capsule, cut off from the earth's biorhythms, is more stress than any human nervous system can tolerate, and so far, all experiments conducted on earth simulating such confined environments have been failures.

With our next group of case studies, then—Ronald Reagan, Gianni Versace, and Princess Diana—we already are beginning to witness the crumbling of the cult of the megacelebrity. For whereas stars like Elvis and Marilyn, Jim Morrison and John F. Kennedy, Andy Warhol, and Elizabeth Taylor had been open and attuned to their public and had rushed out to meet the world with vitality and enthusiasm, with Reagan, Versace, and Diana, we enter a world in which the celebrity has turned inward to a private solipsistic realm of fantasies in which the outer world scarcely figures. They were all moody, introverted dreamers, these latter three, for they inhabited mental landscapes that were distant and remote from what was going on around them, and when reality intruded into their fantasies, it came as a complete shock.

Reagan lived inside a Hollywood dream world in which his mental furniture was made out of black-and-white images from old movies, for he spoke and thought in terms of Hollywood clichés, and when the Iran-Contra scandal broke out, it took him completely by surprise, so removed was he from the daily goings-on of his staff's activities. Versace, likewise, spent his life building a private dreamworld of celebrity fashions and high couture to which the general public was absolutely not invited, and when Andrew Cunanan showed up on his doorstep, he was literally struck by a bolt out of the blue. And Princess Diana—for at least the years of her marriage to Charles—lived inside a Barbara Cartland novel and never could understand why the reality she was experiencing with her Prince Charming would never match up to the novels that she had spent her childhood reading.

Furthermore, a certain routinization of the charisma of earlier celebrities is evident: Reagan was the first American president not to have studied the classics and to derive his figures of speech from Hollywood movies; Andrew Cunanan's murder of Gianni Versace is a clichéd repeat of Mark David Chapman's novel shooting of John Lennon; and Princess Diana's car crash is itself a clichéd rerun of the famous crashes of James Dean and Grace Kelly.

Diana, moreover, pushed the cult as far as it could go, for it is impossible that a human being could ever become more famous than she, or possibly even as famous. She was not only the most famous woman in the world, but may even go down as the most famous woman in history, rivaled perhaps only by Cleopatra, for her life, too, has all the makings of a Shakespearean tragedy. Her car crash, furthermore, differed from all the other famous crashes before it in that it has a certain inauthenticity about it; that is to say, her crash did not originate "organically" from out of her own doings, but was itself brought about by the paparazzi who pursued her. The central irony of the media's reporting on the Diana crash is that it is not a "real" event at all, but one they brought about as a desperate attempt to report on the "event of the century." Diana's crash happened because the paparazzi needed it to happen so that they could report on it.

And so now here they are, the last of the giants.

10

Ronald Reagan: The Celluloid Man Made Flesh

> When elected governor of California, [Reagan] was asked how he thought he would do in such a daunting political role. "I don't know," he replied, "I've never played a governor."[1]

REAGAN STEPS DOWN FROM SCREEN, ENTERS PHYSICAL WORLD

The first point to notice about Ronald Reagan is that whereas the other celebrities who we have studied in this book so far—Jim Morrison, Marilyn Monroe, and Elvis Presley come to mind—were engaged in a life-and-death struggle between their physical selves and their electric stereotypes, Reagan experienced no such struggle, for he was never the least bit disturbed about being typecast and no identity problem ever troubled him. Reagan, unlike these others, was essentially identical with his onscreen selves. Indeed, it might even be said that through some mysterious process (that Reagan welcomed), Reagan's avatars—both onscreen and on television—very early on in his career actually *replaced* the physical Ronald Reagan, like one of those spores in the film *Invasion of the Body Snatchers*. He *was* his onscreen self, made flesh.

Somehow, the process of being cloned via the silver screen had the bizarre side effect of transubstantiating his bones and blood such that their physical matter disappeared and was replaced by *light*. There was no "real" Ronald Reagan, only the projection from another world of what *appeared* to be a physical human being. Thus, like the Docetist heresy that described Christ as merely appearing to be real, so too, Ronald Reagan was an avatar from another reality: that of the celluloid world. In this respect, Reagan differs quite considerably from our other case studies.

An extravagant metaphor?

Perhaps.

But how else to explain the fact of Reagan's basic transparency—in the dual sense of both film and stained glass—for at every turn of his life, he appears to believe that he is inside a movie, and acts, accordingly, in such a manner as to render himself momentarily diaphanous to a celluloid narrative?

When, for example, in a 1980 debate with George Bush in Nashua, New Hampshire, the moderator suggested that he turn his microphone off, Reagan, in a rare outburst shouted back at him, "I paid for this microphone, Mr. Green!" he was actually referencing Spencer Tracy in the 1948 film *State of the Union*, in which Tracy had said, "Don't you shut me off! I'm paying for this broadcast."[2] His embarrassing question to Gorbachev at their first summit meeting in Geneva in 1985, in which he commented that he "was certain the United States and Soviet Union would cooperate if Earth were threatened by an invasion from outer space" is straight out of drive-in B movies from the 1950s like *Earth vs. the Flying Saucers* or *The Day the Earth Stood Still.*[3] And when, after being shot by John Hinckley, he said to his wife, "Honey, I forgot to duck," he may not have been quoting an old movie, but he *was* quoting Jack Dempsey when he lost the heavyweight boxing title to Gene Tunney in 1926.

Indeed, Reagan was a walking museum of American monomythic types out of old black-and-white movies: the football star, the cowboy, the Cold War spy, the World War II hero, the small-town man with big ideals; at one point or another in his movie career, Reagan had played them all, and such filmic ghosts had so fused together with his own persona that he spent the rest of his life quoting and referencing them. The title of his autobiography, for instance, *Where's the Rest of Me?* was a quote from *King's Row*, in which he had played a small-town man who had been victimized by a moralistic surgeon who had amputated his legs unnecessarily. "Win one for the Gipper," which became Reagan's slogan for George Bush's 1988 presidential campaign, was a reference to the film *Knut Rockne*, in which he had played George Gipp, the high school football star who died tragically young. And Reagan's campaign image of the man of the people on his way to Washington to straighten out a corrupt and bureaucratic government—which got him elected in 1981—was a deliberate evocation of Jimmy Stewart's character Jefferson Smith in *Mr. Smith Goes to Washington*, in which a small-town rube heads off to the White House with big ideals, only to find them dashed by graft and corruption.

Reagan constantly behaved as though he were playing the role of leading man in a Hollywood movie, as his biographer Lou Cannon illustrates:

> One White House aide recalls that Secretary of State George P. Shultz, huddling with Reagan in the secure vault of the American ambassador's residence in Moscow during the 1988 summit, coached him for his meeting with Soviet leader Mikhail Gorbachev by telling him what to do "in this scene." Shultz proceeded through a series of precise directions in stage terminology, telling Reagan where to stand and what to say. The aide was horrified that the secretary of state would treat the president as a man who "didn't have the intellectual wherewithal to be able to think or act on his own." But Reagan was not offended. He himself saw the meeting with Gorbachev as a significant performance, and he valued the services of a good director.[4]

Indeed, Reagan had become so mentally entangled in the realm of celluloid, that he often confused his own memories with scenes from old movies. As Frances Fitzgerald writes:

> Speaking to the Congressional Medal of Honor Society in December 1983, he told a World War II story of a B-17 captain whose plane had been hit and who was unable to drag his wounded young ball-turret gunner out of the turret; instead of parachuting to safety with the rest of the crew, the captain took the frightened boy's hand and said, "Never mind, son, we'll ride it down together." Reagan concluded by telling the society that the captain had been posthumously awarded the Medal of Honor. But no such person existed: the story came from the 1946 movie *A Wing and a Prayer*. Within a month of this event Reagan told the Israeli Prime Minister Yitzhak Shamir that the roots of his concern for Israel could be traced back to World War II days, when he, as a Signal Corps photographer, had filmed the horrors of the Nazi death camps. Reagan, however, did not leave California during World War II; he had apparently seen a documentary about the camps.[5]

Although Reagan was a reader—of adventure novels, at least—words apparently did not make anywhere near the impression on him as did images. By his own admission, he first turned to the comic section when reading the daily newspapers, and only after a thorough analysis of the latest strips did he transfer his attention to world affairs. His priorities, evidently, were: entertainment first, politics second.

When his cabinet realized that his grasp of world events was poor, they decided to "educate" him in the medium that he knew best, that of celluloid, by showing him movies made by the Central Intelligence Agency (CIA) about global happenings. This method, at least, kept Reagan awake, for he had a tendency to doze off during briefings and cabinet meetings in which he was easily bored. Furthermore, he rarely read the briefings that were given to him, as White House Chief of Staff James Baker realized one morning when he asked Reagan if he had read the briefing that Baker had given him the night before regarding an important economic summit, and Reagan replied, "Well, Jim, *The Sound of Music* was on last night."

Taken individually, the foregoing anecdotes may be rather harmless—even charming—but cumulatively, they add up to a mockery of the office of the president of the United States, as though a clown or a comedian had been elected to office rather than a competent statesman. As McLuhan pointed out, the clown is someone who tries to solve specialist tasks using generalist methods, and Reagan was the class clown of all the American presidents who tried to be president by sitting back and letting everyone else do the job for him while he drew cartoons on pads of stationery, which he frequently did to pass the time during long and boring cabinet sessions.

Reagan's journey to Washington, then, represents the complete Los Angelization of America, for Reagan, like Walt Disney, was a spore sent out—not from a spaceship—but from the collective Overmind of Los Angeles to attempt an insidious takeover of the United States by becoming its apparent ruler. When he was voted into office in 1981, Americans were essentially casting their vote for movies and entertainment over books and intelligent, reasoned discourse as the new guides at the wheel of the Ship of State. Hitherto, the office of the president had been reserved mostly for educated men, for Kennedy, Eisenhower, and Truman had all been literate men who had studied the classics, but in Reagan's case, he had not studied the classics at all, but rather watched them projected onto silver screens and television sets.

Reagan was the prototype for the celebrity who gets elected into office based on the public's familiarity with his mediatic image and its subliminal associations. In Reagan's case, those associations had to do with myths of conquest, of gunslingers, military heroes, and other solar warriors who save civilization by slaying the dragon. The great irony of the Reagan administration, however, is that while Reagan's imago subliminally projected images of conquest and glory, in reality, he was a fumbling clown who could barely manage to perform tasks unaccompanied by the supervision of his advisors. But he did accomplish one thing: he opened up the pathway to political office for other media stars like Clint Eastwood, Jessie Ventura, and Arnold Schwarzenegger, all men whose public personae conveyed abrasive images of masculine deeds and manly competence.

For a society of the spectacle, such as ours, only the spectacular will do, and ever since the days of Ronald Reagan, we have routinely put electric ghosts and phantoms into public office, for we are a people who easily mistake substance for shadow. Our electronic mirrors have confused and tangled us up with the etheric dimension, for they have unleashed a virtual realm of hungry ghosts and avatars upon the world, tricking us into believing that our phantoms can save us.

Though, traditionally speaking, the dead can have little effect on the physical world except to scare and confuse the living, this is beginning to change, for now our electrically generated ghosts are starting to affect the course of world history, changing it in ways hitherto undreamed of by our forebears.

Ronald Reagan is an illustration of this new phenomenon, as the following story tells us.

REAGAN TRAVELS TO HEAVEN, SHAKES DEATH'S HAND

The whole drama of Reagan, John Hinckley, Jr., and Jodie Foster is symptomatic of a culture in which history is being replaced by virtual images manufactured in silicon circuits. A word or two about Hinckley's psychological situation may not be out of order here, because Hinckley forms such an interesting counterfoil to Reagan, the first celluloid president in history who was nearly assassinated by a man obsessed with a celluloid image.

Hinckley was an introverted youth born into a wealthy Texas oil family. He grew up in Dallas and later attended Texas Tech sporadically for a time before deciding to become a songwriter and move to California. It was in California that he became obsessed with the movie *Taxi Driver*, which was to Hinckley what the novel *Catcher in the Rye* had been to Mark David Chapman, namely, the primary work of inspiration for his deeds. Hinckley identified with the homicidal character of Travis Bickle and fell in love with Jodie Foster's virtual double Iris, a 12-year-old prostitute. (Foster apparently bore a resemblance to his mother Jo Ann, whose nickname had, in fact, been "Jodie.") After returning to Evergreen, Colorado, from California, Hinckley moved in with his parents and started an organization called "American Front," an alternative to the Democratic and Republican parties. The organization included no real members, save himself, for just as he had made up a fictitious girlfriend in California about which he had written to his parents, so too the members of his organization were fictitious. Modeling himself after his heroes, Travis Bickle and Lee Harvey Oswald, he began to collect guns. When he came across a May 1980 issue of *People* magazine that stated Jodie Foster was attending Yale University, he decided to travel to New Haven, Connecticut, to "rescue" her, just as Travis Bickle had rescued Iris in *Taxi Driver* by killing her pimp.[6]

He began stalking Foster, leaving letters and poems in her mailbox. He obtained her phone number and called her, tape recording a couple of conversations in which she strongly discouraged him from calling her again. He decided that the only way he could possibly win her heart was to perform an act that would result in elevating him to a role of notoriety in which she could relate to him as a fellow "celebrity." He began stalking Jimmy Carter for this purpose, with the idea in mind of assassinating him.

He sent an anonymous letter to the FBI that read: "There is a plot underway to abduct actress Jodie Foster from Yale University dorm in December or January. Not ransom. She's being taken for romantic reasons. This is no joke! I don't wish to get further involved. Act as you wish."[7]

After hearing about the assassination of John Lennon in December 1980, he traveled to New York City and considered killing himself on the exact spot on which Lennon had been murdered. He went out and bought a Charter Arms revolver, the same kind of gun Chapman had used to kill Lennon. (Chapman's deed seems to have acted as fresh inspiration, for Hinckley was later found to have a copy of *Catcher in the Rye* in his Washington, D.C., hotel room.) He was unable to go through with the act, however, and so he returned to New Haven, where he left Foster one more note: "Just wait," it read, "I'll rescue you very soon. Please cooperate."[8]

On the advice of a psychiatrist, the Hinckleys kicked their son out of the house in an act of "tough love," and Hinckley decided to head back to New Haven, this time with the intention of killing Jodie Foster. On the way, however, he happened to ride a bus through Washington, D.C., where he took note of Reagan's schedule.

On March 30, 1981—just three months into Reagan's presidency—Hinckley waited at a Hilton Hotel in Washington, D.C., for Reagan to emerge from a talk he had been giving to the American Federation of Labor and Congress of Industrial Organizations (AFL-CIO), and when the president surfaced, Hinckley fired six shots in his direction. The secret service agents immediately tackled Hinckley, but not before the bullets had wounded three men in Reagan's entourage, while a stray bullet had ricocheted off the limousine and plunged into Reagan's chest, where it lodged in his lung, dangerously close to his heart. Reagan was rushed to George Washington Hospital, where doctors proceeded to dig out the bullet as Reagan came close to dying.

Although Hinckley was found to be not guilty by reason of insanity, he never heard voices of angels or demons or Little People telling him what to do, as did Mark David Chapman, who avoided the insanity defense by pleading guilty. Though disturbed, Hinckley was not schizophrenic, and in his case, had no obsession with, or interest in, Ronald Reagan. Indeed, he could just as easily have killed Carter. All that mattered to him was that Jodie Foster take notice of his attempt at slaying the dragon to rescue her from some unnamed evil.

Hinckley's act also differed from Chapman's in its basic aims, for whereas Chapman's assassination of John Lennon had been an iconoclastic assault on a culturally constructed image, Hinckley's was just the opposite, for he was an iconophile in love with the celluloid image of Jodie Foster. And whereas Chapman was essentially phobic of all things virtual, Hinckley actually was seeking a pathway that would enable him to enter *inside* the world of the electroverse inhabited by celebrity icons. It is as though he wanted to see himself painted as a figure inside of a piece of stained glass, as a Judas or a Satan. By metamorphosing into a media personality through his attempt on the life of an icon, he would be enabled to enter into the same virtual landscape inhabited by Jodie Foster's Iris character from *Taxi Driver*. In that iconoscape, he would be able to meet with her and talk to her, exactly like the figures Alice spoke to upon her translation through the looking glass.

There is great irony in Hinckley's attempt to assassinate the first president in American history whose consciousness was just as distorted by the fabrications of hyperreality as his own, for Reagan, too, lived mostly in a world of fantasies shaped by images out of movies. Hinckley merely wished to cross through the silver screen and enter into that same universe of grainy, flickering forms lifted up out of the murky depths of our mythic consciousness by means of electricity. It is therefore one of the supreme ironies of history that though it mattered little to Hinckley which president he shot at, the one he ended up attempting to kill was someone who had been nearly as mentally crippled by the Hollywood dream machine as himself.

Thus, not only is history being replaced—and displaced—by the virtual, but also the etheric ghosts and doubles that live in the virtual world are actually beginning to have an effect on the physical world itself by possessing the psyches of real human individuals and causing them to perform acts they otherwise might not have thought of doing. Jodie Foster's virtual double in *Taxi Driver* very nearly cost American history one of its most popular presidents.

This is something worth thinking about.

REAGAN TAKES EARTH HOSTAGE, SURROUNDS IT WITH SATELLITES

Death enters into Reagan's life and begins to change the morphology of his thinking. Reagan has always seen himself as a savior figure, just as he had saved 77 people from drowning during his time as a lifeguard in Dixon, Illinois, and just as he had saved the country from rising inflation and high unemployment. But now he has been saved, he believes, by a God who has spared *him* from drowning. He has been saved for a purpose, and that purpose, he supposes, is to be the one man in the world capable of ending the Cold War.

God has spared Reagan from death so that Reagan may act as his emissary on earth to spare the world from the annihilation of a nuclear war. This becomes the new myth that shapes the acts and thoughts of Ronald Reagan from henceforth.

He becomes more apocalyptically minded now. He is certain that The End is coming—for he believed literally in the inevitability of Armageddon—and now he begins to worry about it. He suspects that maybe, just maybe Armageddon will be a nuclear war and that God has saved him in order to save the human race from annihilation.

To provide for his people—the good shepherd watching over his flocks—he realizes that some kind of a shield will be necessary, for it has dawned on him that in the event of a nuclear attack, the United States would be all but helpless to watch the missiles fall and the cities evaporate, while launching its own mutually assured counterattack.

And so, on March 23, 1983, nearly two years after shaking the hand of King Death, Reagan unveils his plan to forestall Armageddon: the Strategic Defense Initiative (SDI), a ring of satellites that will provide the United States with a shield of laser defenses to vaporize incoming missiles. The idea, perhaps, has been borrowed from the movies: *Murder in the Air* (1940), in which he himself starred, or Hitchcock's *Torn Curtain* (1966), but it will do the job, nonetheless.

The vision of a planet surrounded by a ring of satellites, as though it were a fortress under siege, reveals a picture beginning to form in Reagan's mind of a sun-soaked earth, its blue curvature marbled by clouds, which he is looking down on from above, as though in a Near Death Experience. He is moving, with this vision, like a satellite himself, circling the earth above the boundaries of nation-state politics and beginning to think globally, for it is a vision that will involve transnational research and development from think tanks and corporations in countries as far apart as Japan, Germany, Israel, and Great Britain. He even volunteers to share the technology with the Russians, much to their bemusement.

The idea, however, is as colossally impractical as Howard Hughes's great Hercules behemoth or Walt Disney's Epcot city. Indeed, it even resembles a larger version of the latter, with its image of the earth protected by a huge dome, as though it were a single, enormous city. With SDI, Reagan is attempting to put the earth inside of a huge glass bottle.

Such a vision is both archaic and futuristic. On the one hand, it is an updating of the old idea of the city as a walled fortress complete with archers stationed at the battlements who are ready to shoot down anything that comes their way. And, yet, it is as schlocky as a science fiction image out of a James Bond movie. The idea makes a mockery out of the notion of a traditional city, for it reveals how the geopolitics of horizontal orientation have given way to the aeropolitics of the orbital space around the earth, which will structure all our postmodern wars and cities from here on out. Satellite technology changes everything, and Reagan's idea was sensitive to the Zeitgeist, for he is already looking ahead to the first Gulf War, with its Global Positioning System and satellite-guided missiles and bombers, which took their directive from pulsating electromagnetic signals beamed to them from the skies above.

Gorbachev objected to the idea on the grounds that it would start a new arms race at precisely the time when he and Reagan had agreed to slow it down and eventually to eliminate nuclear weapons. Reagan, though, would not back down, perhaps sensing that the idea would scare the Russians out of the arms race altogether.

The idea is so gigantic—and seems just barely plausible enough—that it did indeed frighten the Russians. Although their scientists insisted to Gorbachev that it never would work, doubt nonetheless lingered. Satellites with X-ray lasers in outer space to shoot down missiles? Another crazy idea from those Americans with their Hollywood movies! And this from an ex–movie star president!

Eventually, Gorbachev laughed at the idea and told Reagan he could have it.

But the very madness and scale of the vision is enough to demonstrate the kind of "fatal strategy" toward which the Cold War was pushing things, for now it was beginning to give birth to strange, aberrant ideas.

What's next? Gorbachev thought. Things have gone far enough. They must change.

And so they do.

REAGAN GOES FISHING, SAVES SOULS

It is true that under Reagan the gap between rich and poor widened considerably, and so his detractors tended to see him as an uncompassionate man interested only in creating tax breaks for the wealthy. There is no denying that Reagan cut funding for education and social welfare programs such as unemployment assistance, food stamps, federally assisted housing, and AFDC (Assistance for Families with Dependent Children). He even tried to attack Social Security, but he did all these things to reduce government interference in the lives of individuals, for he believed that welfare robbed the poor of self-initiative and made them dependent on government handouts. Cutting taxes and reducing government spending on everything except the military, however, had the side effect of creating the nation's largest deficit in history, for under his administration the deficit reached the almost mythical sum of more than $2 trillion.

From the time he picked his drunken father up off the floor of the front porch as a young man, Reagan had always seen himself as a savior figure. Thus, he saw it as his destiny to save the American people from their own worst predator, the government, and everything he did was designed to put government on a diet and save people money by lowering taxes. He sincerely believed that his supply-side economics would redound to the benefit of all, not just the rich.

Reagan, however, did not have the intellectual wherewithal to think anything through carefully, for he operated mostly out of gut instinct. Thus, he could not foresee the side effects of his own economic policies, for he had a tendency to leave those sorts of details up to others. For him, it was the overall vision that mattered. If people got lost in the details—such as the poor and the homeless, both of which groups increased on his watch—that was not his fault, but rather the faults of his cabinet members who had not sufficiently worked out the details of his plans.

Reagan *was* a compassionate man moved by the sufferings of others. In the case of the Iran-Contra scandal, for instance, Reagan's primary reason for trading arms to Iran was not so much to finance the contras—that was largely Oliver North's idea—but to rescue the hostages in Lebanon, who had been taken captive by Hezbollah in 1983. Rescuing the hostages (at first, there were six of them, but the terrorists, realizing they had a good thing going, kept taking more) was, as far as Reagan was concerned, almost a religious act. Here we see Reagan in the role of the Fisher of Souls, like Orpheus or Christ, the latter of whom says to his disciples, "Come, I will make you fishers of men." Christ had been an avatar of Yahweh who had taken on human flesh to descend into the world and redeem humanity from its subservience to brute, animalistic passions. Reagan, too, saw himself as divinely appointed to save human beings, and the hostages were no different in this respect. They *had* to be rescued, redeemed from the devil's grasp, even if it meant breaking international law to make deals with terrorists. He is once again the lifeguard on duty jumping into the water to save the drowning; once again, the shepherd watching over his flocks, going after those who had strayed into the keeping of the wolf.

But take note: redeeming human beings with gadgets—TOW missiles, specifically—designed to kill and destroy other human beings has a certain irony about it.

Engines of death to be bartered for human souls held in hock.

Once again, Reagan shakes Death's hand who, meanwhile, keeps the other one hidden behind his back.

REAGAN TEARS DOWN THE WALL

On June 12, 1987—nearing his last year in office—Reagan made a speech at the Brandenburg Gate in Germany. Near the end of that speech, he leaned forward to shout into his public address (PA) microphone the words, "Mr. Gorbachev, open this gate!" as though he were standing outside a walled city-fortress at the head of an army siege. After a pause during which he waited for the applause to die down, he then said, more famously, "Mr. Gorbachev, tear down this wall!"

The Berlin Wall had gone up on August 13, 1961, as a delayed response to the Marshall Plan, and the process of its disintegration began on November 9, 1989, just about two years after Reagan's speech. One might gain the impression from this media construction of events that Reagan's words had a delayed effect that resulted, by some wayward principle of magical resonance, in the catastrophic bifurcation of the wall coming down two years after pronouncing his speech through an electric microphone. Indeed, it is as though Reagan's words brought down the wall through a sonic effect like the blowing of the trumpets and the shouting of the Jews, which brought down the walls of Jericho in Joshua 6. Thus, the electric PA becomes the modern equivalent of the rams' horns of the Hebrews in the middle of the second millennium B.C.E.

In Joshua 6, the collapse of the walls of Jericho signifies the beginnings of the process whereby the Jews took possession of the Promised Land, since Jericho is the first city that they assaulted after crossing the Jordan River. The collapse of the Berlin Wall in 1989, likewise, signified the shift into the new Promised Land of the orbital space around the planet—stuffed full of satellites—together with the rise of metanational organizations not tied to any sort of geophysical nation-state politics.

Reagan's assault on the Berlin Wall is the first one made on behalf of the Promised Land created by globalization, for the unification of Germany signifies the slackening of the tension between East and West—communism and capitalism—the careful boundaries of which had kept the dynamism of the energy flowing that had powered the Cold War. But with the fall of the wall, globalization could proceed unobstructed, for there was no longer an enemy to the imprisonment of the planet with virtual technologies. At last, the United States would be able to succeed in fulfilling the capitalist dream of monopolization (of the planet), for with its competitor gone, the planet could now be transformed into a single, global market.

But the fall of the wall was preceded by another omen that was its harbinger: the Soviets' withdrawal from Afghanistan in 1988, which had the side effect of unleashing the Islamist energies of the *mujahideen* upon the world. The efforts of the Islamists now shifted from the Soviet Union to the United States as the empire to bring down, for the very reason that the United States is the single and sole power left to swallow the planet alive and must, therefore, be resisted.

Thus, the conflagration that brought down the World Trade Center in 2001 is the Islamist response to Reagan's public speech at Brandenburg, which had the nonlinear effect of bringing down the Berlin Wall. The toppling of the Twin Towers, furthermore, has *its* own Biblical equivalent in the striking down of the Tower of Babel, that skyscraper that the prehistoric Hebrews regarded as such an affront to the heavens.

The effacing of the Berlin Wall was an act tantamount to wiping away the boundaries of the local and the ethnic and the provincial, while the crash of the World Trade Center—"crash" as though they were bodies in motion which, financially speaking, they were—signified a blow struck at globalization, for the twin towers were its primary economic symbol. The two acts are direct, asymmetric responses to one another and are of equal symbolic significance.

Ronald Reagan may not have single-handedly ended the Cold War—as his hagiographers would have us believe—but he almost certainly was a significant force in its erosion, for at his various summit meetings with Gorbachev, he acted with geological force to apply slow, steady pressure on the general secretary of the Soviet Union to eliminate armaments. By the time Gorbachev stepped into office, however, the Soviet system was already a ramshackle edifice, which Gorbachev knew very well was no longer working and would have to be reformed, at the very least. The moment he came to power in 1985, for instance, he already had made up his mind to pull out of Afghanistan; the difficulty was how to do it without losing face. Reagan's pressure on him was simply one more cause out of a multitude of impinging causes that finally acted with asymmetric force to break the camel's back, as it were. Or, in this case, the bear's.

At least, this would be the perspective from a complex dynamical systems view, but according to the popular view, which is based on a linear, mechanical model of cause and effect, action and reaction, Reagan becomes the Cold Warrior who brought the Soviet Union down with a single karate chop. In this media reconstruction of world events in accordance with mythology, the speech at Brandenburg and the fall of the Berlin Wall become symbolic signs pointing to the rise of the folk myths of Reagan as the Cold Warrior who brought an end to the Cold War. This particular mythology has a great deal to do with Reagan's current fame and admiration, for every year, his popularity increases among the American public, and he is now regarded as the second most popular president after Abraham Lincoln. The reason for this has almost everything to do with the popular (mis)perception of his having ended the Cold War as a lone David standing up to the Goliath of the Soviet Union.

He was no such thing, of course, but at light speed everything collapses into cliché and stereotype, while truths and complexities are crushed into two-dimensional oversimplifications.

From out of the ashes of the Cold War—or the Third World War, as some would have it—Reagan's electronic avatar emerges as a legendary folk hero, a stern, forbidding gunslinger who had no reservations about ordering the invasion of Grenada or the airstrikes against Libya. The real, three-dimensional Reagan, however (if there was one), was Le Mat, the fool who could barely keep awake at cabinet meetings and who was mocked and ridiculed behind his back for being a simpleton even by his own cabinet members.

But in electronic society, it is not the real, physical person who counts; only the electric shadow that lives and grows with a life of its own; a life that becomes enriched with the passage of years by the luxuriant overgrowth of mythology, for it is mythology that makes giants out of dwarves and dragons out of lizards.

11

The Passion of Gianni Versace

THE DISAPPEARANCE OF THE SPECTATOR

As a young child, Gianni Versace liked to play among the scraps of fabric that his mother, who was a Calabrese dressmaker, would discard from her cuttings. In particular, he enjoyed taking these scraps and making little puppets out of them.

When he grew up, these little puppets made out of textile fragments became the supermodels that he cast in his fashion shows, as though to say, aren't we *all* part of the proscenium nowadays? Isn't this global circus just one gigantic play? And that being the case, shouldn't we dress for the part?

After all, Versace took his cues from the streetwalker, designing much of his couture after the fashions of the London punk underground or even the prostitutes that so fascinated him—as they did Fellini—as a young child growing up in Reggio di Calabria.

And the world itself, as both Marshall McLuhan and Jean Baudrillard well knew, has been transformed by electronic technology into a gigantic theater in which there are no spectators, only actors. The spectator is dead. With such interactive phenomena as reality television and YouTube, *everyone* is an actor on display for everyone else. There is no audience anymore.[1]

What has changed all this, of course, replacing the spectator's unmediated gaze, is the ubiquitous eye of the camera, which substitutes an *artificial* gaze for that of our own eyes. We no longer look out on the world with naked eyes, but through electronic appendages, which we pass around like the single eye shared by the Graeae in the Greek myth of Perseus. We can no longer see anything at all for ourselves because the ocular gaze of the electronic eye sees everything for us.

A motif in Renaissance art depicts the Eye of God inside of a triangle always looking out over the world. In the 1525 painting by Pontormo known as *Supper at Emmaus*, for example, we see Christ seated at a table about to break bread with his companions while directly above his head hovers a glowing, radiant triangle with a single human eye inside of it. This was meant to connote the Eye of God as an all-seeing ubiquitous Presence watching over the deeds of humanity.

This motif, however, was a prophecy that has come true, for the all-seeing Eye of God has been replaced by the omnivoyance of the artificial electronic Eye, which gazes down at us from the tops of streetlights, the roofs of Wal-marts, from inside of banks and convenience stores, even from outer space, where it has grown wings and flies, like the Eye of Horus, around the planet, restlessly scanning it for visual information. These eyes even visit other planets on our behalf, where they look pointlessly out over stony red landscapes completely bereft of the metabolic dramas of living forms. No dramas there. At all.

The Renaissance Eye of God was merely a preparation for the coming of Man, who displaced God. Now Man watches over himself, and what He likes to see is a good show.

A spectacle.

THE SPECTACLE OF THE CATWALK

In his famous essay on wrestling, nearly everything Roland Barthes claimed as characteristic of that "sport"—that it is not a sport at all but a spectacle of highly caricatured types who bear strong resemblances to the stereotypes of the Commedia dell'arte—also can be ascribed to the world of haute couture: it, too, is a spectacle filled with stereotypes in which "Good" triumphs over "Evil." In the world of 1950s French wrestling, the "evil" characters were personifications of the values rejected by bourgeois society: laziness, indolence, and effeminacy.[2]

In Versace's fashion shows, the "good" are those celebrities he seated in the front rows as evidence of their having been smiled upon by Lady Fortuna. The supermodels, likewise, which he created by taking already famous models from the pages of fashion magazines (as opposed to merely hiring runway models) and sending them striding down his catwalks, also are "good," for they are genetically blessed and represent "the beautiful people," those human equivalents of the Platonic Forms about which the rest of us can only dream, but never actually become.

The "evil" ones in this catwalk mythology are conspicuous by their absence. They are the excluded Other upon which this system has been constructed and without which it could not function: those *not* favored by Lady Fortuna and who must, consequently, languish in the obscurity of anonymity. These shows are not celebrations of *them*, but of *us*, the ones whom Destiny has chosen to become the celebrity gods of a postmodern Olympus. And those others, the ugly ones who represent the failures of Nature's genetic experimentation are merely banal, plain, ordinary; they represent the unprivileged term of this binary opposition, for were a single one of them to appear within the confines of the cosmos built around the fashion show, the illusion would come crashing down at once, and bring the proceedings to a complete halt.

All of Versace's endeavors were tantamount to the construction of a cosmology, one built on the principle of the excluded Other, in which a realm of pure beauty and good fortune becomes an artificial reality hermetically sealed off from the real world of Time and Becoming, the factual world of the broken, the flawed, and the imperfect. Versace's cosmos is a world of gods: it is eternal and pure and beautiful, and the deprived and the misfortunate must not be allowed anywhere near it.

It is often the case in mythology that when a world of perfection such as this one has been created, and the gods have reached a resting point of satiety, the Other shows up and brings it all crashing back down into Time, where thermodynamically unstable systems go spiraling pell-mell into entropy and chaos. In *Beowulf*, for instance, the moment the great beer hall of Heorot has been constructed and everyone is enjoying themselves is the precise moment at which Grendel shows up. In the Book of Genesis, no sooner has Yahweh rested from his handiwork on the seventh day, than a serpent arrives to go poking about in his carefully cultivated garden. In the Arthurian Romances, likewise, the stories often begin with the immortal company lounging around in the dining hall of their recently completed Camelot, drinking and singing, when a figure of uncertain import abruptly appears through the doorway from the world outside: a strange Green Man, perhaps, or an old hag with boar's tusks. The company falls immediately silent.

And time begins again.

THE GAZE OF THE MEDUSA

Amid all the beauty and opulence of the Versaceverse, one small concession actually was made to the realm of the ugly and the perverse, which became the motto of Versace's company, and the very inclusion of which may perhaps have ensured his success (for a while, at least) through its magical invocation of the excluded Other. We are speaking here, of course, of the famous Versace logo, the Medusa's head.

In Greek mythology, Medusa was one of three gorgons who had been born to the sea creatures Phorcys and Ceto. The gorgons, like so many other fabulous beasts, were composite creatures: they had bronze hands, gold wings, long red tongues that lolled between boar's tusks and snakes in the place of hair. Their power consisted in the fact that they could transform any living creature that gazed upon them into stone.

The appropriateness of the Medusa as a logo for a fashion designer whose career success was based almost entirely on the spectator's gaze is notable. The Versace family states they chose the logo because they thought it would put a spell on the population and make everyone buy Versace products.

Its real import, however, stems from its relation to the realm of the fashion photographer—a figure without whom there very well may have been no Versace, because the supermodels that he created were already well known from the world of fashion magazines. For the Medusa gaze is precisely the gaze of the camera eye, which freezes into immobility the image of the person it captures. Just as in the case of the Medusa, whose reduction of the living back into the realm of the mineralogical is a perfect metaphor for the rigor mortis of death, so too, the photographer "kills" his models, as it were, by removing their images from the temporal flow and fixing them into a permanent rigidity by means of chemical processes. The images of the supermodels that once graced the covers of *Vogue* and *Elle* magazines, then, were actually pictures of corpses, dead things removed from the realm of the living, transformed by the Medusa gaze of the camera eye to a state of permanent immobility.

Hence, the myth of the Medusa is the key myth for that of the fashion photographer, but it is not, strictly speaking, the proper myth for Versace. As a fashion designer, Versace was not "killing" his models, but rather garbing them in fragments of his own mind, for when the supermodels strode out onto the runway, they actually were wearing *him*, like the mind-born sons and goddesses that, in Hindu mythology, spring from the brain of Brahma whenever he meditates. Versace was giving birth to these women as the creations of his own workshop, just as Gepetto created Pinocchio and then wished upon a star that he would become a little boy. The appropriate myth, in his case, therefore, is that of Pygmalion and Galatea, in which the sculptor brings his statue to life by praying to Aphrodite to animate it. Thus, Pygmalion is the antidote to the Medusa myth, for whereas in that myth the living are transformed into statues, in the story of Pygmalion, a statue is brought back into the realm of the living by means of the intercession of the goddess of love and sexuality. Versace's work as a fashion designer was a continual reperformance of the Galatea story, for again and again, with each new outfit that he designed, he brought the dead fashion models whose images had been killed by photographers on magazine covers back to life by garbing them in the vestments of his own mind.

Thus, by building a creature from the realm of shadows and death into his cosmos, Versace (a true Classicist at heart) assured himself of success by mollifying what would otherwise have become an angry deity who would have wrecked his world much sooner. In the *Oresteia*, the wrath of the Furies is checked only by giving them a temple in their honor as part of the official religion of the city of Athens. In the Versaceverse, though, the creature from the world of the excluded Other did not show up until Versace was already dying (of cancer), and thus was ready to be transformed into a god by the performance of the celebrity passion play, the same passion play that deified John Lennon.

VERSACE CONTRA ARMANI

The lineaments of a cosmology often become more clear by contrast with another cosmology. The world of Versace's archrival, Giorgio Armani, for instance, is patterned by *its* own forms, shapes, and laws, and it is a universe that differs in almost every respect from that of Versace's.

Even a cursory glance at Armani's palette of earth tones—browns and tans and coppers—reveals a stark contrast with Versace's peacock spectrum of bright reds and blues and emerald greens, yellows, and pinks and pastels. The contrast recalls the basic Renaissance opposition of Venice and Florence: the dark, syrupy browns of the northern school of Giorgione and Titian as against the visually crisp and chiseled forms of Raphael and Michelangelo. This is no accident, either, since Versace was born in Reggio di Calabria at the very southern tip of Italy, while Armani was a northerner. The imprint of the sunny Mediterranean, with its lime-green palm fronds, gold-flecked seas, and cerulean skies never left Versace, and indeed, formed the visual basis of his entire worldview.

Versace's colors are those of the daytime sky: blue and yellow, white and crimson, pink and gold; hence, the heaven archetype generally. Armani's earth tones, by contrast, are just that, the colors of the ground, of rocks and trees, dirt and hills. Considered thusly, the two designers form the basic dyad of the universe of haute couture: they are the Sky Mother and Earth Father of high fashion (Versace specialized in women's wear, Armani in men's).

Whereas Versace's clothes are directed at the eye—with all their pictographic patterns, *Vogue* magazine covers, Andy Warhol Marilyns, and Byzantine icons—Armani's are not only aniconic, but also meant to be *touched:* they are profusely textured with pleats, rumples, and folds reminiscent of the grain of wood and leaves and rock (they remind one of the highly textured and haptic worlds captured in the environmental sculpture of Andy Goldsworthy). Versace's clothes, on the other hand, provide the eye with a glittering panorama of shapes, forms, and patterns like something out of an Asian court. This basic opposition of country and city is characteristic of the dyad, too, for whereas any of Versace's supermodels would look out of place photographed against a natural background, Armani's models are often shot on beaches and in country scenes, for the patterns on his clothes often reiterate those of the palm trees or jagged, stony landscapes visible beyond the models.

Paradoxically, however, Armani does not wish to reveal the body, but rather to hide it behind layers of clothing. His menswear engulfs its protagonist; his destructured jackets fall and hang loosely, often with pleated folds, while his men's pants are normally baggy. He wraps his male models in dense layers: shirts buttoned up to the collar surmounted by a sweater-vest and covered with a loose-fitting jacket. Only the head is left to swim above it all as the center of the personality. For Armani, the center of being rests in the head, but for Versace—as for the ancient Greeks—it lies within the sternum. To the Greeks, the body *was* consciousness and so all their clothing was designed to reveal its curvilinear beauties and rigid, unyielding convexities.

In the same spirit, Versace's couture is tight and form-fitting; his men's trousers hug the ankles and legs, leaving them clearly defined. He shows off the female form with scandalous visions of crevasses and openings in his dresses that provide momentarily arresting views of unexpected fleshy landscapes. His dresses are high cut, sometimes shockingly so, even daring to open as high up as the pudenda, where they reveal leopard skin panties framed by the inverted V of the cut. There is abundant cleavage, sometimes with only the nipples covered, and airy, diaphanous evening gowns that provide clear views of bras and panties. For Versace, the female form was something to be put on display and showcased like expensive jewelry, not to be hidden away by the square, rectilinear working girl outfits of Armani, whose pleated patterns, carefully placed beading and constant use of lacework invite the hand to explore what it cannot see. Armani's women's wear encourages the hand to travel over the crinoline and silk organza, the crepe and gauze weaves, to explore landscapes of fabric whose poetry can only be unfolded by the sense of touch.

VERSACE BUILDS VAIKUNTHA

Versace's vision was to build an impenetrable dreamworld of opulence and wealth that would be hermetically sealed against traumatic incursions from the Real. He moved to Miami in 1992—that sun-soaked, palm-lined American equivalent of southern Italy—where he proceeded to spend $32 million on the (re)construction of a 20,000-square-foot, 16-bedroom mansion that he named Casa Casuarina. The house was a replica of America's first (European) house, which was built in Santo Domingo by the son of Christopher Columbus, an appropriate choice of model for a man who arrives in South Beach like a mythical colonialist figure out of a William Faulkner narrative. Versace, likewise, constructed his own dream palace, his Vaikuntha,[3] among the palms and pastel buildings and crumbling harbors of sleazy South Beach.

Versace's dreamworld: Moorish tile; Greek marble; Byzantine mosaics and inlaid floors; ceilings adorned with Renaissance art; Roman baths. The busts of Christopher Columbus, Pocahontas, Confucius, and Mussolini—weirdly dissonant—are preserved in the courtyard where he found them. From the roof, he has a view of South Beach and the ocean beyond it.

In his book *The Arcades Project*, Walter Benjamin describes the whole cosmos of capitalist society as it emerged in the 19th century through advertising and department stores and crowds as a huge, phantasmagoric waking dream. "Capitalism," he writes, "was a natural phenomenon with which a new dream-filled sleep came over Europe, and through it, a reactivation of mythic forces."[4] Versace's cosmos, likewise, is a dreamworld of art and beauty and wealth and fame that runs only parallel to the real world, but never at any point actually touches it.

As every dream hides some deeper facet of the soul's darkest regions, regions that one often wishes would remain dark forever, so too,

Versace's dreamworld is an Apollonian façade designed to conceal the reality of waking to a world of temporal metabolisms in which the motion of every system is tantamount to the aging of that system. Versace's cult of the body, his love of beautiful men and women, his need to be seen frolicking with celebrities all are part of an attempt to create a frozen world of the beautiful in which the sublime simply does not exist. It is all a fantasy vision of a world without time in which nothing moves save what is beautiful.

Hence, the irony of Versace having designed the costumes for the 1980s television show *Miami Vice*, which is an image of the very fallen world that Versace built his dream vision to *cover over*: a realm of corruption, crime and death, gutted buildings, and ramshackle harbors and rotting yachts; guns and blood. This is the world that Versace built his castle to escape from, but it is out of the depths of this very world that a creature will escape and begin the long climb up the mountaintop to reach him, a creature who wishes to pull down what Versace has built up, for this creature cannot stand having been excluded from such an attempt to raise a pure dream of marble and ivory in which shadows do not exist.

Versace's dreamworld suffered from a fatal incompletion which this creature attempted to remedy: it is no accident that Versace's favorite color was white, for this creature was a shadow of utter blackness who had come to bring darkness into the Kingdom of Light. He arrived, this being, like the Hindu god Shiva who, angry at being excluded from the great sacrifice of Daksha (to which all the other gods but he were invited), shows up at the party to kill and maim everyone. No god emerges from the sacrifice of Daksha unscathed by Shiva's fury.

And so Versace's dreamworld of timeless beauty and Platonic Form was about to be wrecked by the excluded Other.

CUNANAN TEARS IT DOWN

Whereas Mark David Chapman and John Hinckley were introverted loners, Andrew Cunanan was an extroverted socialite who always had plenty of friends. He grew up in San Diego as the child of two strange parents, a chronically depressed mother and a Filipino father who was a con man always scheming for ways to make quick money. After making a killing, he sold the family's two mortgaged homes, and then went back to the Philippines to disappear from his son's life forever. Before vanishing, however, the father taught his son that the most important things in life were the most expensive and that nothing else mattered as much as appearances.

After graduating from Bishop's School in La Jolla, Andrew went to live for a time in Berkeley with a recently married couple whose newborn daughter he helped raise. He was openly gay and read fashion magazines like *GQ, Vogue*, and *Vanity Fair* religiously. Bret Easton Ellis's *Less Than Zero* was his favorite book, and in many ways functioned analogously to Chapman's *Catcher in the Rye* and Hinckley's *Taxi Driver*, since it provided him with the main pattern for his life: a tale of rich, but decadent kids constantly high on cocaine who pay for their habits by moonlighting as gay prostitutes.

Cunanan was a compulsive liar with an unstable identity, a truly Hydraic ego. His friends claimed that they all knew different Andrews. One Andrew pretended that he was Jewish (in reality, he was Catholic). Another pretended that he was known as "Count Ashkenazy." He would tell people that his father was a Filipino general who flew Ferdinand Marcos around the Philippines, or that his father was gay like himself and in love with one of Andrew's boyfriends. Andrew might have a factory in Mexico or an estranged wife and daughter whose photos he would pass around.

He spent a great deal of time courting lovers in San Francisco's Castro district. In fact, it was there in 1990 that he apparently met Versace for the first time. The maestro had come to the city to design the costumes for Strauss's opera *Capriccio* and Andrew, together with his friend Eli, met the famous designer at a large gay disco called the Colossus. Maureen Orth's description of that first meeting is worth quoting here:

> That night, Eli and Andrew entered the Colossus dance area and went to the VIP room to await Versace . . . After about fifteen minutes of chitchat and waves of young men eager to meet him, Versace began to survey the room. He noticed Andrew standing with Eli, cocked his head, and walked in their direction. "I know you," he said to Andrew. "Lago di Como, no?" Versace was referring to the house he owned on Lake Como near the Swiss border. Reportedly he would often use the Lago di Como line when he wanted to strike up a conversation with someone.
>
> Andrew was thrilled and Eli couldn't believe it. "That's right," Andrew answers. "Thank you for remembering, Signor Versace." Then Andrew introduced Eli to Versace, who made polite talk about whether they had seen the opera. (They hadn't.) Eli and Andrew then drifted back to the dance floor.[5]

As one of Andrew's acquaintances remarks: "Basically . . . there was this sense of 'I've finally met one of the people who's like a god to me.'"

Andrew apparently went clubbing with Versace and his boyfriend a couple of times, but that was about the extent of their acquaintance. He soon returned to live with his mother in San Diego, where he got a job as a clerk in a Thrifty drugstore, which he kept for the next three and a half years. At night, however, he would head down to the bars in Hillcrest, where he would shed his persona of Andrew Cunanan on financial aid (for he had enrolled at the University of San Diego) to become "Yale-educated Andrew DeSilva, Mr. Congeniality, big time spender and heir to any number of fortunes—parking lots, car dealerships, sugar plantations, New York real estate, even a mattress distribution warehouse."[6] He was looking for a sugar daddy, a rich older man who would be intelligent, artistic, and preferably famous.

It was during this period that he became acquainted with the man who would later become his first victim, Jeff Trail, a young Naval Academy graduate whom Andrew admired. Jeff was in the closet, however, and although Andrew was infatuated with him, it does not appear that the romantic feelings were mutual. Jeff remained only a friend.

Andrew began to make his living now as a drug dealer—cocaine, marijuana, Percodan, Valium, and so on—and he bought himself a handgun. According to Orth, he was using crystal meth at this time, although he was extremely discrete about it. Over time, this drug makes the user depressed, irritable, and paranoid.

In July 1995, he moved out of his mother's apartment and into the condo of a sugar daddy in La Jolla named Norman Blachford, who put him on a monthly allowance. Later that same year, he met David Madson, the man who would become his second victim. He went out with David while still living with Norman. He and David were involved in sadomasochistic sex, although David seems to have been rather reluctant about it. He complained to friends of Andrew wanting to dominate too much.

Eventually, Andrew broke with Norman when he demanded that Norman buy him a $125,000 Mercedes SL 600 convertible and Norman refused. At about the same time, his love affair with David crashed, since he had been sending David postcards pretending he was in France while he was with Norman, and David eventually broke it off when he realized that Andrew was playing him. The simultaneous ending of these two relationships, it seems, began to destabilize Andrew's personality. He went to see Jeff Trail, the next most important figure in his life, but Jeff had by this time grown weary of Andrew's lies and Andrew received a cold welcome from him.

David, meanwhile, had found another boyfriend, but Andrew figured out a way to include himself in the picture, going to visit David in Minneapolis and meeting with Jeff, who now also lived there. Andrew had put on some weight, and he was very depressed. A friend who had run into him around this time made the following comment: "He looked bad. His eyes were sunken, he was overweight, not talkative. He was completely different, all by himself. He seemed depressed—he was not running around, not being the life of the party. He was not in a good mood."[7]

As David Madson went through boyfriends, Andrew hovered in the picture, offering David gifts and bribes, which David, to his detriment, accepted. Andrew would often housesit for him when he was gone, taking care of his Rottweiler. At one point, Andrew even offered him a ring, but David turned down his proposal. However, he did accept Andrew's invitation for a round-trip weekend to Los Angeles with him in the spring of 1997, during which time Andrew lavished gifts on him, such as expensive Armani suits.

People who met Andrew at this time claim that he was physically aggressive with them, grabbing them, spinning them around, poking them, picking them up, and even choking them. Apparently the kind of porn Andrew liked involved watching people getting tied up and stunned with Tasers. He could sometimes be heard to mutter to his friends, "Oh, I'd like to electrocute *him*."

On the weekend of April 25, 1997, Andrew bought himself a one-way ticket to Minneapolis from San Diego. In San Diego, he said his goodbyes to friends and gave away some of his personal possessions. He had made plans to stay with both David and Jeff, who were nervous about having him around. (According to Joseph Geringer, Jeff and David may have been seeing each other behind Andrew's back.[8])

Jeff and Andrew were broke, and so Jeff had agreed to meet with him to discuss the possibility of dealing steroids to Midwesterners. On the night of April 27, Jeff left his boyfriend at 9:00 P.M. to meet with Andrew inside David's loft, where he was staying. Because different commentators give contradictory accounts, what happened next is confusing. Geringer says that David and Andrew were there together and that they invited Jeff over to put Andrew's mind at ease about any potential involvement between Jeff and David. When Jeff arrived, an argument ensued, and Andrew supposedly went to the kitchen utility drawer and withdrew a heavy claw hammer with which he then proceeded to smash Jeff's skull apart, bludgeoning it 27 times.[9] However, it is difficult to believe that David, a bodybuilder in peak physical shape at the time, would have just stood by watching Andrew club their mutual friend to death, and so Maureen Orth's account seems more likely.

In her version, Andrew was alone in David's apartment when he called Jeff and invited him over. Soon after Jeff arrived, Andrew grabbed the hammer and attacked him. By the time David showed up, the deed had been done and could not be undone, so David and Andrew together rolled up Jeff's body inside a Persian rug and pushed it behind the couch, where it sat for two days, while the two tried to decide what to do next.

Eventually, they climbed into David's Jeep Cherokee and headed north. After about 45 miles, they pulled over near a lake in Chisago County, where Andrew then shot David three times and dumped his body out of the jeep. Andrew then proceeded to make his way to Chicago, where he arrived on May 4 in the neighborhood of the Gold Coast. There, he killed a 75-year-old business tycoon named Lee Miglin. This crime was especially brutal but it was not, apparently, random, despite the Miglin family's insistence that Lee and Andrew had never met. According to Orth, witnesses have reported seeing both Andrew and Lee talking together in Miglin's house the night before the murder took place, and it was well known in the local gay community that Miglin was gay (or at least bisexual). When the body was found, Miglin had been stabbed several times and a hacksaw had been used to slice open his throat, apparently while still alive. His head had been wrapped like a mummy in masking tape with an opening left for the nostrils and bruises indicated that he was beaten and tortured while still alive. His feet had been bound with orange electrical cord and two bags of cement had been dropped on his torso, fracturing his ribs. Miglin's wife, a host on the Home Shopping Network, had been out of town for the weekend and returned on Sunday to find things amiss. Neighbors helped locate her husband's body. After the killing, Andrew had apparently spent the night, slept in Lee's bed, shaved, showered, ate his food, and then left. There was no sign of forced entry, and the fact that the dog, which normally barked at strangers, was not heard to bark and was not harmed suggests strongly that Andrew and Lee knew one another.

Andrew traveled south on I-95 and, after overhearing through the media that the stolen Lexus he was driving (Miglin's car) had a cell phone that was enabling government agents to track him every time he used it, he came to the conclusion that he would have to swap it for another car. He took the first exit after the bridge in New Jersey to Fort Mott State Park, where he traveled down the long narrow dirt road through deep woods to reach a cemetery, parked the Lexus, and walked up the road to the caretaker's (a man named Bill Reese) stonehouse. The area was remote, and so Andrew entered the house and shot Reese in the back of the head and then stole his red pickup truck. This was his fourth killing in 12 days.

Andrew, during this time, had been making appearances on *America's Most Wanted*, and his name was being cycled through the newspapers and on the nightly news. He might have experienced a certain grim satisfaction that he was beginning to attain the fame that he had so longed for all his life, but it was not enough. To attain the level of fame that he desired, he would have to kill a celebrity, and in doing so, he would become a permanent member of the Electroverse. After all, nobody forgets the name of the assassin who kills the historical martyr: John Wilkes Booth, Lee Harvey Oswald, Sirhan Sirhan, Judas. All these men were as famous as the figures they had killed. From henceforth, no biography of Versace, whether electronic or print, could ever fail to include *him*, Andrew Cunanan, as a vital part of the story.

Stopping only to change license plates, therefore, Andrew traveled all the way to Miami, where he arrived in South Beach on May 11, 1997. That month's issue of *Vanity Fair* happened to feature an article on Versace's new mansion, Casa Casuarina, and it is possible that the article gave him the idea to kill Versace, although it is more likely that he specifically traveled to Miami to kill the rich and famous gay man with whom he had once caroused.

Andrew stayed at the Normandy hotel for almost two months, living an underground life of selling drugs and doing some prostitution. He mostly hid out in his hotel room, where he read books about art and celebrities, sleeping in the daytime and going out only at night.

Then, on Tuesday, July 15, Versace took his customary morning walk at about 8:40 to the News Café, where he bought five magazines. Some employees at the café noticed that he took a slightly unusual path, traveling along the opposite side of the street and walking a little farther ahead before doubling back, as though trying to shake someone. When he returned to the front gate of his mansion, however, Andrew was waiting for him across the street, dressed in a black baseball cap, shorts, and a tank top pulled over a T-shirt. Versace walked up to the gate and started to unlock it while Andrew crossed the street, passing an eyewitness to the murder. Andrew raised the gun and shot Versace in the back of the head with Jeff Trail's 0.40-caliber gun. The bullet traveled through Versace, hit the metal railing and split into fragments, some of which hit a dove in the head and killed it instantly. Versace turned round, and as he did so, Andrew shot him once again, this time directly in the face. The bullet lodged in his head and cracked the top of his skull. Versace collapsed to the street, blood fanning in a vermilion pool around him.

The scenario was an almost exact replay of Mark David Chapman's slaying of John Lennon. In both cases, the assailant waited for his victim to return home to his mansion and simply walked up and shot him. The only significant difference was that Lennon's murder took place at night as his day was ending, whereas Versace's was only beginning. Cunanan was performing a media myth and doing it faithfully.

After the shooting, Andrew simply walked away. Now he lived in a universe free from the power of Gianni Versace.

Several days later, on July 23, at about 3:45 P.M., he killed himself on a houseboat in a South Beach marina. He shot himself in the head with the same gun, as though to imply a curious parallel underscoring the similarity of his own death with that of the man whom he had so admired.

SHADOW PUPPETS

Andrew Cunanan was a living fulfillment of the prophecy made by Andy Warhol with his 1964 mural *Most Wanted Men*, in which Warhol foresaw that under electric conditions, anybody can become famous for doing almost anything, and that the new electric media—such as television shows like *America's Most Wanted*—would be the primary means whereby even criminals could become superstars. Cunanan himself was one of the FBI's 10 Most Wanted fugitives, and he seems to have been a creature imagined by Andy Warhol and projected forward into our time, several decades later.

The criminal is the shadow cast on the physical world from the light of the celebrity's hyperreal one. In a way, they are inseparable, and that is why we in America—the land of the pop star—are so fascinated with outlaws, gangsters, serial killers, and the like, for they are the foil by way of which the brightly lit cosmos of the celebrity can exist. In the world of Gangsta Rap, the two actually begin to coincide, for many rap artists are in fact gang members who continue killing each other off even once they have attained electronic fame.

In our current culture of the celebrity, fame is amoral, for it can be attained by anyone for any reason. The lights shine on Al Capone and Charles Manson just as brightly as they do on Warren Beatty and Madonna. As McLuhan was the first to realize, the medium is indeed the message, for it is electronic technology that makes instant fame possible (and also instantly forgettable), no matter who is being sent beaming through the circuits or for what reason. In a print-based society, by contrast, fame is an achievement, something that has to be worked at. In the everything-all-at-once world of real-time technology, however, fame is not difficult to achieve and requires no prerequisites of mastery or discipline. One simply stands in front of a camera and does something outrageous. No skills are required.

Andrew Cunanan was the shadow cast by Gianni Versace, a shadow that, like the fairytale shadow in Hans Christian Anderson's tale, simply detached itself and decided to do away with the man who had generated it. Versace was the man of the Old World who had accomplished a life based on the mastery of a difficult craft and built up a vertical world—what Deleuze would call "the plane of organization"—of castles and mansions. Cunanan was the New World man who was good at nothing in particular, suffered from Attention Deficit Disorder and moved horizontally—"rhizomatically" in Deleuze's discourse—over the American landscape like a nomad, wandering from place to place and city to city. The one built up structures; the other pulled them down.

In the old world of moral standards shaped by literacy and tradition, Cunanan would have been judged as evil, a reprobate and lunatic, and hence, not even worth mentioning in a literate essay. In the new world shaped by electronics, however, both Versace and Cunanan are equally famous, and no biography of Versace can overlook the man who not only took his life, but who also became famous along with him. The world of print, now doing a slow-motion collapse into the abyss of non-being, was a universe of moral standards and hierarchy; the electronic one that now surrounds us is an amoral flatland in which all comers are embraced.

It is, above all, a world in which neither past nor future exist, but only an eternally present *now*, a homogeneous sameness and dullness spread uniformly across the planet and populated with the momentarily famous. Indeed, Warhol's very phrase "famous for 15 minutes" is a tacit recognition of the steadily diminishing temporal window of this electronic cosmos, in which the rate of vanishing speeds up the vanishing of the famous, who now endure their fame for ever shorter and shorter intervals of time in the media's ahistorical landscape of senility in which events are interesting only until the next one comes along.

Indeed, Cunanan's fame lasted only a month or so, for no sooner was his name a household phrase than Princess Diana's crash occurred in August of that year to displace him.

12

Princess Diana's Media Metamorphoses

Had Diana lived in a pre-Electronic Age, it is unlikely that she would ever have become famous. For her fame rested almost entirely on her relationship with the camera eye, and as it was the camera eye that invented her, so too was it the camera eye that, in the end, destroyed her.

In the Gutenbergian Age, she could not have become famous because she never would have had anything very interesting to say. Diana was not an eloquent person, for words—printed or spoken—were at odds with her highly tactile and visual nature. As Camille Paglia rightly points out, Diana communicated through her body language alone.[1] Her early posture, for example—hunched forward with her head down and eyes looking shyly up at the photographers who circled round her like ringmasters—conveyed the image of a naïve young country girl whose overexposure beneath the spectatorial gaze of the megalopolis was frightening and disorienting. By the end of her days, however, her posture had changed, for her body somehow had become more elongated—like a Giacometti sculpture—while her gaze, staring imperiously from the top of an erect neck, had become a power of self-assuredness all its own. Thus, her apparently facile qualities of gesture, touch, posture, and gaze, when plugged in by the electronic media, were amplified a thousand-fold, and the rich, sensuous display of body language unveiled to the public was essentially that of a gigantic, goddess-size figure.

Far from stripping her of her aura a la Walter Benjamin, the electronic reproduction of her image actually magnified the aura she possessed to Gulliver-esque proportions, reducing the rest of us to Lilliputian-size spectators. As a denizen of the Electroverse, Diana strode about among our model cities and toy cars as a giant, like the woman in the 1958 movie *Attack of the 50-Foot Woman*, a film that weirdly prefigures her advent. In that film, a woman who is exposed to radiation from a fallen alien satellite is enlarged to Godzilla-size proportions. The movie poster shows her straddling a freeway, clutching an automobile in one hand while her other foot crushes a few cars and trucks. Diana, likewise, by exposure to the ELF radiation of the media, was enlarged to enormous proportions, for she strode effortlessly about the globe from city to city as though taking giant-size footsteps.

The image of a gigantic woman with lissome gazelle legs striding through the world's cities evokes a comparison with some of the more physically anomalous goddesses out of ancient iconography. Diana's electric shadow, for example, invites a certain comparison with an image out of ancient African rock art, specifically, the White Lady of Rhodesia, as she has been called, who strides across a prehistoric landscape in which she is the largest entity in the picture, with great long, white legs, bow and arrow in hand, while tiny hunters and animals scurry about in the background. Or we may think of the statue of the Ephesian Diana who stands with hundreds of breasts ready to feed the Amazons who worshipped her. But perhaps the Princess of Wales is closest in spirit to the Chinese folk deity Kuan-yin, goddess of inexhaustible mercy and compassion, who often is depicted with 11 heads that tower, pagoda-like, from the top of her skull (for each hears the cries of the suffering of the world from a different direction) and 1,000 arms (each one reaching out to palliate a different suffering soul).

Hence, Diana's comment that she once made to a reporter, "Wherever it is in the world that someone calls me in distress, I will run to them," presupposes a similar kind of replication of herself, for the reproduction of Diana's image via the camera eye does have a weirdly multiplying effect that is similar to the reiteration of multiple arms, breasts, and legs of these ancient goddesses. By means of the electronic media, Diana had seemed to be everywhere all at once, with a thousand heads and arms and legs all over the world on magazine covers, newspapers, and television programs. Only the deities of the ancient past had such mythical powers of self-proliferation (such as Krishna or Monkey in the Chinese novel *Journey to the West*) and as a result, the public began to attribute magical powers to her as though she were a saint or a goddess.

But now we should consider the evolution of the stages of Diana's media transformations as they occurred. Diana is an extreme case, forming something of a metapattern by way of which all other such mediatized celebrity deformations should be measured as approximating closer to, or further from, the pattern apotheosized by her life. Paying close attention to these stages, we will note the gradually increasing speed of the temporal rhythms of her life, and the attendant sense of increasing isolation and mental illness that results from this electronic acceleration.

Here, then, are the stages as they occurred.

EPOCH I: FROM PARK HOUSE TO ALTHORP

We find Diana as a child growing up under pastoral circumstances in a rural environment. Park House is on the Sandringham estate, the Royal Family's country-seat in Norfolk, and it is located in a secluded area. On this estate, we find her surrounded by animals: horses, hamsters, guinea pigs, cats and dogs, and so on.

The temporal metabolism of this epoch is as slow as the growth of a tree, the spinning of a spider's web or the polishing of the rocks in a river bottom. Rainstorms come and go over the horizon, with lightning flashes snapping like flashbulbs, and the slow, patient processes of photosynthetic plant life are at work everywhere. Gnats swarm in the orange twilight air, and gray, soggy clouds perpetually mottle the blue dome of the sky like the piebald patches on a horse's skin.

From about the age of 13 or so, she begins to hang pictures of Prince Charles up on the walls around her bed. To pass the long afternoons, she reads Barbara Cartland novels of princes and their troubled courtships with ladies, novels that always end in bliss. During this epoch, Charles's image looms gigantically over her and she looks up at him like a small child whose parent has momentarily blotted out the sun.

This epoch concludes in 1977, with her first meeting of Charles at the age of 16 at a shoot organized at Althorp, another family estate. Her sister Sarah had been dating him, but Diana met him in a ploughed field near the village of Nobottle, leaving a strong impression on his mind of her joviality and forthrightness. "I've met him. I've met him at last," she told her school friends, although the real significant meeting would not take place for another few years when, in 1980, he would confide in her his feelings of loss regarding the assassination of his mentor Lord Mountbatten.

EPOCH II: COLEHERNE COURT, LONDON

In this epoch, Diana migrates from the country to the city, where she takes up residence in a flat shared with three roommates in Coleherne

Court in London. This period coincides with that of her courtship with Charles, who now begins taking her with him into the countryside on hunting and fishing outings.

When the press discovers that she is Charles's probable choice for a wife, they begin camping out on her doorstep, following her everywhere. It is at this point that a major increase in the temporal metabolism of her life begins to take place, for now she finds herself living in the city at a pace and a speed that is established by the modern media. She is a country girl no longer, but a denizen of the modern mediatized metropolis, and not only that, but one of its primary fetishes.

She takes a job as a kindergarten schoolteacher, and it is during this time that the first photos of her begin to surface, such as the one in which she is shown holding a child in either arm and looking rather uncomfortable while the sunlight illuminates her legs through a slipless dress. Here we witness the birth of her media doppelganger, at the moment of the division of her body with the creation of a double made out of light opposed to her physical, material self.

At first, her mediatized image is not a threat to Charles, for during the period of their courtship, the media doubles of the two are on about the same size and scale, with hers maybe slightly smaller than his. However, whereas his image has stabilized and will grow no further during the course of his life, Diana's electronic shadow begins to grow steadily larger.

The creation of this mediatic clone was not without its side effects upon her, for it was at about this time that she first began to suffer from bulimia. In her biography of Diana, Sarah Bradford implies that the bulimia began not as the result of a casual remark from Charles, as is usually thought—"Oh, a bit chubby here, aren't we?"—but rather as the result of seeing a huge poster of herself. Here is how Bradford puts it:

> On one occasion in a car with the Queen's press secretary, Michael Shea, she broke down in tears on seeing a huge picture poster of herself. "I can't take this anymore," she sobbed.
>
> From that time, her weight plummeted. According to her later account this is when she began to suffer from the eating disorder bulimia, gorging herself on bowls of cereal and custard and then vomiting.[2]

Apparently, the image feedback of herself, magnified to gigantic proportions, induced a sort of opposite resonance effect in her psyche's own self-image, which correspondingly shrank in response to the size of the huge vision of herself on the poster. Once her interior self-image shrank, she began to physically shrink herself. Here we see the first effects of the change in her body as a result of the media magnification of her image. The bulimia almost seems to be an attempt to flatten herself out, as though to provide less resistance to the speed at which she is being hurled into the media maelstrom.

EPOCH III: BUCKINGHAM PALACE/KENSINGTON PALACE

This period begins with the wedding, in which the couple, for the first time, is replicated via television, as the broadcast was beamed all over the world. The image of the couple inside the church, like Jan van Eyck's mysterious wedding couple in his *Arnolfini Marriage*, bears some scrutiny that, like van Eyck's painting, rewards the cautious eye.

On the small rectangular box of the television screen, with its flickering blue phosphorescent image, Charles stands at the altar with his bride, she in a white dress with an impossibly long tail and he in a blue royal uniform. They are both smiling and waving and they seem very happy. Diana, however, is not what she seems to be, for in reality she is merely the manifest content of his waking dream, a Freudian screening image designed to hide the latent content of the *real* woman of his heart, Camilla Parker Bowles. But since Camilla is already married and has an unsavory sexual history, she is not fit to play the role of the public bride; that is Diana's job, for she has been hired, as it were, to play the two-dimensional role of the screening image that fits the public's expectations of what a young princess ought to be (although she does not yet know this): Diana is young, virginal, shy, and naïve; in short, a perfect fit with the public image. No one can possibly object to her. But Charles is really only marrying an *image* here, for the real three-dimensional woman of his heart is Camilla, the woman whom Diana was meant to *conceal* from the public gaze. Thus, the unspoken pact: if Diana should ever reveal any depth to her two-dimensional role, she will be discarded immediately as unsuitable. It is all in accordance with an electronic medium in which images are flattened out into clichés and stereotypes.

At first, Diana did indeed force herself to fit into the role of this flatland image (the bulimia is part of that attempt), but the problem was that the other unused portions of her personality kept surfacing in the form of mood swings and fits of bad temper, which became increasingly common as the days passed. (Fights over Camilla had begun *before* the marriage, however.) As her biographers Tim Clayton and Phil Craig describe her gradual disillusionment:

> [B]ehind the scenes the jolly girl in green wellies who, a year before, had endeared herself to Charles and his friends with her love of the countryside now made it clear that she wanted no part of it. She took every opportunity to complain about Balmoral—the incessant rain, the muddy barbecues, the ugly furniture, the antique bathrooms. Longing to have her husband to herself, Diana was cross and bored while Charles was hurt and embarrassed by her ill-concealed resentment, and disappointed that she no longer wanted to share the pursuits he enjoyed.[3]

With the public, however, Diana was cheerful and warm, and they, too, in response to her, because her behavior was unusually personable for a member of the Royal Family. She was tactile with them, for she never wore gloves and always shook hands and held people. Soon, the Prince began to realize that he was being upstaged.

> It would be really embarrassing sometimes because she'd be on one side of the road and they'd all be excited and screaming, and on the other side of the road they'd all be going, "Oh, no!" because they'd got him. He'd just turn round and say, "I'm really sorry, she'll be here in a minute."[4]

Thus, during this third epoch, Diana's image began to grow larger and larger, finally overshadowing Charles's, so that the couple were in exactly opposite positions from those in which they had begun: now he stood in *her* shadow, and it was unbearable for him. (He had begun by telling people that whoever married him would have to walk in his shadow, the poor girl.) As a result of the electrodynamics of moving images, however, they are not accelerated *together* in a single reference frame, but rather, each occupies his and her own niche alone, like a sculpted figure in a church. This disproportionality of their images ensures that they cannot exist as a couple occupying the same space (unlike the perspectivally correct Arnolfini couple in van Eyck's Renaissance painting) for they are never the same size as each other. First Charles was the giant and she the naïve little girl; then, for a brief period, they were both the same size, and it is this period of their courtship that notably is the only period in which they were happy together. After the wedding, Diana becomes larger than Charles, and as a result, his ego cannot withstand the pressures of the spatial discontinuity between them. Instead, he flees back to Camilla—an apparent surrogate mother figure for him, as she was older than he and far less attractive than Diana—for he cannot tolerate the imagistic distortions wreaked on his wife as a result of her electric speed.

Diana not only grows larger during this period, but she becomes flatter and thinner, as well. The metabolism of her life speeds up: she meets more and more people and she is called upon to attend more public events. And as she moves faster, she grows lonelier, ever more remote from Charles, and ever more cut off from friends and family. She begins to fall into a deep depression, especially after the birth of her second son, Harry, in September 1984, and begins to exhibit suicidal behavior. She begins cutting herself and is taken to see psychologists, who prescribe Valium to her, which she refuses to take.

EPOCH IV: SEPARATION AND ISOLATION

This epoch begins in 1992 with the serialization of Andrew Morton's biography of Diana in the *Sunday Times*, a project that was undertaken with her full cooperation to even the odds between herself and the Royal Family, whom she regarded as having used and mistreated her. This was her first attempt to make use of the media as a weapon of her own, for it was one of her primary aims to publicly expose the relationship of Charles and Camilla, to reveal the shadowy *hidden* woman by disclosing her presence to the world. In doing so, she made her own image suddenly and abruptly *transparent*, revealing herself for the media ghost she had really been. Thus, with this momentary alliance on her part with the printed word, her persona is immediately deepened and given a third dimension, as though she had stepped inside of a 17th-century painting. Now, she is revealed as having complex feelings of anger and remorse and hatred, things that are utterly inimical to a two-dimensional stereotype, and as a result, the public is at first baffled: they have no idea what to think. This new alliance between Diana and the printed word—for despite her denials to the contrary she was essentially the book's coauthor—is startling and surprising, for no one had any idea that she would attempt an act of demolition upon her own media persona.

> The book told of Diana's psychological problems, the bulimia, self-mutilation and depression—including the Sandringham suicide attempt that never was. Charles's infidelity with Camilla and his unkindness to Diana were similarly revealed. . . . The heir to the throne came out worst of all: a cynical adulterer who mistreated his virgin bride and selfishly ignored his children.[5]

The immediate result of publishing the book, predictably—since it signified her abrupt attainment of a third dimension, something upon which her marriage to Charles had depended on never happening—was to increase her isolation from the Royal Family. Charles at this point withdrew his belongings to Highgrove while she remained at Kensington Palace. Then they announced their separation to the public.

It was around this time, in late 1993, that Diana dropped her police escort because she was seeing an Islamic antiquities dealer named Oliver Hoare and she did not want the police knowing her whereabouts at any given minute. As a result, however, the paparazzi swept down upon her like the birds in Alfred Hitchcock's movie, swarming around her everywhere she went, demolishing her private bodily space. This event marked a further acceleration of her life, and she found herself moving ever faster by means of the intense scrutiny of the camera eye, which now invaded her every waking moment. The collapse of her personal space, paradoxically, however, resulted in a new gigantifying of her electric persona, for now pictures of her doing banal things like shopping and eating and walking down the street commanded a new premium in every newspaper and tabloid around the world. It is during this fourth epoch that her electric persona attains global proportions in direct relation to the collapse of her immediate personal bodily space. It is as though she implodes, becoming the human equivalent of an event horizon that drags the cameramen down with her, very nearly fusing her body with the camera, as though it were a prosthesis.

> There was a demand for pictures of Diana angry or in tears, and so she would be provoked. She said they tried to trip her, and shouted obscenities looking for a reaction—"You're the fucking Princess of Wales, stop carrying on like a fucking tart"; "You're a real fucking loon, aren't you?" . . . One day a passer-by with a home video camera filmed Diana trapped by a crowd of photographers in a London street. Her arms were wrapped around her face and she was whimpering like a wounded animal.[6]

With these invasions, we have an example of a new development in Diana's life as a celebrity in which the media does not so much report the news, but stages it to report on what it has staged as though it were newsworthy. Daniel Boorstin in *The Image* has called this sort of thing the media "pseudo-event." In the present case, the celebrity is deliberately provoked by the paparazzi into an angry reaction and that photograph together with its accompanying story is printed in the tabloids the next day, where it is presented as though something newsworthy has actually taken place, but of course, it has not. The media are interfering with the news and actually manufacturing it and then reporting on what they have manufactured as though it were news, because this is what sells papers. In Diana's time, this was not a new trend, but with her it takes on a new ferocity and intensity, eventually leading to her death.

Also, during this period, she gave an interview for the BBC television show *Panorama* (November 1995) in which she publicly admitted to having affairs and talked about her depression and suicide attempts. She had some nasty words for Camilla, saying that there had been three people in her marriage from day one. In the immediate aftermath of this interview, the Queen sent her a letter advising her to divorce Charles immediately. Diana herself, apparently as a result of the continuing electric acceleration of her life, was becoming increasingly paranoid. "[She] was convinced that her rooms were bugged," write Clayton and Craig, "believing that someone had taken a pot shot at her in the park and telling Jephson that the brake wires had been cut on her car."[7] She also became convinced that a nanny named Twiggy Legge-Bourke whom Charles had hired to look after the children had had an abortion and that the child had been Charles's. This was not true, but Diana at this time was seeing conspiracies everywhere. She would leave disturbing messages on her staff's answering machines and pagers, such as: "The Boss knows about your disloyalty and your affair."

"My husband," she stated in a letter at this time, "is planning 'an accident' in my car, brake failure and serious head injury in order to make the path clear for Charles to marry."[8] Paranoia is a psychological by-product of information overload, a response on the part of the nervous system to attempt to arrange data that is coming at it too fast into meaningful patterns. Diana was traveling around the world in 1997 visiting sites where landmines left behind by occupying troops, many of them British, had remained to cause grief and suffering to innocent children and hapless unfortunates who stumbled across them. She went to Angola and Bosnia, and gave talks in New York and London on behalf of her new cause. She was beginning to move frenetically about the globe now, as though restless with London. Clayton and Craig make the following interesting comment about this period:

> We thought hard about the best way to render Diana's POV in our television series, or whether we should even try. With a video camera set to record three or six frames a second, the perspectives lurch and then settle, a face in a crowd emerges from a blurry background, the lights of passing

> cars smear across the screen. Is this how she saw her world—her worlds? For by now she was moving quickly through so many of them. Thinking of Angola at the Four Seasons, thinking of Manhattan in Luanda. Absorbing the taste and refinement of one, the amputations and shantytowns of the other, her internal camera lurching first one way then another. And all the time, the montage speeding up.[9]

Diana met Dodi Fayed in July 1997, but this seems oddly to have been part of a recent pattern in her life, in which had found herself drifting toward the cultural landscapes of the Islamic world. While meeting Fayed, she had been seeing another Muslim man named Hasnat Khan about whom she had been fairly serious and apparently considered marrying, although Khan's Pakistani family were horrified at the prospect of his marrying a non-Muslim woman. Before Khan, another affair had been with Oliver Hoare, an antiquities dealer specializing in Islamic art. One begins to wonder whether she were not finding herself purposefully attracted to the West's primary cultural "Other," as part of an attempt to cause consternation about these affairs among the Royal Family. In this respect, she was performing something similar to Nietzsche's switch from the Greeks to their primary enemies the Persians, whose great prophet Zarathustra became Nietzsche's primary mentor for a time as part of an attempt to distance himself from the Hellenic world in which he had spent his early years as an academic specialist. Diana seems to have been intent on marrying an Islamic man as a part of her long and unending war against the Royal Family, for after her death, Dodi Fayed's father Mohammed would claim that she and his son had been murdered as part of an attempt by MI6 to prevent an Islamic man from being the stepfather to the future King of England. This seems unlikely, and there is little in the crash scenario to support Fayed's contention. It is not mere paranoia, either, because without question such a marriage would have been met by resistance, in one form or another, by those in power in Britain, especially after the events of September 11, 2001.

THE SIGNIFICANCE OF THE CRASH

Diana's car crash is the ultimate event toward which the logic of her life had been accelerating, with ever greater speed and ineluctability. As the French theoretician Paul Virilio has pointed out, the faster a society moves, the more likely it is that accidents will take place, for accidents are not really "accidental" at all, but by-products of increased speed. At high rates of speed, that is, accidents are inevitable.

Not only does the logic of Diana's life in her last year have the feel of an approaching disaster of some sort looming upon the horizon—for it is clear that she had gotten off on the wrong track with the wrong people—but the culture itself, *our* culture seems to have been manifesting omens pointing the way. David Cronenberg's film *Crash*, for instance, had just been released in 1996 as an examination of the fascination with celebrity car wrecks.[10] Such events as Diana's crash rarely take place without casting warning shadows backward in time.

The crash, it is true, had multiple causes: Dodi Fayed, it seems, bears some responsibility, since Diana was in his care at the time. It is also true that had Diana been wearing her seatbelt, she may very well have survived, so she herself must be regarded as having colluded in her own death. And then, of course, there is the issue of Henri Paul's intoxication. But it is also the case that if the paparazzi had not been chasing them, the crash never would have occurred in the first place.

In a motif in mythology known as the "Wild Hunt," packs of the spirits of the dead, led by a deity or a spirit-hero such as Odin or King Arthur, set off in pursuit of a maiden or some other hapless figure. Wolves and demons rage across the sky in pursuit of their prey, like a storm, and in the end the prey is caught and killed. The paparazzi, it seems, riding on their motor bikes and scooters (which have replaced the horses and wolves of the Asgard pantheon) were performing a modern version of this ancient myth, for they chased her right into the jaws of the Great Beast that lay waiting to devour her and carry her off to the realm of the dead. If we think of the tunnel as a large alimentary canal with the row of pillars as a rudimentary spinal column, then the mythic lineaments of the event become clear, particularly as hell was normally depicted in Medieval art as the open jaws of a great beast.

It was, furthermore, the camera that had created her and it was the camera that hunted her to her death, hungry for more images of her body. Photography and the cinema both were born in Paris, the capital of the 19th century, as Walter Benjamin called it in his famous essay, and so, in a way, it is Paris itself that swallowed her alive, that great literary metropolis of the Old World that seems somehow to have taken affront at her presence in the city and so gobbled her up, just as it had swallowed up Jim Morrison many years earlier.

In this respect, Paris—the great capital of the printed word and of linear reasoning—seems to have sided against her—the image goddess—in her war with the Windsors, for the prince, too, had been essentially a relic of the old Gutenbergian world, with his love of books and tradition, polo and hunting. When he married Diana, however, Charles inadvertently plugged in his wife, causing her to glow like a neon sign so that wherever they went, crowds besieged her because she was so radiant. With her love of pop music and her sense for the latest fashions, her lack of propriety, and her ease with the populace and her alliance with the media, Diana represented the forces of modernization and electronic culture and, as such, had a disintegrative effect on the monarchy. In her television interview on *Panorama*, she had cast doubts on the ability of Charles ever to handle the role of kingship and this may have gravely undermined his self-confidence. The immediate effect of that interview had been to accelerate her divorce and to distance herself from the Royals, who no longer wanted her around because they sensed that she was a dangerous competitor. The people wanted Diana, not the Windsors.

And somehow, one cannot escape the feeling that the ancient literate city of Paris was in league with the Windsors and chose to swallow her up as a sacrifice, as something that was as much an affront to its literary sensibilities as she had been to the Royals.

Remember: the camera was invented in Paris in the 1820s and Diana's car crash was not so much a death by automobile as a death by the harrying, pursuing, winged gaze of the camera eye.

V

The Myth Today (The 2000s)

Heath Ledger and Michael Jackson

INTRODUCTION

In an age, as Jean Baudrillard points out, in which we no longer have shadows—for technology has given us the means by which to overdetermine our destinies at the price of eliminating the Other from our lives (we are all autonomous cyborgs these days, in need of nobody but ourselves and our video screens)—what we do have are celebrities who make use of technology to construct and replace these lost shadows in the form of synthetic Others who exist in a separate reality that runs parallel to, and only tangentially touches, the world of the real.

Two of the most recent protagonists in this experiment of constructing our missing shadows are Heath Ledger and Michael Jackson, both of whom built separate selves and then set them free to roam in ersatz cosmologies, a feat requiring the sacrifice of their own blood. Together with Anna Nicole Smith, they are the most recent manifestations of the myth of the tragically dying and reviving celebrity, for all three created media avatars who were paradoxically more "real" than they themselves.

But there is a lingering sense of déjà vu about this group: Anna Nicole Smith repeats the story of Marilyn Monroe, but as a reproduction that is weaker than the original, for she lacked the wit, charm, and tragic sense of naiveté coupled with grace that characterized Marilyn, a true original (or at least, as "original" as a copy of oneself can be said to be in contemporary postmodernity); Heath Ledger's avatars—which become more complex with time—nevertheless exhibit the same kinds of weirdly contorted internal disfigurations of the soul as was the case with James Dean, as though the strange and misshapen Beings inhabiting both these men were as savagely warped as one of those Bodies Without Organs that haunt the paintings of Francis Bacon; and with Michael Jackson, despite his bizarre idiosyncratic originality, we always sense the ghost of Elvis Presley looming somewhere behind him like a secret and barely perceptible aura subtly distorting the outlines of his anatomy.

There are indeed now more celebrities than ever before, but they are metastatic proliferations of hollow selves like cancer cells that reproduce without regard to the fabric of the body social. Stars like Brittney Spears, Justin Timberlake, Usher, and many, many others are merely self-conscious reruns following the genetic program laid down by Michael Jackson who, in turn, would not have been possible without Elvis Presley. Few 21st-century celebrities are interesting in the kinds of unique and provocatively complicated ways in which it can be said that Marilyn was one of a kind, or Elizabeth Taylor or Marlon Brando.

Thus, Michael Jackson and Heath Ledger are important to consider as modern instances of the myth, although they represent a faded and frayed version of it, since the shadows of Elvis and James Dean loom gigantically behind them. Originality in the cult of the celebrity is now long since a thing of the past.

So here, for your consideration, are two final case studies.

13

The Multiple Selves of Heath Ledger

PINK MOON

On January 22, 2008, Heath Ledger was found dead, aged 28, in his SoHo apartment in Manhattan.

His housekeeper, Teresa Solomon, had arrived at about 12:30 P.M. to find him lying face down on his bed, snoring. A couple of hours later, his masseuse, Diana Lee Wolozin showed up for a 3:00 P.M. appointment. The two women chatted for a bit, but by about 3:10 P.M. when there was still no response from Ledger's bedroom, the masseuse went in and began to set up her massage table. The actor, however, was still lying face down upon the bed, with the sheet pulled up to his shoulders. When she touched him to try and wake him up, his body was cold, and it was at this point that she began to be alarmed.

To avoid a "media circus," Wolozin contacted Ledger's recent girlfriend Mary Kate-Olsen, who responded to the situation by sending one of her private security men over to the actor's apartment. At 3:26 P.M., the masseuse called 911 and within about seven minutes, the New York Fire Department paramedics arrived and began attempting to revive him. But it was too late.

The paramedics declared him formally dead at 3:36 P.M.[1]

The autopsy revealed the presence of six different medications in Ledger's body: two pain relievers (oxycodone and hydrocodone), two antianxiety medications (alprazolam and diazepam), and two kinds of sleeping pills (temazepan and doxylamine). There was no evidence of alcohol or any illegal drugs, and because large quantities of any of these drugs were not indicated in his system, suicide seems unlikely. The combination of these particular drugs in the body is potentially lethal, and so the results of the autopsy suggest an accident. The drugs had been prescribed by different doctors in different locations between Europe and America.

For several years, Ledger had been suffering from insomnia, anxiety, and depression, especially since the period of his work on Ang Lee's *Brokeback Mountain* in 2004. As he told columnist Sarah Lyall during the filming of *The Dark Knight*:

> "Last week I probably slept an average of two hours a night . . . I couldn't stop thinking. My body was exhausted and my mind was still going." At that time, he told Lyall that he had taken two Ambien pills, after taking just one had not sufficed, and those left him in a "stupor, only to wake up an hour later, his mind still racing."[2]

This behavior was confirmed by actress Michelle Williams, to whom Ledger had recently been engaged: "For as long as I'd known him, he had bouts with insomnia," she said. "He had too much energy. His mind was turning, turning, turning always turning."[3]

Ledger had met Williams on the set of *Brokeback Mountain* and it was around this time, according to his biographers, that his sleep deprivation and anxieties began. His breakthrough performance in Ang Lee's film was followed by those in *Casanova* (2005), *Candy* (2005), *I'm Not There* (2007), *The Dark Knight* (2008), and *The Imaginarium of Dr. Parnassus* (2009). The overall impression made by these roles is that of a complete discontinuity with everything that he had achieved before, and so it is no surprise that his physiology was afflicted with a whole new set of problems, which, as it were, ran parallel to the new roles. For Ledger, at the time of his death, had been involved in the construction of a new self, a self that required of him an almost yoga-like effort of concentration on his performances, which had the total effect of improving them immensely and elevating him to the stature of great actors like Jack Nicholson and Sean Penn. But it was also during this "third act" of his career that rumors began to circulate (although still unsubstantiated) of Ledger's abuse of drugs like cocaine and heroin. His relationship with Michelle Williams disintegrated during this time, as well, which was especially painful for him because the two had had a baby girl named Matilda, and Ledger was anxious over the fact that Williams had been given sole custody of the child.

During the last few years of his life, then, Ledger was apparently coming apart at the seams, while simultaneously engaged in the creation of a new mediatic self. This new self was his most ambitious project yet, for it was designed to counter and neutralize the previous celluloid avatar that he had built up during a decade-long career in film. The creation of this new avatar seems to have destabilized his physical body and sent waves of devastation rippling through his personal life.

Thus, as in the cases of Elvis Presley and Marilyn Monroe, Heath Ledger was caught up in a deadly and desperate battle against his own electronic selves, for just as Presley and Monroe had created clones of themselves that had the unintentional—and alienating—effect of trapping them inside the two-dimensional cosmos of media reality, so too, Ledger was battling his own clones in a war of images that ultimately would end with the destruction and death of his three-dimensional physical self.

Ledger's life was merely following the preformed patterns of the myth of the vanishing celebrity laid down by Presley, Dean, and Monroe, and he is, moreover, a contemporary example of a celebrity whose life has followed that myth's contours. Elements of Ledger's life are evocative of James Dean (his young age at the time of death); Marilyn Monroe (ending up dead on a bed from lethally interactive medications); and Rudolph Valentino (as we shall see). It is therefore important to consider him as a recent example of the viability of the myth of the vanishing celebrity, which is still alive and operative within our hypermediatized, real-time world.

Heath Ledger began his career in 1994 as a single, naïve self, full of hope and ambitions.

But now there are *three* Heath Ledgers: a physical (vanished) self and two (immortal) avatars.

What follows, then, is the story of the creation of those avatars, which emerged from the soil of Ledger's body like flowers from the blood of the slain god.

RIVER MAN

The first significant role of Heath Ledger's career was the Australian television show *Roar!* which was broadcast in the summer of 1997 on the Fox Network. At the time it was made, Ledger was only 16 years old, but he was playing a 20-year-old hero named Conor, a Celtic warrior whose task was to unify the tribes in battle against the Romans. Set around 400 B.C.E. in Ireland (although the Romans never went into Ireland), the story was created as an attempt to cash in on the success of the New Zealand television shows *Hercules* and *Xena: Warrior Princess*. However, only 8 of the show's 13 episodes of its first season were aired before being cancelled.

Conor is an example of the traditional monomythic solar hero who defends the values of civilization against the Other. The monomythic hero is always on the side of the Light—as implied by Conor's blonde hair—and he is always against those beings who, in one way or another, personify the Darkness that is ever threatening to disrupt and subvert civilization's most basic values. In this case, the role of the antithetic Other is played by the Romans, who oppress the Celts with unjust treatment.

Thus, it is important to remark that Joseph Campbell's *The Hero With a Thousand Faces* is *not*, as he thought, *every* hero, but only a certain type of hero, for Campbell's monomythic hero is a good-natured, callow young warrior who goes on to discover the presence of evil in the world and seeks to overcome it (in reality, this was but a projection of Campbell's own "good guy" persona onto the literary texts of ancient civilization and in no way representative of *all* heroes everywhere). Ledger's Conor *is* Campbell's monomythic hero, and this role will set the tone for most of his career.

In Ledger's first major cinematic role, the 1998 Australian film *Two Hands*, he plays 19-year-old Jimmy, a street punk who attempts to do a job for the Australian crime underworld—namely, deliver a payoff to a woman in an apartment building—but the money is stolen from him due to his own negligence, and Jimmy winds up on the mob's hit list. He must spend the rest of the film running for his life until he finds the nerve at the film's climax to confront the mobsters with a gun.

We see Ledger once again in the role of the traditional monomythic hero fighting to preserve his integrity against the slick and decadent mobsters who will kill anyone who even slightly inconveniences them. Jimmy upholds the values of decency, of civilized society, against the rogues, thieves, and murderers who are eating away at that society. The viewer identifies with his guilelessness and honesty, and thus Jimmy becomes the perfect vehicle through which the viewer may descend into this landscape of debauchery and witness for himself just how depraved these people are. Jimmy's compassion and decency correspond to those of the ideal viewer's, and so the mobsters become the dark Other who are the enemies of decent society and must be morally punished for their own lack of civilized values.

* * *

In the 1999 Hollywood teen comedy *10 Things I Hate about You*, Ledger plays Patrick, a tough high school kid who is paid to date a girl named Kat. Kat's sister Bianca has been forbidden to date by their overprotective father, but he has stipulated that she can begin dating only when Kat does, the catch being that since Kat is antisocial and a well-known shrew, their father does not believe this will occur anytime soon. However, the boy who wishes to date Bianca pays Patrick to seduce and begin dating Kat, who at first receives him with cold hostility but then gradually thaws as she is swayed by Patrick's evident charm.

The movie is an adaptation of Shakespeare's *The Taming of the Shrew* and once again we find Ledger in the role of a character who represents the values of civilized society, for he must tame and domesticate the antisociality out of Kat, thereby transforming her into a member of acceptable society. Because Shakespeare's play is in turn a late echo of the courtly romances that feature the typical scenario of a man attempting to woo the graces of a frosty (often married) woman for whom he has proclaimed his love, and who sets him on the difficult path of overcoming tests and trials to win her hand, we become aware, once again, of the hand of Campbell's monomyth guiding Ledger's role.

In Mel Gibson's 2000 Hollywood melodrama *The Patriot*, Ledger plays Gabriel, the son of the American war veteran Benjamin Martin (played by Gibson). Gabriel has grown up in the shadow of his father's legendary heroism and now wishes to become a soldier himself to fight off the British during the American War of Independence. Gibson's film—as is always the case when he directs—is sentimental, manipulative, and historically inaccurate—but it features Ledger once again in the role—as in *Roar!*—of the hero who defends a society against colonial oppressors, only in this case the Romans as the Other have been exchanged for the British as the Other.

If his role in *The Patriot* was, in essence, a reprise of his role in *Roar!* then Ledger's next film *A Knight's Tale* (2001) was a retrieval of the troubadourian subtext of *10 Things I Hate about You*. In this film, Ledger plays a knight attempting to win the hand of a lady through participation in jousting contests. The film is painful to watch (and not because of the jousting scenes, either), but the casting of Ledger was a significant event in his career, because this film made him really famous for the first time. It also began to bring to his conscious awareness what he had been doing unconsciously all along: namely, constructing the template for an archetypal action hero. This dawned on him when he was subsequently offered the title role in the 2002 Hollywood movie *Spider Man*, which he turned down.

> "People kept telling me I had to do big popcorn movies," [Ledger remarked], "they kept talking about 'opportunities.' I refused to put on tights and play a superhero. I don't want to be a 'mega-dude,' there's too much baggage that goes along with those kinds of roles. And besides . . . I didn't feel like I deserved it," he lamented. "I didn't really know how to act properly. I started to feel like a bottle of Coke. There was a whole marketing scheme to turn me into a very popular bottle. Coke tastes like shit, but there's posters everywhere so people will buy it. I felt like I tasted like shit, and I was being bought for no reason."[4]

Ledger's response to this dilemma was to take a role in a "serious" film, the Merchant and Ivory–style 2002 period piece *The Four Feathers*, in which he portrayed British officer Harry Feversham, a man who resigns his commission from his regiment just as it is announced that Sir Garnet Wolseley will march on Egypt to suppress the 1882 uprising of Urabi Pasha. Feversham's peers believe him to be guilty of cowardice and so, together with his fiancée Ethne, they send him four feathers, the symbol of cowardice. To redeem himself in their eyes, Feversham travels to Egypt on his own, where he fights on the side of the Muslims. One by one, however, he saves the lives of his friends in heroic battles and eventually creates an image of himself in their eyes as a great war hero.

In an odd way, the film parallels Ledger's attempts to prove to the world that he was more than just a Hollywood popcorn action hero but that, in taking upon himself a difficult role in a narrative with highbrow pretensions, he would redeem himself as a serious actor after all. The film, however, bombed at the box office and generally was panned by critics despite its being, in fact, a very good film.

What Ledger failed to take into account is that the distinction between highbrow and lowbrow no longer matters: an action hero is an action hero, whether he is embedded in a respectable 19th-century narrative or one in which he is slinging from webs in the middle of a forest of Manhattan skyscrapers. The character of Harry Feversham is yet another example of the monomythic hero—in this case, as archetypal soldier—who is defending the values of civilization against the Other, here represented by the Muslims. While fighting alongside Muslims, Feversham nonetheless remains thoroughly British in his intentions of restoring the image of himself as a member of respectable British society. He is bent on reintroducing himself into that society, where the heroism of his deeds will be esteemed by his friends and his reputation thereby restored. He is, in other words, motivated primarily by egoistic concerns and represents nothing more than an avatar of the British empire.

Pausing a moment to look back at the tracks that we have laid, it is evident that throughout the course of his career thus far, Heath Ledger was engaged in constructing a second self, a celluloid self as the monomythic hero always defending the values of civilization—that is, cities, states, empires—against the powers of darkness and uncivilized brutality that threaten to erode its organization. Thus, he actually was composing, out of the scraps of each of these roles, a sort of composite self, or Master Avatar, as the image of the great solar hero who *builds up* and then *defends* microworlds against the corrosive forces of ancient Chaos. In this sense, his avatar exactly opposed that of Jim Morrison's, who identified not with the hero of civilization but with its great antagonist, the Lizard Man or Dragon King who tears it down.

In creating this avatar, furthermore, Ledger was simultaneously looping back to the origins of the cult of the male movie star and essentially *folding in* to his body of work the previously constructed monomythic avatar of silent film star Rudolph Valentino, an actor whose films correspond structurally to Ledger's. Valentino, too, spent his career building the first Master Image in celluloid of the monomythic hero, which is confirmed by a glance at his many roles: the Sheik, the World War I soldier, the Spanish matador, the aviator, and so on. And let us not forget the further coincidence of the fact that Valentino, too, died suddenly at a young age, in his case, of complications arising from a perforated ulcer at the age of 31.

In the remaining four films of the first period of Ledger's career—*Monster's Ball, The Order, Ned Kelly,* and *The Brothers Grimm*—we see him finishing and completing the construction of this hero myth: in *Monster's Ball*, though his role is only a supporting one, he is a corrections officer (that is, defending the state against criminality); in *The Order*, he plays a Catholic priest who is a member of the Carolingians, a mysterious group that dedicates itself to fighting demons and performing exorcisms; in *Ned Kelly*, he portrays a real-life Australian cowboy who was mistreated by the Victorian police and sought revenge on them through the staging of a Maccabean-style revolt in which he became the center of a band of outlaws who plunder, pillage, and rob wherever they can, while redistributing the money back to the poor. In the lame Terry Gilliam film *The Brothers Grimm*, he portrays Jakob Grimm who, together with brother Wilhelm, fights monsters and wicked witches.

Thus, the general lines of Heath Ledger's career up to this point are clear, for over and over again he is cast in the role of the defender of civilization. This is the image of himself that he was constructing in the electric ether and it is very likely that had he died at this point, he would not have been remembered at all. This particular avatar was not only a two-dimensional construct—as are all electric avatars—but a clichéd image that is found in all the mythologies of the great world civilizations. It is not really very interesting, in spite of Campbell's celebration of it in his book *The Hero With a Thousand Faces.*

But then a singularity happened. Ledger suddenly reached a gap, a lacuna of darkness into which, rather mysteriously, his hero avatar disappeared. When he emerged from the obscure darkness of this mysterious gap—this fundamental discontinuity in his life and career—he set to work again, but now with a new image that began guiding him to choose different sorts of roles from what he had been used to.

He began to work on the creation of a *second* avatar, a *third* self, one who not only would cost him his life, but also would ultimately immortalize him as a permanent shade in the electric underworld where the revenants of dead celebrities take up their abodes.

THINGS BEHIND THE SUN

The 2005 film *Lords of Dogtown* is the first film in which Ledger begins construction on his new self. He plays Skip Engblom, the real-life owner of a surf and skateboard shop in 1970s Santa Monica, a dilapidated neighborhood scattered with the rusted, hulking ruins of Venice Beach carnival culture. Engblom's teenage protégés later became the famous Z-Boys captured in the pages of *Thrasher* magazine who reinvented the art of skateboarding by transplanting surfer moves to their skateboards and, with the introduction of polyurethane wheels, created a whole new art form out of skateboarding in Los Angeles's empty swimming pools.

Thus, from out of the ruins of Venice Beach carnival culture, Skip Engblom surfaces in Ledger's career as a new and complex three-dimensional character who is anything but a hero, for Engblom is an angry and aging alcoholic who watches the young boys who work for him leave to find lucrative offers with corporate sponsors who transform them into celebrities. Engblom gradually loses everything until he winds up designing surfboards in the back room of somebody else's shop.

For the first time in his career, Ledger portrays an individual who gradually fails while everyone else around him succeeds. This is no longer the archetypal hero who saves civilization, but rather a man who can barely save his own life. Thus, the role is homologous in Ledger's career with that of Marilyn Monroe's frayed character in *Bus Stop,* in which she attempted to project a new avatar that would dismantle her previous image as a glitzy showgirl. Ledger's Engblom represents the beginning of his attempt to destructure his hero myth avatar by portraying the first in a series of misfits, failures, and clowns who would compose the remainder of his acting career.

In *Brokeback Mountain* (2005), Ledger portrayed another three-dimensional and complex man named Ennis del Mar, a cowboy living in Wyoming in the 1960s who falls in love with another man almost by accident and much against his own will. The other man, played by Jake Gyllenhaal, is Jack Twist, also a cowboy, albeit one who is much more comfortable with his life as a gay man. Jack has affairs with other men over the years, but Ennis does not, although both men attempt to lead lives of "normalcy" with wives and children. Their affair continues for many years until one day Jack is beaten to death by homophobes in Mexico.

Ennis is a complex, shambling wreck of a man whose marriage disintegrates and who never remarries while he watches his daughters grow up. He is an image of the archetypal cowboy turned upside down and inside out, for the representation of a gay cowboy is tantamount to something of a sin against the Western genre, which prides itself on being the last bastion of rugged masculinity and bravado.

Ledger has returned to the image of the hero figure, but with the conscious purpose of transforming it into something almost unrecognizable, twisting and torquing the archetype as though it were a topological object in non-Euclidean space. Ledger's third self is a new and strange avatar that represents a defiant rupturing of all the traditional lines of flight of the hero who saves civilization by exiling its chaotic elements. Here, Ledger is beginning to create a screen double that no longer expels chaotic elements from civilization, but rather begins to fuse with them to create an avatar that is much closer to the bizarrely contorted and grotesque bodies of Bakhtin's carnival culture that seek to disrupt all the sculptural lines and traditional canons of Classical aesthetics.

With the 2005 film *Casanova*, Ledger suffers a momentary relapse and returns to the hero myth, this time playing the archetypal and (very) two-dimensional character of the paramour who is always in trouble with the ladies. However, in the film which follows, the 2006 *Candy*, he returns to his project of dismantling his previous electronic self, for in this film Ledger plays Dan, a frustrated poet who is addicted to heroin and who, together with his wife, Candy, embarks on a lifelong odyssey of drug abuse and depravity. Over time, Dan watches his wife transform into a prostitute to support their habit, while he himself resorts to thievery and criminality. Slowly, the couple slide down into hell with Candy winding up in a mental hospital, although the film does end on a hopeful note with Dan refusing to take her back after she has come out of the hospital, thus refusing to replay his outworn life patterns.

Dan's descent into heroin addiction is not comfortable to watch, for the camera's gaze is unflinching and present even in the most horribly intimate moments, such as when Candy is forced to give birth to a dead baby. Dan is no archetypal hero at all, but rather a man who is slowly dissipating himself into the abyssal waters of the vortex of altered consciousness.

In the 2007 film *I'm Not There*, Ledger plays another antihero, loosely based on Bob Dylan, a character named Robbie Clark who is an actor struggling to achieve a stable sense of identity while his marriage falls apart. Contrary to the general drift of critical opinion, however, this film does not work: it is a contrived and confusing mess of pretentious references and self-conscious acting that delivers one of Ledger's weakest performances.

It need hardly be said that playing the Joker in Christopher Nolan's 2008 comic book masterpiece *The Dark Knight* did not kill Heath Ledger. According to a belief from the Middle Ages, the pelican nourished its offspring by cutting into its own breast so that they could drink from its blood, and thus the pelican was thought to be the perfect allegory for Christ. But it is an even better allegory for what Heath Ledger was doing with his cinematic roles ever since taking on the difficult challenge of Ennis del Mar in *Brokeback Mountain*, for these roles were almost literally living off Ledger's blood. His self-taught method acting of deeply identifying with, and then internalizing, these new and complex characters was having the effect of slowly destabilizing his body's circadian rhythms, rendering him unable to sleep at night.

> "You're affected by whatever you're portraying," he acknowledged. "Your body has a memory of the experiences you have in life. If you're tricking yourself to feel anger every day, you go home angry. Then you get home, and you're like, 'Argh! Fuck me, why am I angry? I've got no reason to be angry.' And you wind yourself down again. But you do carry it. The mood of a film always takes me over."[5]

Hence, if the rumors of his experimentation with heroin usage while filming the movie *Candy* should ever turn out to be true, then no one would be at all surprised, given Ledger's newfound intensity.

Although the Joker is not a three-dimensional character, Ledger's performance is nonetheless one of the best and most memorable of his career. In the vision of Gotham according to the Batman comics, the city is essentially an underworld flooded with astral spirits: the Penguin, Scarecrow, Raz al-Ghul, Catwoman; all are creatures out of ancient myth and folklore, and it is Batman's job to combat them and keep the grid of Gotham free and clear of their sticky ectoplasm. These criminals are not actually criminals at all, but shades and revenants from the underworld that, if allowed free reign, would gum up the works of Gotham and transform the entire city into the megalopolitan equivalent of Alzheimer's, in which it would exist in an eternal present, its inhabitants wandering like zombies through a fog of twilight awareness. This is, in fact, what the bad guys of Christopher Nolan's first Batman film, *Batman Begins,* had attempted to do.

But Nolan's vision of the Joker is one degree more complicated than the Joker of the comics. Nolan's Joker is really a disguised allegory for the modern terrorist who wishes to blow up the system and prevent the world from being sealed off beneath a dome of late-capitalist hyperreality in which the planet becomes a gigantic shopping mall and where everyone is forced to become consumer zombies with no higher aims than participating in the circulation of signs.

But terrorism—and hence, also Nolan's Joker—is an objection to all this, whether we think of the Aum Shinrikyo nerve gas attacks in Tokyo in 1995, the Oklahoma City bombing also in 1995, or al Qaeda's 2001 attack on New York. These attacks share in common the rejection of a flatland consumerist paradise at the end of history in which nothing any longer has any meaning in favor of a reversion to an archaic vision of the passionate, vendetta-ridden human, drunk on his idols and prepared to sacrifice his life for the gods of his tribe. This is a very old way of human existence, and it is not one that is going to disappear easily, if ever.

Nolan's Joker, it is true, has nothing to do with religion, except insofar as he represents a vestigial survival from the realm of ancient myth, in which tribal beings such as the Australian aborigines painted their faces white to illuminate the human skull beneath as a recognition of the survival of the tribe's dead ancestors into the present. Nolan's Joker, stripped of religious references, however, is nonetheless the archetypal modern terrorist who resists Batman's overarching systems of technocratic manipulation and control. Thus, in Nolan's vision, Batman becomes an image of the technocrat whose solution to every problem is to build newer and more efficient machines with which to batten down the dome of consumerism.

Thus, Nolan's vision in *The Dark Knight* is actually a dramatization in miniature of what is going on across this planet right now, for it perfectly distills the two great forces that are struggling for possession of it: the bloodless consumer world of shopping malls, airports, and business parks at the end of history; or the violent, abysmal depths of the human psyche in which life is thought to be worth living only in servitude to ideals that are higher than the mere consumption of goods.

Ledger's performance is so haunting because he plays the Joker as though he *were* a three-dimensional character. *This* Joker is almost real: his hysterical and iconic laugh is cut to a minimum; he has nervous tics and mannerisms like a real person; and he is quite serious about his motives. This is why his iconic face paint is rendered as though it were carelessly applied and already beginning to smudge and wipe off, for the paint is a mask that flattens the supervillain into a two-dimensional stereotype. Ledger's Joker mask is falling off in direct proportion to the degree to which he attempts to put as much flesh onto the bones of a walking cliché as it is possible to do.

We can imagine how Ledger's project of creating a second avatar might have continued by considering a couple of the projects he was considering in his last years. For instance, according to his biographer Brian J. Robb, Ledger had expressed interest in playing the role of Satan in a $130 million adaptation of Milton's *Paradise Lost*, a role that would have been homologous in the Christian cosmos to that of the Joker in comic book cosmology.

He wanted to direct and possibly to star in a biopic of the 1970s British folk singer Nick Drake, a man who, like Ledger, also died young and in a similar manner, for Drake was found dead at the age of 26 of an overdose of antidepressants. Though Ledger never made the film, he *did* cast himself in a music video of Drake's song "Black Eyed Dog," which concludes with an image of Ledger drowning in a bathtub.

Thus, by the end of his career, Ledger had come exactly 180 degrees from where he had started with the monomythic hero of *Roar!* to a Jim Morrison–style avatar dissolving into a watery abyss.

Which brings us back, full circle, to the beginning.

Ledger's project of creating a second avatar seems to have somehow destabilized the metabolic processes of his physical body, rendering him anxious, depressed, and unable to sleep at night. This new process of concentrating so intensely on his characters that he managed to fuse with them at an almost molecular level seems to have been responsible for his use of the pain killers, sleeping pills, and antianxiety drugs that eventually killed him.

But by the time of his death in January 2008, he had already more or less completed his life's task, that of downloading himself into the electronic universe of mediatic reality that runs parallel to our physical world, and in which he took on this incarnation in the form of *two* avatars: a heroic savior of civilization, and a more complex and twisted misfit that defies categorization and stereotype.

The task was complete.

He had played his role in the larger task that has become the primary obsession of our entire civilization, namely, that of constructing a gigantic double of the physical world via satellite, Internet, television, film, genetic engineering, and the construction of theme parks.

Ledger had descended into the plasma pool of electric technology and had reproduced two copies of himself. In the end, he lay dead on his bed of drugs that he had taken to slow it all down, because the acceleration to light speed had made his own metabolism speed up too fast for him to live comfortably in the physical realm.

He was ready to go.

But his doubles had already hatched from their eggs and would carry on the "Heath Ledger" identity without him, bearing it with them into the reaches of the electronic immortality that stretches beyond the frontiers of biology into an unknown and unforeseeable lost highway of the future.

14

Michael Jackson's Macrosphere: Genesis, Evolution, Disintegration

Michael Jackson was a modern incarnation of the Boy in the Plastic Bubble, although he did not literally inhabit a laminar airflow room insulated and isolated by plastic. His bubble was more figurative, more of the imaginary domain, like those ancient crystalline spheres that once encased the earth in a protective etheric envelope, sounding musical notes as they revolved. Jackson's bubble was his creation of a kind of womb-spherical cosmology that not only surrounded him, but also replaced the world of three-dimensional material reality—the world that you and I inhabit—with a more subtle world, one made out of light and visions and dreams. If it is true, as theoretician Peter Sloterdijk claims, that the habitation in which one lives is essentially an extension of the immune system, then we may say that Michael's entire universe was a physical projection of his own psychological immune system, specifically designed as a kind of mental greenhouse that allowed him to thrive and create his music videos and record albums.

This was not a man who could function without such a greenhouse, however—unlike, say, Elvis, who *was* able to function, albeit *dys*functionally, in the real world—for once this greenhouse had been invaded by the cold and pitiless gaze of forensic science and the intrusive Eye of the media, he was no longer able to survive as an artist. By the time his immunosphere had shattered and lay in ruins all around him, his life as a creator of mediatized avatars and digital clones was over. His final days were a slow, creeping seepage of the reality that had come to infect him with a viral proliferation of banality that caused his body to implode and his inner eye to wilt, ceasing to produce visions any longer.

But by that point, it did not really matter, for although the macrosphere that he had created had collapsed in on him, a thin, visionary outer layer—as of an etheric epidermis—was shed by this macrosphere as it deflated. This outer layer survived to become a layer of hyperreality, in which the illuminated imago of Michael Jackson survived into the media Afterlife, where it joined the eternal icons of Elvis Presley, James Dean, Marilyn Monroe, and all the others spinning in their perpetual electromagnetic orbits about the earth.

TO BEGIN, THEN, AT THE BEGINNING, WITH AN IMPORTANT AND EARLY REALIZATION . . .

Shortly after Michael Jackson and his four brothers—Tito, Jermaine, Marlon, and Jackie—had signed on with Motown in 1968, Michael, who was 10 years old at the time, was instructed by Berry Gordy, the man who owned and operated Motown, to inform the press that he was only 8 years old. He was also told that he must say that it was Diana Ross, formerly of the Supremes, who discovered him and his brothers, although this, too, was a fabrication, since the Jacksons had already been signed to the label by the time they were introduced to Ms. Ross.

The 10-year-old Michael had not the slightest difficulty adjusting to this new state of affairs, in which he now had to inhabit not just *one* world, but rather *two*. As he later told his biographer J. Randy Taraborelli, "I figured out at an early age that if someone said something about me that wasn't true, it was a lie. But if someone said something about my *image* that wasn't true, then it was okay. Because then it wasn't a lie, it was public relations."[1]

This moment was Michael's first intuition that he would no longer be living in the same world, phenomenologically speaking, as the average human being, but rather in multiple worlds, simultaneously. And these worlds would require multiple selves to inhabit them.

AND TO CONTINUE WITH A MYTH . . .

The story that the Jacksons had been discovered by Diana Ross is worth remarking on, because she is the prototype for the many subsequent spiritual foster mothers—from Jane Fonda to Elizabeth Taylor—who will give birth to, and nurture, Michael's media avatars.

When the Jackson 5 appeared on television for the first time, it was on *The Hollywood Palace* hosted by Diana Ross, who introduced them as "Michael Jackson and the Jackson 5." Their first album, likewise, released on December 19, 1969, was entitled *Diana Ross Presents the Jackson 5*. Michael even lived for a short period with Diana Ross in Los Angeles, just after moving from Gary, Indiana, along with his brothers, in the summer of 1969 (Berry Gordy lived just up the street and was seeing Diana romantically at the time). Thus, she functioned for him in the role of a mother figure, displacing and replacing his biological mother Katherine, who was then still living in Gary.

So, in other words, Diana Ross and Berry Gordy (whom Michael regarded as a father figure) function as displaced parental figures for Michael, and thus played roles in the very ancient myth of the birth of the hero, in which the hero's original parents are swapped out for a new set who happen to stumble on the child in the wilderness, where he has been abandoned, and then raise him. In the typical example of this myth, the hero's original parents are nobility who, for one reason or another, have had to get rid of the child and so abandon him in the wilderness where he is later discovered and raised by lowly shepherds or peasants. In Michael's case, the story is the other way about, for his true parents are from humble Gary, Indiana, while the second set of parents—the fantasy parents—who "adopt" him are of nobility, or in this case, its modern equivalent, celebrities.

Thus, Diana Ross and Berry Gordy become the parents not of Michael's biological birth, but of his etheric second self, his mediatic shadow. This is the prototype for Michael's later disavowal of paternity in "Billie Jean," and his rejection of descent by biological evolution in favor of the intervention of science, which will create children for him via artificial insemination.

Michael's cosmology will involve the creation of a parallel universe in which science and electronic technology have usurped the role played by traditional biology. In such a universe, biology becomes superfluous, and in this sense, and for this reason, Michael Jackson will become the direct (spiritual) descendant of Walt Disney.

NEXT, OUR HERO IS RAISED BY TELETOPIANS . . .

Their first appearance on television, on *The Hollywood Palace* with Diana Ross, shows the Jackson 5 standing in a row singing before microphones, all dressed in identical lime green suits with gold shirts.

On *Ed Sullivan* in 1969, they are dwarfed by a large maroon-colored backdrop shot through with multicolored spikes like lightning bolts. Later, on *The Carol Burnett Show* in 1974, they are dressed once again in lime green, where they perform with Carol on a stage that engulfs them.

When watching these shows, one has the impression of looking through the individual viewer of one of Thomas Edison's kinetoscopes of the 1890s, in which miniature figures dance in black and white on a tiny screen, as though peering through the aperture of some secret laboratory experiment involving the production of tiny homunculi brought to life by the miracles of chemistry and set dancing in a test tube.

Indeed, it can be said that television has a miniaturizing effect on the Jacksons who appear as tiny humans born out of a glass tube, in this case the cathode ray tube that brings them into jittery life. Television has a derealizing effect on anything that travels through its circuits, and the Jacksons as they appear are shorn of depth and significance of any sort, very much resembling toys that have been homogenized for mass consumption. In the cosmology of television, the world of perspectival, three-dimensional space—in which all objects must conform to the laws of a single spatial field organized by the eye—is absolutely irrelevant, for people and objects can appear to be any size in any place (or even multiple places) at any time.

The subliminal effect of transforming the Jacksons into toys is that they are rendered harmless, depotentiated by electronic technology and safe for beaming into the living rooms of the average American middle-class home. Thus, Michael Jackson's "Wonder Child" persona at this time is that of an innocent and pure boy with the best of intentions, desiring only to perform for middle America with middle American values. The sanitization of his image means no trouble: no trouble for you, no trouble for me. *This* young black boy is cute and harmless: he is not yet "bad."

AND KEPT LOCKED AWAY IN A CAGE BY A FEARSOME GIANT . . .

The image of the Jackson 5 conveyed by television as dancing homunculi is not all that far off from the truth of their lives at this time. Their career had been managed by their violent and tyrannical father Joseph, who made them rehearse while holding a leather belt in one hand, like Pinocchio captured by the Italian puppeteer who forces him to perform. At Motown, they were not allowed much in the way of creative input by

Berry Gordy, their second "father," whose staff of professional musicians wrote all their songs and played all the instruments on their records. The only thing demanded of them at this time was that they sing . . .

And indeed, their Motown songs were huge hits that broke one chart record after the next: they were the first band in history, for instance, to have their first four singles—"I Want You Back," "ABC," "The Love You Save," and "I'll Be There"—become number-one hits on the Billboard chart.

But as our comparison with Pinocchio suggests, their lives during this time have a fairy tale quality: the story of five brothers who have been captured by a giant who keeps them locked up in a cage, taking them out only to sing and dance and make money for the giant, could just as well be any standard fairy tale out of the Brothers Grimm. The goal, then, is to escape from the giant, which normally would be accomplished by the youngest brother, the only one clever enough to find a means of escaping and setting the others free.

THEN HIS MICROSPHERE COLLAPSES . . .

The brothers at this time—throughout most of the 1970s—constitute a tribe of their own and, to Michael, they are his only defense against the strange world beyond the cage, where people—also giants—stop and stare through the bars with their large and frightening visages, gaping at the exotic creatures on the other side. Michael's days with his brothers were largely, though not of course entirely, happy ones, and the tribal environment they created was a sort of "second womb" for Michael, a familial microsphere that acted as a membrane protecting him from the world outside.

As Michael, however, later told the British interviewer Martin Bashir, new traumas began to disturb the functioning of this microsphere when Michael's brothers started bringing women home with them and having sex with Michael in the same room. He would be forced to listen to their bewildering activities, which apparently caused him an early aversion to sexuality. This period also taught him that women were disposable and not to be trusted.

And then, as his brothers got married one by one, the tribal bonding that had held them together in a steady state began to fall apart, especially when their father Joseph negotiated a new contract for them with CBS that allowed them to leave Motown and its creative restrictions behind—all of them, that is, except Jermaine Jackson, who had married Berry Gordy's daughter.

AND HE IS BORN YET AGAIN . . .

The title of Michael's 1979 solo album, *Off the Wall*, is subliminally suggestive of the nursery rhyme of Humpty Dumpty, the eggman who took a fall off the wall and could not be put back together again. Indeed, the advent of Michael's fifth solo album signifies the shattering of the egg that had contained him as a nurturing vessel up to this point. For years he had pretended to be just another member of a five-member pop band, but by the time Jackson and Quincy Jones put this album together, it was evident that he was a megastar in the making, with the capability of standing on his own two legs and venturing forth out beyond the iron gates of his father's compound in Encino.

In the history of biological evolution, the reptilian egg was superseded by the mammalian womb—itself a sort of involuted nest that is sealed off inside of a warm-blooded epidermis—and so now, the advent of the new soniscape that will be laid down in his next three solo albums, *Off the Wall, Thriller,* and *Bad*, Michael will begin the process of moving from the egg inside of which he had been nurtured together with his brothers to building his own womb-sphere with an independent cosmology and a geographically isolated world of its own at Neverland Ranch, located high in the hills north of Santa Ynez, beyond the reach of the banalities of Los Angeles.

On *Off the Wall*, over which CBS had promised him complete creative control, Jackson wrote most of the songs and hired Quincy Jones to help him produce the music. The result is a smooth, stream-lined album, the musical equivalent of a 1950s rocket-finned automobile. "Its rhythms," according to *Rolling Stone* magazine, "are smooth but propulsive, charged but gracefully syncopated; the melodies are light as air but immediate and unforgettable."[2]

Michael appears on the album cover dressed in a black tuxedo, hands in his pockets, smiling, standing with his back against a brick wall. He is alone and we presume his brothers must still be somewhere on the other side of the wall. At the age of 21, he is now mature and self-confident. The tuxedo, furthermore, is suggestive of a graduation or a wedding, and hence of a rite of passage of some sort.[3]

This photograph is significant for showing the results of his first nose job, since after having an accident while dancing, he had broken his nose and had had a plastic surgeon thin it out slightly.

Thus, his birth through a hole in the wall to another world comes along with a physical alteration marking that rite of passage.

IN THE LAND OF THE GARGANTUANS . . .

Michael's first music videos begin with this album, and since he later becomes *the* great master of the music video (rivaled, perhaps, only by Madonna), it is worth pausing to remark on the significance of his first video for the song "Don't Stop Till You Get Enough." In it, we see Michael Jackson dressed in the same tuxedo in which he appears on the cover of *Off the Wall*, for he intuitively understands that the music video is essentially an album cover that has been plugged in and turned on. The video shows him dancing alone against an ever-changing backdrop of colors and shifting geometries. Not much else happens, yet we note something interesting.

We have already pointed out the miniaturizing effect that television had on the Jacksons, but with Michael's first video, it is evident that the music video as a new medium has exactly the opposite effect, although it uses television as its primary means of conveyance: for the music video does not miniaturize, but rather gigantifies, its performers. Released from the confines of the dollhouse-like television studio, the music video, with its borrowing of filmic editing techniques, enlarges and magnifies the performer's imago. Michael appears in this video very much like a giant in relation to the shifting landscapes around him. He has, indeed, not only broken out of the cage, but actually become one of the giants who had once peered down into it.

This effect finds further confirmation when we glance at the music video that Michael helped his brothers make for their song "Can You Feel It," from the Jacksons' album *Triumph*, which was released on July 3, 1980. The video perfectly captures the sense of a 1980s album cover in motion, for in it, Michael and his brothers are literally the size of giants who go striding over cities sprinkling stardust on them, which is eagerly received by fans on the ground below as manna from heaven. The five brothers erect a rainbow arch in the sky, which is presumably meant to bridge their world in the heavens with that of their merely mortal fans who dwell in the tiny cities on the ground below. The video thus not only demonstrates the inherently gigantifying effect of the new medium of the music video on the imagos of its performers, but also makes visible the role played by celebrities in our society, who have taken over the niche once occupied by the gods of ancient myth and religion.

Celebrities are not just stars, they are whole constellations in the religion of pop culture.

AS MICHAEL JACKSON BEGINS TO BUILD HIS COSMOLOGY, BIOLOGY IS LEFT OUT OF ACCOUNT . . .

With the advent of *Thriller*, released on December 1, 1982, the rudiments of Michael Jackson's cosmology begin to take shape.

The origins of the song "Billie Jean" are instructive in this regard, for as his biographer J. Randy Taraborrelli tells it, the song was an attempt to exorcise a demon that had come to haunt him in the form of a fan who had sent him dozens of letters in 1981 claiming that Michael was the true father of her child. She sent photographs insisting that the child obviously had his eyes, and she even mailed him a gun with a note that asked Michael to kill himself on a certain day after which she would do the same thing upon killing her baby: this way, the three of them could be united in heaven. Michael was terrified by this fan and had her picture framed and placed in the dining room on a coffee table so that he could memorize her face in case she ever showed up in his life.[4]

What is fascinating is how Michael is once again troubled by the problem of biological apparentage. The very possibility of being the father of a child seems to horrify him, and it is significant that the song is based entirely on a denial of his taking any part in such a process. Later on, when he decides to have his own children, he will hire a surrogate mother, Debbie Rowe, whom he will have artificially inseminated to produce two children for him and then, when she can have no more, he hires another woman, whose identity remains unknown, to bear him a third child. And since all of these children are thoroughly white, it is unlikely that Michael's own genes are even involved.

In the cosmology that Michael is beginning to build, then, biology must be escaped from at all costs. His utopia is a world of the spirit that is dominated by the heaven archetype and it is in fierce opposition to the earth archetype, which is traditionally identified with the Mother. As in the case of the Buddha, whose mother dies soon after bearing him as a way of signifying Buddha's rejection of the earthly world in favor of Nirvana, or in the case of the mythology surrounding Christ, whose mother, upon her death, is borne up to heaven as a way of assimilating all earthly powers to the heaven/Father/Spirit archetype, so too, in Michael Jackson's cosmos, women are not allowed to be the bearers of the magical powers of procreation.

It was said of Michael's subsequent plastic surgery operations that his face came more and more to resemble Diana Ross's, and this is perhaps no accident, for it is symbolic of his appropriation of the creative powers of the Mother. In Michael's cosmos, he will become a god whose identity is transgendered, simultaneously male *and* female. In ancient myth, the Great Mother had given rise to the dying and reviving male god as a mere appendage from her own body, but in Michael's case, it is the other way about: the Great Mother will become implicate in *his* own body, for his creative powers will be almighty and can be rivaled by nothing and no one.

AND THE MACROSPHERE BEGINS TO ASSUME ITS CONFIGURATION . . .

Peter Sloterdijk, in his *Spheres* trilogy, argues that the history of humanity is based on an attempt to create living spaces that are replacements for the womb. Civilizations build "macrospheres" around them as articulations of the uterine space once occupied by the embryo in the womb, where the original "companion" of the fetus was the placenta. Thus, much of human social bonding, according to Sloterdijk, is an attempt to replace this original "microsphere" of fetus plus placenta as a dyadic unity with new social groupings.[5] In a sense, while with his brothers, Michael Jackson had done just that: he was part of a social organism in which his brothers functioned for him as a sort of second womb protecting him from the world outside.

But with the shattering of the egg that had once enclosed him, starting with his album *Off the Wall*, Michael was born into a new environment in which he was no longer part of a tribal unity, but a loner standing in difficult terrain. The attempt to create a new cosmology that would substitute as a uterine environment for the loss of his primal unity with his brothers begins almost immediately with *Thriller*. In both the songs on the album and the three music videos for "Billie Jean," "Beat It," and "Thriller," he begins to refashion his Wonder Child avatar as a being with god-like powers over time and space.

At this time, however, he is still living with his family at the house in Encino and, in fact, it is not until after the release of his album *Bad* in 1987 that he finds a proper geographic location for his new macrosphere. In 1988, he buys the property he called "Neverland Valley Ranch."

In this new environment, he proceeds to ground his cosmology in a geographic location in which he attempts, like Walt Disney before him, to construct a mini-utopia that features children as its primary inhabitants.

These children are, of course, replacements for the lost tribe of the Jackson 5.

THE WORLD IN A BOTTLE . . .

To understand the vision of Jackson's cosmology, then, which is complex and multitiered, we must begin by examining the topography of Neverland Ranch, which serves as a world-island unto itself.

Laid out on a roughly north-south axis, the 2,600-acre property is organized like a park designed by Frederick Law Olmsted with winding paths and scenic views like Central Park or Prospect Park in Brooklyn. And like Disneyland, its periphery is bounded by a railroad track on the western side, which then loops down into the park from the north and eventually out the eastern side, so as to nearly encompass it.

The park is laid out into three distinct regions: at the southern end, where the entrance gates are located, Michael's private residence looks out over a lake where he dreamed up many of his later songs. Farther north, in the middle of the property, lay the amusement park, with its Ferris wheel, roller coaster, merry-go-round, and bumper cars. At the northern end, toward the mountains, there lay the area of the zoo: a petting zoo, an elephant compound, a crocodile zone, and other such displays.

Hence, time in this world is frozen to a standstill: only children have any ontological status at all. Adults drift through this world like ghosts, utterly irrelevant. Because they are relegated to a peripheral status, sexuality is forbidden here, for sex is tantamount to an admission of aging and temporality. Thus, Jackson has constructed the world as he would have liked it to remain before his brothers started having sex with women and moving on into the difficulties of adulthood. This is precisely why he has named the place "Neverland," after J. M. Barrie's utopia in *Peter Pan*, for this is a place where children never have to grow up, grow old, or die, including Jackson himself, the leader of these lost boys, as he had been the leader of the Jackson 5.

When Jackson hires Debbie Rowe to be the surrogate mother of his children, it is as though he were regressing to a presexual epoch of biology, in which bacteria reproduce simply by splitting themselves in half, rather than engaging in the biological shuffling of genetic difference that generates the metabolisms of higher life forms. Bacteria do not die of old age; in fact, they do not age at all. They can live as long as something untoward does not happen to them.

The lack of discrimination between children and adults in this cosmos means that it is a matter of complete indifference who sleeps where. Children can sleep with adults in the same bed because only children inhabit this utopia. People who seem to be as large as adults are really only optical illusions, for in substance, they are identical with children.

Thus, if you think that Jackson sexually molested children, then you are failing to understand the sacrality of his cosmos, in which children are the holiest of objects. Jackson would no more molest a child than a devout Hindu would eat a cow.

AND THEN THERE'S MICHAEL'S UNDERWORLD . . .

In this cosmology, sex and death are banished to the Underworld of Jackson's music videos, which function in relation to the cosmos of Neverland Ranch in a way that is analogous to the functioning of hell in the Christian cosmos. Indeed, from the start, Jackson's music videos have the quality of a *nekyia* about them: the graveyard of awakening zombies in the *Thriller* video; the descent down the staircases into the New York subway in the "Bad" video; the fascination with the people of "Nighttown," as it were, in the form of prostitutes ("Dirty Diana") and street gangs ("Beat it"). Indeed, everything that is banished from Neverland Ranch—sex, death, violence, criminality, aging, and disease—resurfaces in the music videos, which are a veritable Dantesque journey through the circles of the Inferno.

Even Jackson's famous dances, with their sexual ambiguities, have a vague air of death and the crypt about them, for their jerky movements and syncopated, machine-like rhythms remind us of the skeleton dances of the dead in the famous Medieval depictions of the Dance of Death that first surfaced in the imagery of Paris cemeteries in the 15th century. These images typically depicted a dancing skeleton leading members from every social niche in a jubilant line of ecstatic, dancing death. Indeed, Jackson's body, with its long, Giacometti-like legs and thin, gaunt face, resembles a skeleton, and of course, the zombie dance that he performs in the "Thriller" video is an obvious retrieval of the Dance of Death. But in the later video for "Ghosts," Jackson actually metamorphoses into a dancing skeleton, as though to reveal to us that he merely had been Death wearing the mask of Life all along.

Jackson grabs his crotch for the first time in a dance move in Martin Scorsese's video for "Bad" as a way of reminding us that, Neverland Ranch aside, he has not forgotten about the realm of the genitals altogether.

He is acknowledging the presence of the sex drive in his Underworld cosmology, for contrary to what anyone may think about his relationship with Lisa Marie Presley, the two apparently *did* have a passionate, sexual relationship.

So the complicated semiotics of his dance moves are neither merely sexual nor morbid, but simultaneously both / and. Indeed, everything in Michael's cosmos is both / and: he was both male *and* female; white *and* black; young *and* old; and so on. As in the case of "Death and the Maiden," wherever the erotic impulse is found, death, too, cannot be far behind, especially since sexual reproduction was invented by multicellular organisms as an exchange for their mortality.

In the cosmos according to Michael Jackson, then, everything transcends and yet simultaneously embodies its own opposite. It is a strange, science fictional universe, a world that was, for a time anyway, completely closed off from the real one.

But then, one day, a virus landed on the outer membrane of this macrosphere, a virus that began to inject and proliferate bits of the "reality" that lay beyond the dome.

THE FIRST IMPACT . . .

It was a couple of years after the release of his best album, *Dangerous* (1991), when one of Jackson's child friends accused him of sexual molestation. This was Jordy Chandler, a 13-year-old boy Jackson had befriended one day when his stepfather Dave Schwartz came to Jackson's rescue after his car had broken down on a Los Angeles highway.

Jackson was introduced to the boy and given his phone number, and while on tour for his new album, called the boy often, developing a long-distance friendship with him. When he returned to the United States, he invited Jordy and his sister Lily and their mother June to Neverland, just as he had been doing with children all along. They played games, rode the rides, ate cotton candy, and generally had great fun.

One morning, when the mother found out that Jordy had slept with Jackson in his bed, she frowned on the behavior and confronted Jackson, who denied any wrongdoing. The mother apparently was convinced by Jackson's sincerity, for she allowed the relationship to continue, including sleepovers at Neverland. Sometimes, Jackson would even sleep at the boy's house, where his father Evan Chandler, a dentist, soon took a disliking to him, feeling that Jackson's influence over Jordy was greater than his own.

Eventually, Evan hired a sleazy attorney and claimed that his son confided to him while under the influence of sodium amytal—which Evan had used (bizarrely) as an anaesthetic while extracting a tooth from the boy—that he and Jackson were having sexual relations. Sodium amytal has been widely discredited as a "truth serum," functioning more often instead as a means of implanting false memories in the subject's mind.

When word of this accusation got out, the police descended on Neverland Ranch in 1993 and raided it, searching for traces of child pornography, a sure sign, it was felt, of a pedophile. But they found nothing.

At one point, they even strip searched Jackson himself, carefully examining his genitals for marks Jordy insisted would be found there. The results were inconclusive (for whereas Jordy had said that Jackson was circumcised, in reality, he was not). Jackson's associates, including Elizabeth Taylor, then advised him to settle with the Chandlers and keep out of court, for fear of tarnishing Jackson's image with a long-drawn-out court battle in which a jury might or might not find him guilty. Jackson agreed to pay the settlement, a figure somewhere around $20 million so that he could move on with his life.

According to Jackson biographer Ian Halperin, the Chandlers were actually a father-son screenwriting team (they already had one screenplay produced for the Mel Brooks movie *Robin Hood: Men in Tights*) and were most likely looking for big money to finance the production of their other screenplays.[6] Jackson was the perfect target.

AND THEN ANOTHER . . .

The crisis of the early 1990s was the first blow to the integrity of Michael's protective dome, which continued functioning for another decade or so. The cosmology of Neverland had been built on the idea that children, as he once put it, "don't wear masks," and thus are incapable of the kinds of duplicity and avarice that characterize adults. Children were his religion, and when a child that he had loved and cared for turned against him with false allegations designed to extort money out of him, he began to have the idea that he should have his own children, because that way he could bond with children who he could trust and who would never turn on him. (It is ironic that it was precisely these children that he would later always insist wear masks whenever they went out in public.)

But when the second allegations of molestation surfaced in 2003, this time the dome that covered Neverland finally would shatter, precipitating the greatest and, ultimately, final crisis of his life.

This time, the allegations were leveled by a 13-year-old boy named Gavin Arvizo, who appeared in a character-assassinating documentary constructed by British journalist Martin Bashir, which was broadcast in February 2002. At the time, Jackson's career was at its lowest ebb, for he had just produced a beautiful but slow-selling album entitled *Invincible* (2001)—his last album, incidentally—an album that sold only a couple of million copies and had only one hit single. Bashir had conducted the famous interview with Princess Diana in which she had confessed that her marriage with Charles was really a threesome, and Jackson, who was so fascinated with Diana, thought that Bashir might be able to do something to resurrect his fading image. So he gave Bashir permission to stay with him at Neverland for eight months, trusting that the producer would portray him in a favorable light.

The documentary as it aired, however, focused on Michael's worst eccentricities: the obvious fact, for instance, that he was lying on camera when Bashir asked him whether he had had plastic surgery, and Jackson denied it, saying that he had only a little work done to touch up his nose, and that his skin had lightened by itself. But the documentary also featured Michael sitting on a couch holding hands with Gavin Arvizo, a child who had been diagnosed at the age of 10 with cancer and who was told by medical authorities that he would soon die. Michael took him in, spent a lot of money cheering him up, and soon, the cancer had dissolved. Unfortunately for his image, though, Michael admitted on the documentary that Gavin occasionally slept in his bed, while he slept on the floor. The public reaction in America to this was an outcry, although, interestingly, it did not seem to bother the British any.

In a rebuttal documentary entitled *The Michael Jackson Interview: The Footage You Weren't Meant to See*, the Arvizos went on camera to deny any improprieties and insisted that Jackson had treated them well. Soon after the documentary aired, however, the Arvizos came forward and insisted that Jackson had molested Gavin from February 20 to March 12, 2002, *after* the Bashir documentary had aired. We are asked to believe, in other words, that after the documentary had aired and caused a public stir, Michael *then* proceeded to molest Gavin.

Furthermore, the Arvizos had a shady history: in November 2001, JCPenney had caught the mother giving clothes to the boys and sending them out the front door. When arrested, the mother claimed she had been sexually assaulted by security guards for seven minutes while they detained her. She was able to get the store to pay her a settlement of $137,500 to end the lawsuit. The psychiatrist hired by JCPenney to evaluate her found her to have "rehearsed" her children into supporting her story.[7]

When the case went to trial in 2005, Jackson was fully acquitted of all charges.

AND SO THE SPHERE SHATTERS . . .

But the ultimate effect of the two sets of allegations was to cause Michael Jackson's protective womb, made out of visions and dreams, to disintegrate. The police had raided Neverland twice; its sanctity had been violated. And children whom he had loved and cared for had turned on him.

Like the slaughter of the buffalo that the Native Americans of the western United States depended on as a religious icon, which destroyed their cosmology and caused them to turn inward toward the apocalyptic Ghost Dances and the peyote cults, Michael Jackson's cosmos lay in ruins, and his drug addiction had accelerated out of control. He had begun taking painkillers in 1984 when he had been injured during the filming of a Pepsi commercial in which a mistimed explosive caused his hair to catch on fire, and during the 1993 allegations, his drug use had increased to a point that required him to go into a rehab center. But during and after the 2005 trial, his drug abuse was once again on the rise.

And children, moreover, could no longer be trusted.

Neverland must be abandoned.

After the trial, he fired the staff and let Neverland rot for three years. The ranch soon lay empty and silent, and was "'in shambles,' according to a court declaration filed by Darren Julien, founder of Julien's Auctions, which had been hired to sell off pieces of the property. 'Buildings, amusement rides, industrial equipment, personal automobiles and Jackson's personal zoo and Tipi village were falling apart,' he said."[8]

Jackson had spent his life constructing his own private universe, but the gaze of the media and the forensic eye of the police had caused it to collapse, just as the gaze of analytical science had caused the Biblical cosmology to collapse and give way to the scientific picture of life evolving over a planet whirling about a tiny sun in an almost infinitely gigantic universe of colliding galaxies. In both cases, Reality, sponsored by analytical science, destroyed the complex truth-lies of Myth.

Jackson refused to return to the United States after the trial was over, and instead became a global nomad. He took his children and spent three years with a sheik in Bahrein who had befriended his brother Jermaine, a recent convert to Islam. Michael had begun life as a Jehovah's Witness, the religion of his mother, but during the 2005 trial, the Nation of Islam had come into his life, providing him with private bodyguards. Islam, the West's great antithetical religion, may have held some appeal to him at this time—as it had for Princess Diana—during which he had lost interest in the United States and its media cult and culture of shame and victimization.

At any rate, he considered moving either to Britain or Germany, but eventually decided against them as a result of his declining finances. He spent some time in Las Vegas, where he was often seen being pushed around in a wheelchair and wearing a surgical mask. Drug addiction and poor health besieged him at this time. Eventually, he ended up back in Los Angeles, living in a rented mansion in Holmby Hills.

Thus, during his final years, Michael had performed a sort of Deleuzian shift from building a vertically tiered and hierarchically organized cosmology to a horizontally oriented axis of global nomadism. A vague alliance with the nomadic religion of Islam may have assisted him in becoming his own "war machine," as it were, bent on building cosmologies no longer, but only on tearing them down.

By then he was carrying his own cosmology with him, since the various drugs that he was on—Ativan, Valium, Xanax, Demerol, morphine, and so on—functioned to replace the shattered womb-sphere that had once allowed him to build his own miniature civilization. Lacking the external protection of his macrosphere, he now tried to replace it artificially with the oceanic feeling that drugs induced in him. The exterior womb-sphere became internalized, in other words, made up now only of bizarre, conflicting chemistries that played havoc with his immune system, instead of acting as an extension of it.

IMPLOSION

In the last year of his life, Michael had agreed, under a great deal of pressure due to his mounting debts, to attempt to stage a comeback with a series of concerts that would be given at London's new O2 arena, beginning in July 2009. The rehearsals for this concert comprise the footage shown in the movie *This Is It*, which reveals him singing and dancing, apparently in presentable shape. However, according to a member of his household staff, he was "terrified" at the prospect of the London concerts:

> He wasn't eating, he wasn't sleeping and when he did sleep, he had nightmares that he was going to be murdered. He was deeply worried that he

> was going to disappoint his fans. He even said something that made me briefly think he was suicidal. He said he was worried that he was going to end up like Elvis. He was always comparing himself to Elvis as long as I knew him, but there was something in his tone that made me think that he wanted to die, he was tired of life. He gave up. His voice and dance moves weren't there anymore. I think maybe he wanted to die rather than embarrassing himself onstage.[9]

Although he had promised 50 shows, it was suspected by many of those close to him that he probably would have enough stamina only for the first one or two of them. His health was failing due to drugs and an anorexic disorder, which caused him to avoid eating, so that he had lost a huge amount of weight.

On June 24, 2009, the last night he was alive, Jackson had rehearsed at Staples Center in Los Angeles for six hours after arriving late.

He had hired a new personal physician, a cardiologist from Houston named Dr. Conrad Murray, who had been administering an anaesthesia known as propofol (also called Diprivan) by injection in 50-milligram doses. In the week leading up to his death, Murray had begun to fear that Jackson was becoming addicted to the drug and so lowered the dosage to 25 milligrams and replaced the balance with less powerful sedatives, such as lorazepam and midazolam.

But on the early morning of June 25, Michael complained that he still could not sleep after Murray had given him Valium and two other drugs. Jackson instructed him to give him more of the dangerous propofol.

"I want it to hit my vein and I want to be asleep," he had earlier told a nurse regarding the drug. "I don't even want to wait a second for it to get into my system. I want to be knocked out, asleep."[10]

Murray obliged by administering a 25-milligram dose of propofol at 10:40 A.M. Murray reportedly left Jackson alone to make some telephone calls for about 47 minutes. When he returned, Jackson was not breathing and the paramedics were called at approximately 12:21 P.M. When they arrived, they wanted to pronounce him dead on the spot, but his body was rushed to University of California–Los Angeles Medical Center, where doctors spent another hour trying to revive him with defibrillators.

But it was over.

According to doctors, propofol is not a sleep aid, for it actually induces coma, not sleep. It is extremely dangerous and should be administered only in the context of a hospital, where its effects can be monitored.

"Propofol slows down the heart rate and slows down the respiratory rate and slows down the vital functions of the body," according to one doctor. "You will die if you give yourself, or if somebody will give you, propofol and you're not in the proper medical hands."[11]

Thus, in the end, Jackson's death was a replay of the myth of the dying celebrity, the very myth he had feared would shape his final days, rough hew them how he would. He told people close to him that he was worried he would end up like Elvis, and he was correct.

Like Howard Hughes, Marilyn Monroe, Heath Ledger, and many others before him, Jackson had dissolved his physical body into a chemical soup and replaced it with an eternal icon made out of radiant electrons and photons, like a stained glass image about which, slowly, ever so slowly, gather the creeping tendrils of religious piety and saintly devotion.

Afterword: On the Otherworldly Nature of Electronic Culture

So what does all this mean?

As of this writing, the most recent celebrity deaths to occur were those of Anna Nicole Smith (2007), Heath Ledger (2008), and Michael Jackson (2009). Similar to Marilyn Monroe, Smith was found dead as the result of an (accidental) mixture of drugs in her body, including the sleeping sedative chloral hydrate (the same drug, combined with Nembutal, that had killed Monroe) and a kaleidoscope of benzodiazepines.

As the reader who has read through this book by now realizes, the pattern is clearly recognizable, for Elvis Presley and Marilyn Monroe, too, had died in similar ways as the result of a lifetime of undergoing transformation through integrated circuits. All five of these celebrities, moreover, both the recent ones as well as the "classic" ones, had left the material world behind only after having successfully created virtual substitutes for themselves made out of light and electrons. Once their virtual doubles had taken on secure identities, the real celebrities could then leave their mortal coils behind like snakeskins, for their eternal existences within Electrotopia had been ensured, and their physical presences in the real world were no longer required.

It appears that the French philosopher Jean Baudrillard had it right: we are becoming specialists in the crime of murdering off reality and replacing it with hyperreal duplicates. Indeed, this endeavor seems to be the West's primary preoccupation nowadays, the secret goal that underlies almost everything it does. The creation of electric doubles at the expense of real physical human beings is just one example of a more general process that is ongoing throughout our entire civilization, for we are involved in a gigantic project of replacing *everything* with hyperreal substitutes: Egyptian pyramids are replaced by Las Vegas hotels; the canals of sinking Venice are replaced by Venice Beach, California; history is replaced by Disneyland; Lascaux is closed down to the public and then replaced with a replica; the printed page has been replaced by its virtual image on a laptop; and so on.

We *are* being replaced, and in the case of the cult and culture of the celebrity, we are engaged in a willing process of the replacement of our real selves with electronic avatars. We are in love with the virtual and the hyperreal and we are apparently willing to die for it. Our celebrities are attracted to screens—silver screens, television screens, video monitors—like insects to fluorescent lighting, and the tiny brittle corpses of dead insects that line the insides of these lights find their analogues in the corpses of dead celebrities left behind in the wake of the history of electric media.

There are, furthermore, religious overtones to this process, for the celebrity who gives up his life for the screen is performing a variation of the ancient myth of the willing sacrifice. The celebrity sacrifices his own real three-dimensional existence to bring into being a two-dimensional virtual avatar, thus disappearing into the replaced image and then vanishing from the physical world. Human beings, apparently, are currently undergoing a mass exodus into virtual reality, for the real world—the world of objects, of chairs and tables and trees and mountains—is to be escaped from at all costs so that one may take up one's "real life" in the Electroverse as soon as possible.

An implicit denial of the physical is implied by such a strategy of escape, an almost neo-Gnostic ethic of downloading one's consciousness into cyberspace in an attempt to leave the body behind, like those hapless souls of Marshall Applewhite's Heaven's Gate cult who drank poison to exit their bodies and catch the next spacebus to the galactic dimensional opening that would carry them away to another, better world.

For the past 3,000 years—since the age, that is, of the Axial prophets—human beings have been inventing mental strategies for leaving the physical world behind, and the world that they have escaped into has gone by any number of names: nirvana, Brahman, the Yonder Shore, the One, Heaven, and so on. Such worlds, furthermore—as Nietzsche pointed out—typically have been regarded as *more real* than this one, and as therefore representing the realm of ultimate Truth. It is an interesting irony, however, that the world of the hyperreal into which the celebrity currently escapes is fully known and recognized as "less real" than the world that we inhabit, as terms like "virtual reality" imply. It is, in other words, an ersatz world—and also a meaningless one—into which the celebrity escapes by duplicating himself, a fake world of the "hyperreal" and the "virtually real," but one that is nonetheless the preferred mode of being. Everyone nowadays, in one form or another, wishes to escape into it, and the doorway by means of which this becomes possible is the camera eye.

Indeed, looking back over the various biographies of the celebrities we have covered in this book, it becomes clear that they represent the pioneers, as it were, of the current mass exodus into hyperreality in which every one of us, in the 21st century, is engaged. Nowadays, you are not hip if you do not have a page on Facebook or Twitter or your own Web site (a sort of "cult of me") or else one or two videos on YouTube, for the creation of a virtual version of the self is part of the larger project of our technological construction of the world's double. All our current endeavors from cloning to the Internet to the Las Vegas theme park city are part of one huge labor to remake the world as a double of itself. And, thus, the celebrities who suffered the various tragedies of their lives by creating virtual doubles of themselves through electric media are the prototypes for the rest of us who are just now catching up with them via the Internet.

Andy Warhol, with his cult of the famous nobody, knew just what he was talking about and can be regarded as *the* prophet of where we're at now.

Thus, the camera eye becomes the new gateway into a parallel universe, the modern looking glass through which Alice once upon a time transposed herself. We are completely enraptured by the cold gaze of the camera, just as the mystics of Sufi love poems were intoxicated by their love for the radiance of God, with whom they desired to become One.

Thus, virtual reality has become, in essence, the new religion of the postmodern age in which all other alternate and "better" worlds have been eliminated as escape routes. The "Light from Another World" now emanates from our laptops and television screens just as once, long ago, that light suffused the interiors of cathedrals with the jewel-like radiance of stained glass. Tomorrow, one can be equally certain, it will emanate from something else, for the Light never disappears; it only gets shifted around.

But then, who's worried about tomorrow?

Notes

INTRODUCTION

1. Edgar Morin, *The Stars* (Minneapolis: University of Minnesota Press, 2005), 57.

2. Tim Clayton and Phil Craig, *Diana: Story of a Princess* (New York: Pocket Books, 2001), 347.

3. Though Jones survived the crash, he maintains he has no memory of it beyond the group's pulling away from the curb of the Ritz with the paparazzi in hot pursuit. He also claims that he, in any event, would never have worn a seat-belt, since it would have limited his movement within the car which he, as the bodyguard, would have needed at all times.

4. Kenneth T. Jackson, *Crabgrass Frontier: The Suburbanization of the United States* (Oxford: Oxford University Press, 1985), 248–251.

5. Jeffrey M. Hardwick, *Mall Maker: Victor Gruen, Architect of an American Dream* (Philadelphia: University of Pennsylvania Press, 2004), 81–82.

6. Compare Gilles Deleuze and Felix Guattari's notions of the rhizome, the multiplicity, schizoanalysis, and the acentered self.

7. Daniel J. Boorstin, *The Image* (New York: Penguin Books, 1963), 55–85.

8. Peter Brown, *The Cult of the Saints: Its Rise and Function in Latin Christianity* (Chicago: University of Chicago Press, 1982), 92.

9. Ibid., 58.

CHAPTER ONE

1. Paul Virilio, *Pure War* (Los Angeles: Semiotexte, 1997), 67.

2. Peter Harry Brown and Pat H. Broeske, *Howard Hughes: The Untold Story* (Cambridge, MA: Da Capo Press, 2004), 94.

3. Donald L. Barlett and James B. Steele, *Howard Hughes: His Life and Madness* (New York: W. W. Norton, 2004), 83.

4. Brown and Broeske, *Howard Hughes: The Untold Story*, 151.

5. Barlett and Steele, *Howard Hughes: His Life and Madness,* 140.

6. Brown and Broeske, *Howard Hughes: The Untold Story*, 328.

7. Barlett and Steele, *Howard Hughes: His Life and Madness*, 492.

CHAPTER TWO

1. Marshall McLuhan, *The Gutenberg Galaxy* (Toronto: University of Toronto Press, 1997), 263.

2. Neal Gabler, *Walt Disney, The Triumph of the American Imagination* (New York: Alfred A. Knopf, 2006), 533.

3. Gabler, *Walt Disney*, 534.

4. Gabler, *Walt Disney*, 610.

5. For example, see Jean Baudrillard, *Screened Out* (London: Verso, 2002), 151–152.

CHAPTER THREE

1. Peter Guralnick, *Last Train to Memphis: The Rise of Elvis Presley* (New York: Back Bay Books, 1994), 437.

2. Likewise, the red and white colors of the stage allude, if only subliminally, to the red jacket over a white T-shirt worn by James Dean in *Rebel Without a Cause.*

3. Gail Brewer-Giorgio, *Is Elvis Alive?* (New York: Tudor Publishing, 1988), 49.

CHAPTER FOUR

1. Joe Hyams and Jay Hyams, *James Dean: Little Boy Lost* (New York: Warner Books, 1992), 3.

2. In an alleged interview in 1995, Mario Moretti claims that Turnupseed admitted that he *had* seen Dean coming, and became momentarily confused about what to do, since he was listening to Doris Day and Jo Stafford on the radio. However, Turnupseed's son David denies that the interview ever took place. In any event, I prefer Turnupseed's rough draft version of the crash, because it presents a mythological scenario in which Dean had become invisible, instead of the later, rewritten version, which is merely prosaic.

3. David Dalton, *James Dean: The Mutant King* (New York: St. Martin's, 1974), 317.

4. Louis Crompton, *Homosexuality and Civilization* (Cambridge, MA: Belknap Press of Harvard University Press, 2003), 109.

CHAPTER FIVE

1. Donald Spoto, *Marilyn Monroe: The Biography* (New York: Cooper Square Press, 2001), 324.

2. Ibid.

3. Jean Baudrillard, *Simulacra and Simulation* (Ann Arbor: University of Michigan Press, 2006), 95.

4. Walter Benjamin, *Illuminations* (New York: Shocken Books, 1969), 230–231.

5. Ibid., 229.

6. Donald H. Wolfe, *The Last Days of Marilyn Monroe* (New York: William Morrow, 1998), 231.

7. And yet, these photographs of her rolling about entwined in sheets on a bed rather eerily foreshadow the circumstances of her coming death.

8. Although Donald H. Wolfe points out that the call to Lawford must have occurred around 10:30 P.M., since guests at Lawford's dinner party recall him contacting them after they had gone home at around 10:30 P.M., claiming anxiously that Marilyn had just faded into silence on the phone with him.

9. Wolfe, *The Last Days of Marilyn Monroe,* 462.

10. Note that in Wolfe's theory we have a "true" and original crime scene that is disguised by a secondary Freudian screening one that is entirely mythical. The second crime scene is designed to perpetuate the myth of the celebrity suicide by drug overdose to conceal the "real" crime scene of a politically motivated assassination. Thus, in the media enshrouded culture in which we live, truths are carefully concealed and enwrapped, mummy-like in the shrouds of fantasies. Wolfe's theory, then, whether true or not, is true in the sense of its fidelity to the Hollywood realm of fantasies, where lies and dreams are contrived to make the unbearable tawdriness of life in late capitalist consumer society tolerable. Hollywood does this for us on a daily basis, and Wolfe's theory is a miniaturized version illustrating the function of Hollywood and therefore suits poetically the circumstances of Marilyn's death.

11. Wolfe, *The Last Days of Marilyn Monroe*, 90.

CHAPTER SIX

1. I have borrowed the phrase "electronic stained glass" from the culture historian William Irwin Thompson.

2. William Gibson, *Neuromancer* (New York: Ace Books, 1984), 3.

3. Robert Dallek, *An Unfinished Life: John F. Kennedy, 1917–1963* (New York: Back Bay Books, 2003), 336.

4. Norman Mailer, *Oswald's Tale: An American Mystery* (New York: Random House, 1995).

5. Jean Baudrillard, *America* (London: Verso Books, 1989), 76–77.

6. E. H. Gombrich, *Art and Illusion* (New York: Pantheon Books, 1961), 72.

CHAPTER SEVEN

1. David Bourdon, *Warhol* (New York: Harry N. Abrams, 1989), 123.

2. Andy Warhol and Pat Hackett, *Popism: The Warhol Sixties* (New York: Harcourt, 1980), 83.

3. Bourdon, *Warhol*, 143.

4. Warhol and Hackett, *Popism*, 95.

5. Victor Bockris, *The Life and Death of Andy Warhol* (New York: Bantam Books, 1989), 234.

CHAPTER EIGHT

1. Bob Spitz, *The Beatles: The Biography* (New York: Back Bay Books, 2005), 582.

2. Andru J. Reeve, *Turn Me On, Dead Man* (Bloomington, IN: Author House, 2004), 29.

3. Robert Rosen, *Nowhere Man: The Final Days of John Lennon* (New York: Soft Skull Press, 2000), 94–95.

4. Marina Warner, *Phantasmagoria* (Oxford: Oxford University Press, 2006), 173.

5. Slavoj Zizek points out that there is a rumor to the effect that North Korean dictator Kim Jong Il died in a car crash years ago and that a double has replaced him in his rare public appearances. See his book *The Fragile Absolute* (London: Verso, 2000), 35–36. Interestingly, there actually is a Kim Jong Il lookalike named Kim Young-Shik who happens to be a denizen of South Korea and who runs a stationery shop in eastern Seoul. He is a dead ringer for Kim Jong Il, and has played him in movies and dramas and is often the cause of many double takes by passersby who catch glimpses of him on the street.

6. Larry King, "Larry King Live Weekend: A Look Back at Mark David Chapman in His Own Words," CNN.com, September 30, 2000, http://transcripts.cnn.com/TRANSCRIPTS/0009/30/lklw.00.html.

7. Rosen, *Nowhere Man*, 194.

8. James R. Gaines, "In the Shadows a Killer Waited," *People Magazine*, March 2, 1987.

9. James R. Gaines, "The Killer Takes His Fall,"*People Magazine*, March 9, 1987.

CHAPTER NINE

1. Peter Allen, "The Shocking Truth about How My Pal Jim Morrison REALLY Died," Mailonline.com, July 7, 2007, http://www.dailymail.co.uk/tvshowbix/article-466947/The-shocking-truth-pal-Jim-Morrison-REALLY-died.html.

2. Jerry Hopkins and Danny Sugerman, *No One Here Gets Out Alive* (New York: Warner Books, 1980).

3. The Doors, *The Doors* (Elektra/Asylum Records).

4. James Riordan and Jerry Prochnicky, *Break on Through: The Life and Death of Jim Morrison* (New York: Harper Entertainment, 2006), 92.

CHAPTER TEN

1. John Patrick Diggins, *Ronald Reagan: Fate, Freedom, and the Making of History* (New York: W. W. Norton, 2007), 116.

2. Lou Cannon, *President Reagan: The Role of a Lifetime* (New York: Public Affairs, 2000), 98.

3. Ibid., 41.

4. Ibid., 34–35.

5. Frances Fitzgerald, *Way Out There in the Blue: Reagan, Star Wars, and the End of the Cold War* (New York: Simon & Schuster, 2000), 22.

6. Denise Noe, "The John Hinckley Case," truTV.com, http://www.crimelibrary.com/terrorists_spies/assassins/john_hinkley/1.html.

7. Ibid.

8. Ibid.

CHAPTER ELEVEN

1. Jean Baudrillard, *The Intelligence of Evil or the Lucidity Pact* (Oxford: Berg, 2005), 76.

2. Roland Barthes, *Mythologies* (New York: Hill and Wang, 1972), 19.

3. Vaikuntha, which means "no hindrance," is the palace of Vishnu in Hindu mythology, located at the top of Mount Meru.

4. Walter Benjamin, *The Arcades Project* (Cambridge, MA: Harvard University Press, 2002), 391.

5. Maureen Orth, *Vulgar Favors: Andrew Cunanan, Gianni Versace, and the Largest Failed Manhunt in U.S. History* (New York: Dell Publishing, 1999), 80.

6. Ibid., 84.

7. Ibid., 200.

8 Joseph Geringer, "Andrew Cunanan: After Me, Disaster," truTV.com, http://www.trutv.com/library/crime/notorious_murders/mass/cunanan/index_1.html.

9 Ibid.

CHAPTER TWELVE

1. Camille Paglia, *Vamps and Tramps* (New York: Vintage, 1994), 168.

2. Sarah Bradford, *Diana* (New York: Viking, 2006), 85.

3. Tim Clayton and Phil Craig, *Diana: Story of a Princess* (New York: Pocket Books, 2001), 91–92.

4. Ibid., 96.

5. Bradford, *Diana*, 222.

6. Clayton and Craig, *Diana: Story of a Princess*, 270.

7. Ibid., 290.

8. Bradford, *Diana*, 289.

9. Clayton and Craig, *Diana: Story of a Princess*, 329.

10. William Irwin Thompson, *Coming Into Being: Artifacts and Texts in the Evolution of Consciousness* (New York: St. Martin's, 1998), 308.

CHAPTER THIRTEEN

1. Brian J. Robb, *Heath Ledger: Hollywood's Dark Star* (London: Plexus, 2008), 191–192.

2. "Heath Ledger," Wikipedia, http://en.wikipedia.org/wiki/Heath_ledger.

3. Ibid.

4. Robb, *Heath Ledger: Hollywood's Dark Star*, 76.

5. Ibid., 111.

CHAPTER FOURTEEN

1. J. Randy Taraborrelli, *Michael Jackson: The Magic, the Madness, the Whole Story, 1958–2009* (New York: Grand Central Publishing, 2009), 54.

2. The Editors of Rolling Stone, *Michael* (New York: HarperStudio, 2009), 82.

3. Ibid., 86.

4. Taraborrelli, *Michael Jackson: The Magic*, 223–224.

5. Although Sloterdijk's *Spheres* trilogy has not yet been translated into English, his lecture entitled "Spheres Theory: Talking to Myself about the Poetics of Space" synopsizes the main ideas and can be found online at http://www.gsd.harvard.edu/research/publications/hdm/current/30.Sloterdijk.html.

6. Ian Halperin, *Unmasked: The Final Years of Michael Jackson* (New York: Simon Spotlight Entertainment, 2009), 108.

7. Ibid., 176.

8. Editors of Rolling Stone, *Michael*, 194.

9. Halperin, *Unmasked*, 220.

10. Taraborrelli, *Michael Jackson: The Magic*, 697.

11. Ibid., 697.

Index

About the Author

JOHN DAVID EBERT is an independent scholar and author of two previous books: *Celluloid Heroes and Mechanical Dragons: Film as the Mythology of Electronic Society* and *Twilight of the Clockwork God: Conversations on Science and Spirituality at the End of an Age*. He lives in Boulder, Colorado.